THERE WAS ONLY ONE MARILYN MONROE.
YET THERE WERE SO MANY.

There was the unhappy little girl who would
do anything to be loved. There was the teenage model who learned how her fabulous body
could make important men want to give her a
boost up the ladder. There was the passionate
woman who reveled in sex with either men or
women, or both. There was the star who enjoyed
absolute power and the terrified human being
dependent on drugs. There was the wife who
first idolized her mates and then tore them
down. There was the rapturous romantic who
spoke poetry and the creature of ambition who
used the language of the gutter.

You will come to know all of her, just as Ted
Jordan did, in—

NORMA JEAN
My Secret Life with
Marilyn Monroe

"Fascinating—especially previously unpublished
photos . . . a great gift for M.M. collectors."
—*Babylon Monthly*

NORMA JEAN

My Secret Life with Marilyn Monroe

Ted Jordan

A SIGNET BOOK

SIGNET
Published by the Penguin Group
Penguin Books USA Inc., 375 Hudson Street,
New York, New York 10014, U.S.A.
Penguin Books Ltd, 27 Wrights Lane,
London W8 5TZ, England
Penguin Books Australia Ltd, Ringwood,
Victoria, Australia
Penguin Books Canada Ltd, 2801 John Street,
Markham, Ontario, Canada L3R 1B4
Penguin Books (N.Z.) Ltd, 182-190 Wairau Road,
Auckland 10, New Zealand

Penguin Books Ltd, Registered Offices:
Harmondsworth, Middlesex, England

Published by Signet, an imprint of New American Library, a division of
Penguin Books USA Inc. This is an authorized reprint of a hardcover
edition published by William Morrow and Company, Inc.

First Signet Printing, March, 1991
10 9 8 7 6 5 4 3 2 1

 REGISTERED TRADEMARK—MARCA REGISTRADA

PRINTED IN THE UNITED STATES OF AMERICA

To Norma Jean

They cannot undo the thing that has been—
Though it may never again be.

To my mother

Born an orphan, a victim of child abuse
in five foster homes.
Her young life was hell on earth,
comparable to Norma Jean's

To Dr. Benjamin T. Friedman

My brother, for whose help I give my
sincere thanks. Without him
this book would not
have been written.

And to Lili,

whose rare beauty has never been equaled.

Acknowledgments

This is a book of memories, and like most other people, my own memory is not infallible. For that reason, I owe an eternal debt of gratitude to a long list of people who graciously agreed to search their memories for details that either expanded or corroborated what I had remembered.

That debt can, in no measure, ever be repaid, for their willingness to interrupt busy schedules and aid me in this project were kindnesses I shall never forget. The list of those who helped me in the two years it took to produce this memoir is quite long, and it would take an undue amount of space to offer my personal thanks. However, I do want to pay special tribute to several friends, acquaintances, and fellow moviemakers whose help was particularly valuable.

Among them are: Harry Brand of Twentieth Century-Fox; Charles Goldie of Fox's Stills Department; the still stunningly beautiful June Haver, a wonderful human being and even better friend; Harry Hayden, whose drama school Norma Jean and I both attended; my close friend John Hodiak; Helena Sorell, Twentieth Century-Fox drama coach; Walter Lang, a musical director at that studio; actors Fred

Libby and Lon McAllister; agent Jules Stein, a dear friend of my family; Charles Mapes, Jr., driving force behind the Mapes Hotel in Reno; and Jane Russell.

My gratitude also goes to several people whose untimely deaths occurred sometime after this project began, most especially Henry Fonda and Lloyd Nolan. Aware of my struggles during the early phases of this book, they were characteristically generous with their own memories. My gratitude to them remains eternal.

Contents

Introduction

★

NORMA JEAN

Even to this day, she appears regularly in my dreams: she moves with that sinuous glide, those eyes gazing at me in the special way she looked at people she knew well, the mouth slightly open, the voice all breathless little girl, and her words interrupted by the distinctive giggle that could disarm even her greatest enemy.

It is an image that has haunted me all of my life and will continue to haunt me until the day I die. It is the image of a woman I knew first as Norma Jean Baker, later as Marilyn Monroe. I knew her first as a lover, then as a friend, and for nearly twenty years I was among a small circle of trusted friends to whom the lady I always called Norma Jean acted out the Greek tragedy that was her life.

I was drawn to her during every act in that long tragedy—from the moment I first met her, when she was a scared teenager trying to scrape up modeling jobs, to the final curtain, a lonely death in the bedroom of a small Hollywood house not far from my own.

And I loved this bewitching enigma, always.

*   *   *

Long after her death she continues to occupy my thoughts. Often I'll hear a woman laugh, and a certain way she throws her head back will suddenly remind me of Norma Jean. Or I'll hear a whispery voice, and the memories suddenly come flooding over me of another woman's voice on the telephone, the breathy half-whisper I came to know so well.

In death, as in life, the woman who was Marilyn Monroe continues to exert a power I've never been fully able to understand or explain. Occasionally I'll take a walk past the forecourt of Mann's (formerly Grauman's) Chinese Theater in Los Angeles, watching the tourists gawk at the handprints and footprints entombed forever in the cement. The roster of stars immortalized there is a long one, but I'm always struck by the fact that the one that attracts the largest crowds is a gold-colored block in the center containing the footprints and handprints of Marilyn Monroe, made in 1953. I've seen many of these people trying to match their own handprints with Marilyn's. Most seem to be young teenage girls who have worked hard to imitate the Monroe persona, including the clothes, posture, and way of speaking.

It's eerie to me, but what is happening is simply another reflection of the powerful grip she retains on our popular culture. As perhaps only a few of the gawkers realize, Marilyn Monroe was the only real love goddess produced in this century—and perhaps of all time. I have often argued that the word *star* does not exactly sum up what she was all about. Perhaps, as somebody once suggested, *Aphrodite* is the only word that can summarize the life and career of the former model and bit player who appeared in only thirty movies (including one film left unfinished at her death) and died at the age of thirty-six.

And yet even *Aphrodite* doesn't quite manage to encompass all that she was. After all, only two of the films she made are considered to have any artistic merit, so it is difficult to cite any acting triumphs to account for the extraordinary dimension of her impact. Certainly, her thin acting reputation doesn't even begin to explain why there is a flourishing industry that still surrounds her name, nor why, more than two decades after her death, her name remains magic among a whole new generation.

My own book represents, I suppose, still another contribution to that burgeoning industry. But as we shall see, what follows is not another of the standard Monroe biographies, now apparently legion. As the subtitle suggests, it is a love story and is meant not only to tell the story of a relationship that changed my life forever but to delineate and understand just what the Marilyn Monroe phenomenon was all about.

It should be understood right at the outset that this is no starry-eyed love memoir. As much as I loved her, it was not a blind love; what you will read about here is the *real* Marilyn Monroe. She is portrayed as she really existed: the extremely vulnerable child-woman incapable of hurting a fly who was also a hardheaded bitch consumed by ambition; the innocent ingenue moving through life in a kind of daze who was also petty, vindictive, and cruel; the woman consumed by a need to be loved who was also manipulative and uncaring.

In short, she was Norma Jean / Marilyn: completely unique, probably never to be equaled. And it was a uniqueness that, contrary to popular impression, was not created by a movie studio. What you saw on the screen was fairly close to real life; in her presence I always found myself magnetized by a kind of timeless existence encased in her luminous presence. She simply transferred that to the screen and was able to project it outward, into the audience. And as on the screen, I often found myself totally captivated by the endless contradictions of her strong sexual projection and little-girl, whispery voice; her outrageous behavior and air of vulnerable innocence; and her voluptuous figure and suggestion of frailty.

For a long time I have been urged by friends and others who knew of my relationship with Marilyn to set down the details, to present a full-scale portrait of her. For just as long I have resisted the temptation. Part of the reason had to do with my belief that writing about her intimately would amount to some sort of betrayal of the great secret we both shared. Then, too, I thought that enough had been written about her; it was time to let her rest in peace at last.

But the more I read about Marilyn Monroe, the more I became convinced that it was time for me to reveal the real Marilyn Monroe. Most of what I read simply bore no resemblance to the woman I knew. Aside from gross inaccuracies, it seemed to me that the authors had presented her through the prism of their own prejudices and beliefs. Most often I got the impression they were so busy trying to use her as a symbol of the decline of Western civilization or some such, they really hadn't taken much effort to find out about the main subject in the first place.

To be sure, she was always an elusive character, very difficult to summarize. Yet so much of what I read was so wildly inaccurate, I was convinced that nothing short of my own insights would set the record straight. However, what really finally convinced me to break my silence of more than twenty years was the ghoulish attempt by several Monroe biographers seeking to dig up her body to prove their various unique theories of how she met her death.

I was especially bothered by these highly publicized attempts (thank God, the Los Angeles district attorney quashed them) because I felt strongly that they diminished her; they made her a pawn in a larger game rather than the arbiter of her own destiny. It was the same image of her that had often been presented, and it's quite wrong. The fact is that whatever she was, Norma Jean Baker / Marilyn Monroe was very much herself, exceptionally so.

No one manufactured the often bizarre but very spontaneous sense of humor she had, which inspired her to tell producer Darryl F. Zanuck, when he complained about her lateness on the set, "Oh, I'm not late, Mr. Zanuck, everybody else is too early." No one manufactured her astonishing joy of life, the sheer exuberance that caused her to squeal with unrestrained delight at even simple little pleasures. No one manufactured that walk, the one that literally stopped Groucho Marx in his tracks and left the master of a thousand quips speechless.

And above all, no one manufactured the combination of qualities and deficiencies—some of which would ultimately destroy her—that constituted a very luminous human being.

This is the Marilyn Monroe you will meet in the following pages.

Chapter one

★

A GIRL AT
THE POOL

I am not a child of Hollywood. Not, that is, in the sense Marilyn Monroe was: she was born, bred, and died in the place that was always a state of mind as much as a spot on the map.

But, as both she and I discovered, we shared a susceptibility to Hollywood's powerful force, that captivating attraction that destroys some people, changes others forever, and permanently marks in some way anyone who has ever tried to deal with it.

The younger you are, the more powerful the impact, the more irresistible Hollywood's lure. And in 1940, when I first went to Hollywood—the time of the movie business's so-called golden age—the impact was very powerful indeed. I was all of fifteen at the time.

For the Friedman family of Lancaster, Ohio, times were tough in 1940. Edward Friedman, my father, was looking for a job, but work was a scarce commodity in a small midwestern town just barely recovering from the Great Depression. He had started out in show business with my uncle, the famed entertainer Ted Lewis, but that hadn't worked out. After the brothers split up, Dad studied engineering in college and became a qualified draftsman.

One day my father announced he had found a job—in Los Angeles. We sold the house and all our furniture, packed what was left into a car, and drove Route 66 all the way to the city I knew only vaguely as the place where they made those wonderful movies I used to watch every Saturday.

However much my father, mother, and older brother might have been looking forward to this new adventure, I was not. I was leaving my friends and the town that I loved. Most of all, I was leaving my beloved mountain, Mount Pleasant, a gentle pile of stone that overlooked the town of Lancaster and the Ohio River valley. I had spent many hours up there, on the mountain the Indians used to call Old Standing Stone long before the white man came and settled the valley.

On the day we were scheduled to leave for California, I climbed that mountain for what I thought might be the last time. As usual, it was quiet, a golden silence; only the sound of a bird could be heard as a warm breeze blew from the west. No matter what would happen from then on, I vowed aloud to the mountain I regarded as my personal property and private sanctuary, I would never forget this lofty rock and the great sense of peace it brought to me. Someday I would return.

The sense of loss gradually receded as we headed west, finally arriving at the place my father had rented, a small, two-bedroom apartment in a section of Los Angeles called Beverly Hills. For a kid of sixteen from the Middle West with straw still sticking out of his ears, everything looked as though I had entered some kind of magic fairyland. I saw the oranges growing on trees (I'd had no idea they grew that way), miles of beaches with all those beautiful girls, the big houses and the palm trees, all wrapped in the kind of bright, sunny weather that never seemed to change.

The people who wrote *The Beverly Hillbillies* must have had us in mind. There we were, poor little hicks from Ohio, gawking at this strange world. I felt it most acutely, for my new school was Beverly Hills High School, and if there was ever a place to make a kid feel poor, it was that place. Each morning I would watch as the students either arrived in their own Cadillacs and Mercedes or were dropped off by chauffeur-driven limousines. Most of the students were the sons and daughters of actors, actresses, producers, and directors. And it showed: they were spoiled rotten, and money to them was just something to be spent.

Seeing one of these brats pull up in front of the school in a brand-new, gleaming Cadillac always reminded me that I was now living in a world in which I did not quite fit. The closest I'd ever got to wheels in Ohio was my bicycle, the one I worked all one summer to buy. In Beverly Hills a bicycle was something the Western Union messenger used to deliver telegrams.

I felt like a duck out of water. Although some of the kids deigned to speak to me because I was the nephew of Ted Lewis—then America's most famous entertainer—most did not. The snubs bothered me, and I treasured the kids who became my friends, most notably a beautiful young blonde named June Haver, who later became a star in her own right, and Jerry Paris, eventually a director of note.

There were, of course, compensations for the misery I felt, and they had everything to do with the magical kingdom I now inhabited. Just down the street from our apartment building, for example, lived a luscious neighbor named Rita Hayworth, a wonderfully earthy and friendly woman who served as my first introduction to Hollywood stardom. She was not only approachable, she also turned out to be as openly friendly as the good folks back in Ohio. Possibly aware of the homesickness all the Friedmans were suffering, she went out of her way to make us all feel welcome—even to the extent of teaching me how to dance in the Spanish flamenco style.

"So what do you want to be?" she asked me one day in that throaty voice.

"An actor," I replied unhesitatingly, thinking of the flashy cars so many of my classmates had been given by their film-star parents.

She laughed. "Great," she said. "You've come to the right place for it."

She said nothing to me about the work required to be an actor or the kind of odds stacked against anyone trying to break into the movies. Possibly, she assumed I wasn't really serious, and there was no point in being too realistic with some teenager's fantasy that he'd forget the next morning.

But I *was* serious, for the Hollywood bug had bitten me. It had bitten me by the odd means of a hole in a fence, which bordered the back lot of Twentieth Century-Fox. The lot, used for outdoor location shots, was on the other side of a golf course across the street from our apartment building. One day my friend Jerry Paris and I cut across the golf course and cautiously crawled through a hole in the fence.

As in a fairy tale, I entered a completely different world. It was a set for a South Seas movie: There was a large artificial lake surrounded by palm trees stuck into the ground. They were preparing for a shot, and the place was a madhouse of technicians, cameras, and crew getting ready. At one end of the lake I saw monstrous machines that were making waves in the water; on the other side, Tyrone Power was being made up.

It was the most incredible thing I had ever seen: if you could blot out the sight of the cameras, lights, and the crew, it was as though a beautiful South Pacific island had been transported whole, right there to that small lot in California. Absorbing all this and watching as the star, Tyrone Power, suddenly switched into his role as swashbuckler, I decided then and there that this is what I wanted to do for a living. I would be the next Tyrone Power.

My reverie was interrupted by a studio security guard, who threw us out, but the remarkable image I had seen on the other side of that fence stayed with me for a long time afterward. It remained with me right through the next year, when Pearl Harbor suddenly interrupted all such career plans. I enlisted in the navy, was injured in a gun explosion, and wound up in a hospital, where I had plenty of time to think about Hollywood and what I really wanted to do with the rest of my life—and how I would use my GI Bill education benefits.

"*Acting school?*" My father was almost beside himself with rage. It was now 1943, the civilian economy was booming, and here I was, telling him I had decided to forgo all that by going to acting school in Hollywood. He knew enough about the business to realize that I was almost totally out of my mind: the chance of breaking into the movies in a city fairly swarming with aspiring young actors was a long shot, at best. Besides, aspiring actors starve; how did I propose to support myself while waiting for the proverbial big break?

I really had no answer to that, of course, save to insist I would manage somehow—the eternal answer of youth to doubting elders. It was not a very satisfactory reply, and my father was perfectly aware that the meager savings I had managed to accumulate wouldn't last long. Not in Hollywood, certainly.

The argument ended as expected: I left home, a nineteen-year-old know-it-all determined to become a movie actor (and star, eventually), who did not have a job or the benefit of a single acting lesson.

I didn't really deserve it, but I got two very lucky breaks almost immediately. One came from a woman I remember only as Mrs. Fenton, a motherly old lady who had a particular fondness for young, struggling actors. She ran a small boardinghouse, an ancient three-story Victorian-style sprawler that housed several actors and assorted other California characters. One of them was an old gold prospector who would disappear for six or seven months at a time into the desert, and come back with gold. His return was unmistakable: we knew he was back when we'd nearly faint from an overpowering smell of mentholatum, which for some odd reason he smeared all over his chest before going to sleep.

Still, since room and board was only eight dollars a week, a bargain even in those days, I was not about to complain. Besides, I developed close friendships with some of my fellow would-be actors, particularly one of Mrs. Fenton's favorites, a towering man six feet six inches tall named James Aurness—a name he later changed to Arness.

Then, too, none of the actors who lived there spent too much time in the boardinghouse, for all around there was a magic kingdom to play in. In that year of 1943 the war seemed very far away. It was still Hollywood's golden age, years before smog, pollution, and overcrowding; every evening you could smell the night-blooming jasmine. During the day, miles of uncrowded beaches with white sand beckoned, and each daylight hour was a gem of bright, sunny weather. There was hardly any traffic on the streets.

We all lived in what was really a glittering company town, much like something out of the feudal ages. The big studios were the great castles of this kingdom, surrounded by the much more modest small hotels and boardinghouses in which the hopefuls worked and dreamed for the moment when they would be ushered into the royal presence. In this dreamworld there was a timelessness, for time was marked only by the latest picture, who got what role, and the casting call for the next movie.

My own time was spent, first, at an acting school at the Ben Bard Theater, run by its namesake, an old-time movie actor and leading man. Jim Arness, who had recommended it to me, was a classmate, and he joined me at the school's big hangout: the Open House, just a half-block away. A bar and dance hall, the Open House was the place all the Ben Bard students met at noon to have a drink and endlessly discuss the art of acting. Three nights a week we put on plays, hoping against hope that an agent or talent scout might be in the audience and would think we were studio material. On two other nights we also put on plays at the Geller Theater and studied scripts, radio acting, and some strange new thing called television.

We were all remarkably alike—young, burning with ambition, and willing to live on the verge of poverty just for a chance at a studio contract. It was a form of lunacy, but all our hopes were fueled by the success of some of our predecessors, who now strolled around Hollywood like barons and baronesses. (A number of my classmates did finally make it, including Tony Curtis, Harry Guardino, Gil Stratton, Stu Whitman, and, of course, James Arness.)

In one sense I was more fortunate than most of the other young actor-aspirants, for I had a good job. That had come about through the second good stroke of luck to befall me that year. It came after I had begun swimming regularly at a place called the Lido Club, just behind the old Ambassador Hotel, where people paid fifty cents to swim in the huge Olympic-size pool for an hour. The club was run by a man named Milt Silverstein, who liked and encouraged athletes and struggling actors. By happy coincidence, I was both, and when Milt found out that I had not yet been able to get my Screen Actors Guild card—the necessary ticket for any acting job in a studio—he offered me a job. It was just about a dream job: eighty dollars a week to serve as lifeguard, swimming instructor, and part-time masseur, along with a daily lunch of chicken sandwich and a glass of milk. Considering the tips I got from some of the tired old bodies I massaged, I was making pretty good money, more than enough to pay for acting lessons and have enough left over to sample Hollywood's booming nightlife.

There was an extra little fringe benefit with the job, and it went under the name of the Blue Book Modeling Agency, which had an office in the hotel right near the pool. It so happened that the Blue Book had some of the most beautiful models in Hollywood, and it was not long before I decided to strike up an acquaintance with the agency's owner, a lady with the unlikely name of Miss Emmeline Snively. Miss Snively, about as forbidding as her name suggested, used the pool and adjacent golf course as a backdrop for magazine shots. She guarded her beautiful charges like a cautious mother hen, but she seemed to like and trust me. So much the better, for I used my relationship with her as an entree to make dates with some of her models.

The arrangement was satisfactory for a nineteen-year-old libido, but most of the models, empty-headed beauties desperately seeking any route they could find into a movie contract, failed to leave a lasting impression on me.

Until the early afternoon of a warm summer's day. That's when I saw her.

From the high vantage point of my lifeguard's chair above the Lido Club pool, I saw, just over the other side of the fence guarding the pool, a group of twenty girls clad in bathing suits. Evidently they were preparing for a photo session on the season's new women's swimsuits.

They were all very good-looking women, but one that struck me, even from my high vantage point, really stood out. She was wearing a blue version of what was then a daring new swimsuit style, a French design of two pieces that left the midriff exposed. In a word, she was stunning. She had an hourglass shape, with large breasts that jutted out firmly, as though defying gravity. This bore further reconnaissance.

I dove off the diving platform, swam to the end of the pool, and as I dried off, casually asked my newfound friend, Miss Snively, about the model with the remarkable figure. While I was smitten by the woman's charms, apparently Miss Snively was not, for she answered, almost absent-mindedly, "Oh, she's one of the new girls."

Try as she might, Miss Snively could not remember the woman's name, but added "It's her first modeling job; she's quite nervous. Why don't you wait until they're finished taking pictures, then go over and introduce yourself?"

So I waited as the photographer posed the models in those typical 1940s-era poses, all innocent sex and dramatic backdrops. It gave me the opportunity to study the model whose name Miss Snively could not remember. I was struck by a number of things about her. There was, of course, the incredible figure, which looked as though she had been poured into that swimsuit. Yet there did not appear to be anything else that distinguished her physically: she had light brown mousy hair down to her shoulders; very curly, it looked somewhat frizzy. Her face, while pretty enough, was not especially beautiful. In fact, many of the other young women there that afternoon had much more striking faces.

And yet there was *something* about her, something so intriguing and vibrant, I couldn't take my eyes off her. One reason may have been that she positively radiated sex, despite the fact that she appeared to be barely eighteen. Even while she was just standing around, the aura of sex was almost palpable. But she also had a number of mannerisms that struck me as somewhat odd. The most striking was her habit of constantly licking her lips while performing eye-catching gyrations with her mouth. The mouth itself seemed to be very tight, and she would throw her lips forward and backward, uncertain of herself when she was asked to smile.

Still, this was a woman I wanted desperately to meet. After the modeling session was finished, I walked over to her. "Hello, I'm Eddie Friedman," I announced, deciding that the direct attack would be best. "I noticed you from up there"—I pointed to my usual perch above the swimming pool—"and I thought I'd like to meet you. I'm the lifeguard here."

She appeared totally unimpressed. "Hi," she replied, in a high-pitched, breathless voice, "I'm Norma Jean Dougherty."

I wish I could say that the earth heaved and the heavens parted with thunderclaps at this moment of meeting the woman who would later be known as Marilyn Monroe, but nothing like that happened. We stood there, like two awkward teenagers (for that, essentially, is what we were), trying to make conversation. I tried hard not to stare at her body and concentrated on looking into her blue eyes.

"I've been here about a year," I said, trying to get a conversation going, then proceeded to sum up my life at that point. It did not require much time to summarize nineteen years, including my family's move to Los Angeles, my brief navy stint, my wound, and then my decision on a career as an actor, for which I was now studying while supporting myself at the Lido Club.

She smiled noncommittally during the brief monologue, and seemed to brighten up only when I mentioned the word *actor*.

"Oh, that's great," she said in that little-girl voice. "What a coincidence: my greatest ambition is to become an actress." She went on to explain that she had started modeling to earn enough money to pay room and board at the home of her "Aunt Grace" (a relative with whom she was staying) and hoped, somehow, to begin an acting career. As if anticipating my next question, she mentioned that she was married but now separated from her husband, a navy seaman named James Dougherty.

So far, so good, I thought. Clearly I hadn't exactly bowled her over, but at least she hadn't given me the quick brush-off. Pressing my advantage, I moved to the conversational gambit that still plays well today in California: astrological signs. I told her my birthday —May 23, 1924—and asked hers.

"Oooh!" she squealed, "we're both Geminis! You know, twins! I was born June 1, 1926." This last piece of intelligence gave me some pause: good God, I thought, this voluptuous creature is all of seventeen years old—or, put another way, pure jailbait.

The pause was only momentary, for I was completely smitten by this creature, a child-woman who radiated, I felt, some sort of force field. And, like a piece of iron being drawn toward a magnet, I was hopelessly hooked. I had to have her.

"Listen," I said, deciding on a desperate gambit, "how about if we go out tonight?"

"Tonight?" she said, frowning, as though undecided. She did not seem thrilled with the prospect. "Gee, I don't know."

"We'll take in the show at Slapsy Maxie's," I pressed, naming one of Hollywood's more noted nightspots. She appeared impressed somewhat. "We'll go see my uncle's show."

"Your uncle?" she asked, confused.

"Right, my uncle is Ted Lewis."

The mention of that name abruptly caused a dramatic change in her reaction to me; the reluctant teenager suddenly became practically bursting to go out with me. "Your uncle is *Ted Lewis?*" she said, her eyes widening. "*The* Ted Lewis?"

"Sure," I replied, trying to sound casual. "His real name is Friedman; he changed it when he got into show business."

"Wow," she said, breathlessly. "Yeah, let's go see his show."

I was so overjoyed at her consent, I hardly paid any attention to the rest of our conversation, which centered almost exclusively on Norma Jean's questions about Ted Lewis. "I really want to meet him," she cooed, and when I airily replied that would be no problem, she nearly lit up like a light bulb. There followed even more questions, including which agency represented him.

"The William Morris Agency, I think," I said, failing, in my infatuation, to notice the oddity of a seventeen-year-old neophyte model wondering which agency represented a famous entertainer. The same temporary blindness prevented me from noticing a few other curious details, particularly the question of the extent of her innocence.

I wanted to believe, of course, that I was dealing with an almost totally innocent girl, the better to impress her with my limited knowledge of the Hollywood nightlife. At nineteen years old, already a veteran and on the threshold of what I was convinced was certain Hollywood stardom, I had no doubt that I would sweep this beautiful woman off her feet; she would melt in sheer awe at my sophistication.

I told her I would pick her up that night at her Aunt Grace's house in my Model A Ford, the one I had bought for the magnificent sum of sixty dollars some time before. (There was gas rationing then, but when I couldn't get gas, I would use kerosene; she backfired a lot on that fuel, but she still ran.)

"No, it's best we meet somewhere," Norma Jean said, nervously moving her lips.

"How about the Haig?" I asked, mentioning the name of a popular small bar right near the Ambassador. I was about to explain the choice, when she interrupted.

"Oh, yes, the Haig is good," she said, "better than the bar at the Chapman Park [Hotel]." She named a few other places.

Again, in my smitten state, I was not paying too close attention and thus did not wonder how a seventeen-year-old model knew the ins and outs of Hollywood nightlife. If I had bothered to probe further, I would have discovered that Norma Jean Dougherty was not nearly as innocent as I thought. Not by a long shot. It took some time before I would discover that I was dealing not with an innocent and

naive girl with stars in her eyes but with a multifac-
eted personality of extraordinary complexity.

It also took me some time to realize that I was
dealing with a woman who was doomed by that very
same personality.

Chapter two

THE CHILDREN OF PARADISE

Unless you count the punk-rock palaces and other such strange things, there's not much in the way of nightlife in Hollywood anymore. Just as it did the movies, so television also changed forever the way we occupy our leisure time.

But back in 1943 Hollywood came alive at night, and within a relatively small area now dominated by office buildings, there were several watering holes that glittered from the unmistakable talent of the people who appeared there.

Even the ones supposed to be the fanciest had a certain down-home atmosphere, a shared intimacy between audience and performer. In fact, their main function seemed to be as showcases for up-and-coming stars, who traveled the nightclub circuit. In the war years it didn't cost an arm and a leg to hang around there; a few dollars to nurse a few drinks were enough to allow you to see some pretty impressive talent.

Thanks to my job, I always had a few extra dollars, which I spent hanging around these places, absorbing the show business atmosphere that I loved so much. Possibly it was a genetic strain handed down from my uncle's side of the family. Whatever the reason, I liked nothing better than to sit by the hour, watching and listening: the actors exchanging studio gossip; the women preening, hoping to be noticed by a producer or director; the performers on stage, chatting with the audience; and the occasional soldier or sailor wandering in, wondering if there really was a war on out there someplace.

My easy familiarity with this world of Hollywood nightlife—actually there were only five nightclubs of any dimension there those days—made me, I thought, a man of the world. To impress the new girl, Norma Jean Dougherty, I carefully considered a sort of whirlwind tour of all of them.

First would be the Haig, across the street from the Ambassador Hotel. I especially liked it, for the Haig was known as an "in" place for actors, and I could spend hours there just listening to the shoptalk. It was a small place, with a tiny dining room, a bar, and a platform for the entertainers who appeared there regularly. It featured music, and most of the entertainers played piano, occasionally alternating with a jazz group of stunning talent led by an unknown saxophone player named Gerry Mulligan. His group often played until the wee hours to a devoted audience of afficionados listening to the sound that would revolutionize American music. (The piano players who worked the Haig weren't bad either: Erroll Garner, Nat King Cole, and Bobby Short.)

As I had hoped, Norma Jean was suitably impressed with my tour of the night spots and seemed to come alive when she spotted anyone even remotely famous. We didn't get to see my uncle, Ted Lewis, that first night, but there was plenty else to gawk at. At Slapsy Maxie's, for example, there was the comedian Ben Blue (very famous then) on the bill, along with some struggling new comics named Martin and Lewis and a dancer named Jackie Gleason. And there were similar delights everywhere in this little kingdom: the Earle Carroll Theater, the Florentine Gardens, the famous Ciro's, the Trocadero, and the most famous of all, the Mocambo, where many big stars gathered to be seen.

There were also the places not so famous: the Zephyr Room, whose size made its name almost literal, and where a curious duo did a nice little act. Called Doodles and Spider, they were immensely talented, mostly because of the Spider half of the act, a dancer-singer named Dick Van Dyke. And one of the real "in" places in Hollywood, a nightspot called the Brothers Club. Located in the black district of Los Angeles, it was an after-hours club that operated like a Prohibition-era speakeasy. You would knock on the door, and after a mean-looking man glared at you through a porthole, you would say, "Brother, let me in." If he liked you or knew you, he'd open the door. The place featured black entertainment and an audience of Hollywood sophisticates bored with the usual nightclub circuit. Here actors like Orson Welles, Errol Flynn, John Hodiak, and John Ireland, among others, could relax and carouse until dawn.

Norma Jean loved it all. She loved the glamour and the excitement, the sheer thrill of being near all those celebrities. She was a star-worshiper of the first order, I quickly divined, a trait I put down to her own ambition to became an actress. I have to admit I did not take that ambition very seriously. After all, *every* girl in Hollywood those days wanted to be a queen of the screen. Then, too, with that little-girl voice and all those nervous habits, I simply could not picture this seventeen-year-old as a movie actress. She'd need twenty years of work, I reckoned, to acquire the cool beauty and poise that marked the then-reigning queens of the movies, such as Joan Crawford or Katharine Hepburn. True, she had that voluptuous body, but there were plenty of stunning female bodies in Hollywood, a town that has always had an endless supply of them.

By our third date I was so completely captivated by her, I could hardly even think straight. I had taken to spending long periods of silence with Norma Jean, staring into those blue eyes that always appeared to be restless somehow; at any given time I would be looking into the eyes of a woman, a little girl, a frightened young woman, a personality alive with life, a listless person devoid of life, someone who had been badly hurt, a woman of great depth, an innocent young girl. It was all there, and part of my infatuation had to do with the supreme puzzle she represented. I had never encountered anyone quite like her.

It was on the fourth date that I decided that I must have her, that absolutely nothing else mattered in this world. This was a moment of some delicacy, for I was not quite certain how to approach her on this subject. I hoped she felt the same depth of passion I did, but obviously there was no litmus test I could give her before making my move.

As things turned out, events anticipated me. Sitting in the Haig, downing Cuba Libres, we both began to feel no pain. Casually, as though discussing that year's fashion styles, Norma Jean began to talk about sex.

"God, Eddie," she said, breathlessly,"isn't fucking just the greatest thing that ever was?"

"Sure is," I replied, trying to hide my shock. This was 1943, remember, when women were not supposed to talk about sex openly—certainly not to the extent of how much they liked it. But Norma Jean began discussing sex with a stunning openness and naturalness I had never experienced with any other woman. It had an air of innocence about it all the same, and at a time when sex was considered something "dirty," not really a fit discussion topic for polite company, Norma Jean's approach was quite something else.

"Can you imagine," she said, with an air of total innocence "that the greatest thing in life is free—orgasm. All those great feelings are free. You know, that feeling when there's a cock in your cunt and you're just laying there, and like these waves of wonderful feeling come over you. To me, that's the most beautiful sight in the world, Eddie: two people fucking, just reaching inside each other for their souls."

"You're absolutely right, Norma Jean," I said, almost swallowing my glass. It was time, I decided: I would take her someplace—anyplace—and make mad, passionate love to her. I felt almost faint.

"Come on, let's get out of here," I suggested, rising a little unsteadily from too many Cuba Libres.

"Great," she said, smiling. I noticed that she was also a little wobbly.

We went outside and got into my Model A. It had begun to rain, and water was leaking inside from the torn roof. Norma Jean didn't seem to mind. I kissed her, putting my arm over her right shoulder and cupping one of her breasts in my hand. "Let's go down to Chinatown, Eddie," she half-whispered. "You'll just love it down there."

In the Chinatown section of Los Angeles, she directed me to a restaurant called the Red Dragon—where, to my surprise, I discovered she had worked as a waitress briefly. We had a drink there, then moved to a bar called the Buddha, where we began to drink rice wine. By this time I felt as though I was floating on a cloud. Madly in love, my senses dulled by a little too much drink, I was ready to make love to her right in the middle of the street.

Even the bucketfuls of rain that were now pouring down failed to diminish the passion. We walked, arms wrapped around each other in that downpour, oblivious of everything but the presence of each other. I suddenly stopped, grabbed her with both hands while spinning her around, and yelled, "Hey, you know something, Norma Jean? We're flat broke!"

She laughed, a wonderful throaty laugh as she stood there in the rain, her dress becoming plastered to her body. "Who gives a fuck?" she yelled back. "Hell, I don't care, I'm having a ball!"

For some odd reason I wanted to take her to another place for a nightcap of sorts, but had suddenly realized I had spent all my money. For equally odd reasons, I was suddenly consumed by the desire to get some more. An inspiration struck.

"You've got a job," I told her. "Come with me, I'll show you." Still laughing, she followed.

Just down the street I stopped before a large Chinese restaurant (at that moment closed). On the restaurant grounds there was a man-made pond of sorts, in the center of which rested a Buddha statue. The statue's multiple arms had hands outstretched to take the coins tossed by people who believed the local legend that if the coins managed to stay in the hands, their wishes would come true. Thus my sudden inspiration: I would fish in the water for the unrequited wishes, for it was rare indeed for any coin-tosser to succeed in putting money into those hands.

Praying that the restaurant's owners hadn't cleaned out the water for a while, I began to take off my shoes and socks. "What are you doing, Eddie?" Norma Jean asked, amid more laughter.

"I have two wishes," I said. "One is to find enough money in here so we can go out some more. The other is that I don't get caught. You act as lookout. If you see anything that looks like a cop, yell out."

"Sure," she said, hardly bothering to look, for she was more struck by the sight of a man, already soaked to the skin by the downpour, carefully taking off his shoes and socks, then rolling up his pants before entering the water. I began to pick up coins and heard the sound of uncontrolled giggling from behind me. It was Norma Jean. She was literally cracking up at the sight of me fishing around in the water for coins and trying to jam them into pockets soaked by rain.

"What the hell are you laughing at?" I asked her, momentarily annoyed that she did not show proper respect for my brilliant money-making scheme.

"Move over," she replied, "I'm coming in." She waded right in, and like two little children, we laughed and giggled as we scooped up coins. There were enough retrieved for a few more drinks at a local bar, where the puzzled bartender wondered about this odd, water-logged couple that couldn't stop giggling.

Afterward, we headed back toward Hollywood in

my jalopy. I was trying to think of a place where I could make love to her—my boardinghouse forbade female visitors—when she suddenly said, "Why don't we go over to where you work?"

On the way, with one arm wrapped around her, I got the idea of stopping at the local park, known as West Lake (now called MacArthur Park). The rain had stopped momentarily. It was steaming hot, perfectly suitable for the passions that I felt were about to overwhelm me.

Around the large lake that gave the park its name there were palm trees and large weeping willows, slouching low from all that rain. We took a boat out across the lake, and on the other side I pulled it under a large weeping willow. What happened next seemed to run in some form of slow motion, as in a dream. I began to kiss her, and both of us explored each other's bodies. I opened the front of her dress and exposed the most beautiful pair of breasts I had ever seen.

"Do you believe in fellatio?" she asked, with that air of innocence that was so disarming.

"Hell yes," I replied, trying to sound sophisticated, although I was astounded by a question that I had believed no "normal" woman would ever ask.

The subsequent act revealed a young woman who obviously knew something about the subject, and when she had finished, she just as disarmingly asked if I would do the same thing to her. It was an experience that further convinced me that however innocent I once thought this girl, she was very far ahead of me.

"You don't think there's anything wrong with this, do you?" she asked, again all innocence.

"Oh, for God's sake, *no!*" I shouted in reply. She

had asked the question after making love to me, the most passionate, fulfilling sex I had yet experienced. Obviously I didn't see anything wrong with it. Certainly not in my condition: my feet dangling in the water, the rest of me cloaked in sweat, and the moisture dropping on us from the weeping willow above us, my head almost dizzy with desire.

"Come inside me now, please," she said with that characteristic directness. "Hurry."

At last, when we had finished in a blaze of passion, I assumed she was now finished. It turned out she was just getting warmed up. Incredible, I thought to myself. I never knew that women could really like sex that much. At least this woman did.

After what seemed like hours at the lake, I told her I would take her home. To my surprise, she said, "No, let's go over to the pool where you work." The rain had begun again, and the sky was crackling with lightning. In that charged atmosphere of electricity and passion, I felt energized. There was something almost ethereal going on.

As luck would have it, I had a key to the club. Upstairs, where the massage rooms and showers were, I gave her a robe and some towels. "You better dry off," I said, looking at her soaked dress that was now wrapped around her like another skin. "I'm going to take a shower." Outside, the thunder rumbled.

In the shower I had just soaped up from head to toe when the shower door slowly opened. Before me stood the sight that has remained permanently etched on my memory: Norma Jean in the nude. She looked like a perfect, beautiful statue.

"Do you like what you see?" she asked, smiling. "Will I pass the qualifications? Do you like it?"

I was too overwhelmed by the sight to reply. She

calmly walked into the shower, closed the door behind her, and began to touch my body. I was instantly rearoused. I was also somewhat embarassed, since I had never heard of boys and girls taking showers together (they just didn't do that sort of thing back in Ohio).

But Norma Jean acted as though it was a perfectly routine thing to do. Just as casually, she braced herself against one wall of the shower and, lifting a leg, pushed me inside her. It was another incredible experience. A new world I had never even dared to dream about had suddenly opened to me.

"I have to rest awhile," I told her, trying to hide my chagrin that like all men (even at the lusty age of nineteen), I had my limits.

"For a while," she giggled. She looked deep into my eyes, and in a voice that was not the voice of a seventeen-year-old teenage girl, said throatily, "I hope I've made you happy and I hope I can always make you happy."

"I love you, Norma Jean," I said.

"I've never really felt love like I have with you," she replied, suddenly frowning as she noticed some blood on my lip. She had bitten me there during lovemaking. "I didn't hurt you, did I?"

"Oh, no," I answered breezily, not bothering to tell her that if she had cut off my right arm, I really wouldn't have noticed—or minded.

"Let's go for a swim," she said brightly, and began to walk downstairs in the nude. She noticed my momentary hesitation. "Oh, come on. There's nobody around now, Eddie."

The thought crossed my mind that I might lose my job if we were caught swimming nude in the Lido Club pool. The thought faded almost immediately as it was replaced by the sight of Norma Jean's body walking ahead of me as we moved toward the pool. Actually "walking" doesn't even begin to describe it. She had large, round buttocks, and when she walked, everything seemed to move at once in some kind of symphony.

"Don't look at my ass," she said, giggling. "It's too damn big."

"Not to my way of thinking," I said, staring at what was almost a perfect hourglass shape. It was the kind of shape I used to stare at as a boy in the museums, which always had at least a few of those old Grecian statues showing the perfect female form. Alas, I discovered when I later began to look at girls more seriously, it seemed that no woman had that kind of shape. I began to become convinced that women simply did not meet that Grecian ideal—until I saw Norma Jean.

She entered the pool at the shallow end, her body lit by the flashes of lightning. In my rapture, I chose to overlook a significant scientific fact: in a lightning storm, just about the most dangerous place you can be is a swimming pool, since its water functions as a large conductor. As an experienced swimmer, I was perfectly aware of that, of course. I had chased enough people out of the Lido Club pool on just the imminent threat of a thunderstorm not to know there's a good chance of being killed in pool when the lightning starts to flash.

But on this steamy night, I would have gladly died in that pool, having achieved what I thought was pure heaven. I was more happily alive than I could ever have imagined as I watched Norma Jean paddle (to my surprise, I discovered she couldn't swim a stroke) to the deep end of the pool. When she reached the far end, I dove in and swam toward her.

As I surfaced, I noticed that she had her back to the ladder and was holding on to it, with both arms behind her. I also noticed that she had her legs spread wide apart. Oh, my God, I thought, she's ready to go again.

"Fuck me, fuck me!" she said loudly, her voice echoing throughout the club complex. I suddenly had visions of hotel guests, awakened by the noise, throwing open their windows and staring at these two rutting teenagers in the pool. Maybe somebody would call the cops; I'd be in big trouble for having sex with a girl under eighteen.

Fortunately, the crash of thunder and the pounding rain drowned out all noise from the pool, for Norma Jean was not only passionate, she was *loudly* passionate.

"Oh God," she said, looking like a wild woman, "please let this last, never let it end! I want this feeling to last forever!" I was finding it difficult to keep up with her appetite and found myself in the odd position of the hunter now being the hunted. Only hours before, I remembered, it was me, the libidinous nineteen-year-old male, smitten by the voluptuousness of this young woman, scheming to find some way I could have her. In that era of man-initiates-sex, I had been trying to figure out some clever plan that would overcome her innocent inexperience and get what I wanted. Now, ironically enough, I was riding a tigress who was very much the aggressor; I hardly had a chance to catch my breath.

"You know," she half-whispered after her latest outburst of passion was spent, "everytime the lightning strikes, it's like an orgasm lighting up the sky, and every time the thunder booms, it's like someone up there yelling and screaming in ecstasy. Then, every time the raindrops fall harder and harder, it's as though the heavens were having a huge orgasm. Sweetheart, if this is really what heaven is like, then I want to be closer to it up there. From this moment on, I'll never be afraid to die."

Suddenly she seized me in both arms, held me close, and whispered in my ear, "Darling, in life we weep at the thought of death. Perhaps in death, we weep at the thought of life."

I really had no idea what she was talking about, but the mention of death chilled me. I stared at her; rapturously, she was staring at the stormy skies above us, while the rain poured down. She's a strange girl, all right, I thought. In my smitten state, however, it hardly seemed to matter. I was so madly in love with her at that point, I would have hung on every word even if she'd recited the phone book.

The rain finally stopped, and a chill came up. We left the pool and hurried back upstairs. Laying out a small mattress on the floor, I suggested we take a nap. I was exhausted; judging by her own exertions, I assumed she was too.

But she wasn't. While I nodded off, she recited poetry to me. She was crazy about poetry, she told me, and had memorized huge chunks of many poems. Through a daze I heard her reciting her favorite stanzas as she lay there, beautifully naked and unashamed.

Some time later, I awoke, realizing I had dozed off. She was still wide awake, staring at me. Outside, the first faint rays of dawn were breaking. We dressed and prepared to leave.

"Isn't it great to be in love?" she asked as I drove her back to her aunt's house. We snuggled together in the front seat, oblivious of the fact that we both looked like drowned water rats.

When she got out of the car, she paused a moment. "We have to find out all about each other," she said. I noticed that she was moving her tongue over her lips, the unmistakable sign of her nervousness.

"Sure," I told her, "let's really get to know each other."

"Gee," she said, her tongue darting, "I hope you'll still like me when you find out all about me."

I laughed. How many skeletons, I wondered, could possibly lurk in the closet of a seventeen-year-old girl?

Quite a few, as it turned out.

Chapter three

THE
WHITE PIANO

"How come you never invite me into your aunt's house?"

It was a perfectly natural question, I thought. But Norma Jean seemed bothered by it. She made that little nervous mannerism with her lips.

"It wouldn't work out," she said, frowning.

"What wouldn't work out?"

"You coming into my aunt's house."

I was more puzzled than put out by this odd circumstance. In the months since I had first met her, Norma Jean and I were practically inseparable. Yet she never once invited me into her aunt's home.

"What is she, some kind of drunk or something?" I asked one night. I assumed Norma Jean was hiding some deep, dark family secret.

"No, nothing like that," she said, compressing her lips, the signal that the topic of conversation was closed.

I dropped it, figuring that every family has its black sheep they don't want publicly displayed. Still, it was odd: Norma Jean never spoke about her father or mother, never mentioned one thing about her Aunt Grace, didn't say a word about the rest of her family, and generally acted as though everybody in her family was dead. Having turned my back on my own family to run off to Hollywood, I was hardly a paragon of family togetherness myself, but at least I acknowledged they existed. Why would Norma Jean be so mysterious about her own family?

It took some time for me to learn what Norma Jean was concealing: she came from a family of ghosts.

When Norma Jean finally began to allow a few peeks into her family and her past, I understood why she had taken such pains to conceal them. First of all, she told me, her maiden name was Baker, in fact her mother's married name. So her father was named Baker?

"No, there isn't any father," she said. "Or at least a father I'm sure about. All I know for sure is that it wasn't Baker."

I sat fascinated as the rest of the story came out, piece by piece. Her mother, Gladys—whose maiden name was Monroe—suffered from bouts of insanity, as did her own mother. Married at fifteen to a man named Baker, she came home early from work one day and discovered her husband having intercourse with another woman. Baker then abandoned his wife, in the process kidnapping their two children (Norma Jean's half sisters). Ultimately he wound up in Kentucky, where he remarried. Gladys, his former wife, hitchhiked all the way from California to Kentucky to see her two children. Seeing they were happy in their new home (and with their new mother), she quietly turned around and left. She never saw them again.

Suffering from periodic bouts of insanity, Gladys

Baker had a tenuous grip on life. "You know, she never kissed me," Norma Jean said. "She never held me. In fact, during the times when she was, you know, okay, she hardly said a word to me. When they would let her out of the hospital, she'd come home. She was in a kind of a daze all the time, not quite knowing what was going on. Then she'd get a little better, and then a little better, and pretty soon I'd think she would be okay. But then would come the night when she'd go haywire. I'd hear screaming and everything, and the next morning she'd be gone. They would tell me she got sick again and had to go back to the hospital."

My heart ached for her as she unfolded the story of her childhood and her mother's problems. She seemed so fragile and alone as she told me—sometimes haltingly—about a childhood nobody should have.

After a while I became aware that inside Norma Jean there was an obsession that just about totally dominated her psyche. It wasn't her dream of becoming an actress—she talked about that ambition often enough, Lord knows—but the urge to find out where and how her father was.

"When I was little," she told me, "my mother told me that my father's name was Mortenson, but that shortly before I was born, he went to New York City and was killed there in a motorcycle accident. I don't know why, but I just didn't believe it. Maybe just instinct or something. Anyway, when I got a little older and my mother was living with me during one of her good periods, I used to go into her bedroom. Way up on the wall, where I could hardly see it, there was this picture of a man. Somehow, I thought, This is my father.

"I pestered the hell out of my mother about that

picture. Finally one day she put me up on a chair so that I could stand high enough to see the picture. He was a nice-looking man, with a thin little mustache. Oh, he looked so handsome! I looked a lot like him. In the picture he was wearing a slouch hat and smiling. You know, he looked a lot like Clark Gable."

"Did you ever hear from him?" I asked.

"Nope," she answered, shaking her head. "Never did. But someday I'm going to find him, Eddie. I'll just walk in on him one day and say, 'Hi, Dad, I'm your daughter, Norma Jean.' And then everything'll be okay. Or maybe I won't, I don't know."

At such moments she would begin to cry. "Oh, Christ, Eddie," she wailed, "why didn't he ever come to see me? Was it too much just to come around and see what his little girl looked like? He wouldn't have had to bring me candy or anything, just come and say hello."

I wept too. I wept for this beautiful creature as she sat there, telling me of the pain that tore at her. "Oh, my heart hurts sometimes," she said.

Her act of sharing her heartache with me brought us very close together. I had no childhood like the horror she had experienced, but I could share with her some of my mother's own heartache. Like Norma Jean, my mother was a foster child. I repeated to Norma Jean my mother's stories about the hurt of living in hand-me-down clothes, in being at the tail end of everything, and the stab of pain she would feel every time she would see a "normal" family of mother, father, and children. She nodded in recognition as I told her, the tears running down her cheeks.

"Oh, yes, Eddie, that's right, that's right," she said.

"Ask her about the bath water. All foster kids remember that, I guarantee you. Ask her about how on Saturday night, when it was bath time, all the other kids took their bath first; by the time the foster kid got a chance, that water was dirty and disgusting. Nobody would want to bathe in it. See, that's the kind of things you remember."

Norma Jean had been in a half dozen foster homes from the time she was a little girl. To relieve the hurt she felt, she lived in a fantasy world: the movies. Norma Jean went to the movies a lot. "When I got home after the movies," she said, "I used to act out all the parts in my room. You should have seen me, Eddie; I was really very good. That's when I started to dream of being in the movies myself one day."

I began to understand why she was so intent on becoming an actress; to her, movies were a fantasy world, the one to which she wanted to escape the terrible drabness and sadness of her own real life. And I also began to understand why she loved with such fierce passion: she needed love desperately and hoped that the harder she loved somebody, the more they would love her back.

That desperate urge was not only the result of her longing to see her father; it also stemmed, I discovered, from two separate stays in an orphanage. Her stays there had apparently been really shattering to her, for the very fact she was there was an admission that she had no father. That she could never admit, and when the other little girls there asked her when her father and mother died, she would vehemently insist that her father was still alive.

"I'd tell 'em my father was Clark Gable," she told me. "They would laugh at me, but the more they laughed, the more I insisted it was true. And you know, after a while I said it so often, I began to believe it myself. Besides, whenever I thought of that picture my mother showed me in her bedroom, I thought of Clark Gable. He looked just like him."

Who was "he"? At first Norma Jean was reluctant to tell me, claiming she couldn't remember the name. When I laughed in disbelief, she admitted she knew. "Gifford," she said. "C. Stanley Gifford. He was a guy who lived in the same apartment building as my mother. After she got back from Kentucky, I guess she was lonely or whatever, you know, and she took up with him. The next thing you know, here comes Norma Jean, illegitimate as hell. A real little Holly-wood bastard."

She laughed. "You know how I got my name? Well, the first part of my name is for Norma Tal-madge. You remember her? She was a big star dur-ing the silent days. My mother used to work in this film-cutting outfit, and she told me she worked on the Talmadge films. She thought Norma Talmadge was just about the most beautiful woman ever on film. So that's how I got the first part of my name. Jean, the second part, comes from Jean Harlow. My mother figured that this little blond girl she had was going to be another big blond bombshell like Harlow was. Ain't that a hoot?"

In those hours that we sat around the Hollywood nightspots and hangouts, nursing our drinks as she poured out her heart to me, there was a consistent theme. She was in search of her father, the one central drive that dominated her psyche. I don't mean in the literal sense. Gifford, her real father, had moved up north someplace and was running a few businesses, but she made no move to go see him.

No, what she wanted was for her father to come to see her, to walk into her life and at least legitimize her.

Often she mentioned a recurring dream she had. "It's a long dream," she said. "I'm in this hospital, having a tonsillectomy. One day he comes to see me. The other patients are just about falling all over themselves that I have so distinguished a visitor. He stands by my bed. I make him bend down over and over again and kiss my forehead. He says to me, 'You'll be well in a few days, Norma Jean. I'm very proud of the way you're behaving, not crying all the time like the other girls.' God, I'm almost busting with pride that he's with me! I ask him to sit down and take off his hat, but he just smiles at me and keeps standing there. He just keeps standing there smiling, not saying a word, and I keep begging him. Then the dream ends."

At such times she would cling fiercely to me, holding on as though I were a life raft in a stormy sea. I had begun to understand that behind all those nervous mannerisms was a girl who had absolutely nothing in the way of family. Her marriage to Jim Dougherty, she admitted, was not really a marriage at all. Fearful of being sent back to an orphanage, she had agreed to a virtually arranged marriage to the boy next door.

"He's okay," she said of her husband, "but I don't, you know, really feel anything. He's just there, and now that he's away overseas most of the time, he's out of my mind. I don't even think about him too much, to tell you the truth. I guess I'll have to do something about it one of these days. I don't think he cares that much, either, because he likes me well enough, I guess, but I'm just another girl to him. I don't think he was ever really in love with me. He was just there, and I was just there, and I guess everybody figured if we got together, that would solve everything."

As for the rest of her family, there was not much there, either. The "Aunt Gracie" with whom she now lived, she admitted, was not an aunt at all, but the latest in a string of foster parents. The woman, a nice enough lady named Grace Goddard, had worked with Norma Jean's mother; when Mrs. Baker had another of her relapses, Mrs. Goddard agreed to take in Norma Jean. Her real aunts, Norma Jean added, were all Christian Scientists who were so rabidly devoted to their faith that they would occasionally wander into bookstores, ripping up anything they considered critical of Christian Scientists.

"Some group, huh?" Norma Jean said, with a sardonic laugh. "You don't know how much I envy you, Eddie, having a real family. Jesus, what I would give for that! Well, if you don't have one, you can't buy one, that's for sure. There's no such thing as a family store, where you can buy one or rent one, that's for sure." She laughed again, a bitter little laugh.

"I'll tell you about two other dreams I always have," she went on. "One is a real nightmare, the kind, you know, that makes you wake up in a sweat. There are these guys in white suits with blank faces. They put me in a white car. The car drives to this brick building, like the orphanage. We go through one black iron door after another, and each one of those doors is locked behind me. They lock me in this room with barred windows and put a straitjacket on me. I want to get out, but they won't listen to anything I say. 'I don't belong here! I don't belong here!' I keep screaming, but nobody listens to me. And I keep screaming until, finally, my voice gives out. Then I wake up."

The second dream turned out to be much less horrifying, and in a way, much more revealing. "I used to have this dream when I was much younger," she said. "There's this big church, with a lot of people sitting around. I walk into the church, stark naked. Everybody turns around to stare at me. I don't feel any embarrassment or anything. In fact, I feel real good, almost comfortable."

The dream made a great deal of sense to me, for in the time that I spent with Norma Jean, I was constantly amazed at how casual she was about such matters as nudity. She loved to walk around naked whenever she could, and I can't remember an instance that she showed even a twinge of shame. She was perfectly natural, the same way she approached anything sexual. If she wanted to do something, she would simply announce her wish, much like an innocent child.

And like a child, she needed constant loving. Largely, the sex was part of that hunger. She loved seeing me practically lathered with excitement, worshiping at the temple of her body. She would come alive then, clearly overjoyed at how easily she could make someone adore her. "Gee," she often said, "all I have to do is take my dress off."

As we grew more intimate during those magic nights of wartime Hollywood, more secrets came tumbling out. One of them concerned what she called "one of my deepest, darkest secrets."

It happened, she related, when she was nine years old. She was in a foster home run by people who also took in boarders. One of them was a nice old man who went out of his way to treat Norma Jean kindly. One day, he asked her into his room and closed the door behind her.

"I didn't feel any fear," she said. "I figured he wanted to talk to me, or give me a little present, or something. He sat on the bed just staring at me. Finally, he asked me to take off my dress. I didn't know any better, so I did. I stood there in front of him, with my dress off. He went on and on about how beautiful I was, the most beautiful thing he had ever seen, and how he'd love to touch my beautiful skin. He touched me; his hand was trembling. I was totally confused, because I couldn't figure out why he wanted to touch me. Nobody I knew wanted to have anything to do with me, and here was this guy, acting like he was in some kind of an ecstasy, touching me. I got even more confused when he pulled my underpants down. I just didn't know what to do. I wasn't sure if that was okay, or maybe he was doing something bad. Now he started to go really crazy. He touched my cunt and kept whispering how beautiful I was. Beautiful! I was this skinny, ugly little girl, I thought; why does he think I'm so beautiful? He kept stroking me, and I began to get the feeling something wasn't quite right here. I pulled up my pants, put my dress back on, and ran out of there. I told the woman who was my foster mother, but she told me to shut up the minute I mentioned what he had done to me. I also told other people, but nobody believed me. You know, he was this nice old guy, and here's this little brat, the little foster brat, telling this story on him. Who was going to believe that? I stayed away from him after that, though."

"That's a terrible thing to happen," I said sympathetically. "Then it's even worse when nobody believes you."

"Yeah," said Norma Jean, "but you see, that's not the really strange part. You know what it was? The really strange part was that I *liked* it in some ways. What I found out for the first time was that somebody would really pay attention to me if I did one thing: take my clothes off. Also, when I took my clothes off, I had this power, you know, real power. And it was so goddamn easy! Stand there without anything on, and they'll do just about anything. That's what I liked, that feeling of power I had. It was a *thrill,* I'm telling you."

Norma Jean had a habit of long monologues that amounted to self-psychoanalysis. She would go on and on about her childhood, the search for her father, her mother's mental illnesses, and all the rest of it. If I hadn't been in love with her, I would have been bored. But I hung on every word, weeping when she wept, feeling the pain when she felt pain. I adored her, and in the moment of her greatest vulnerability, when she felt that no one loved her or would ever care for her, I would take her in my arms and vow to take care of her forever.

In a sense, of course, we were living out some kind of storybook fantasy straight out of a Hollywood script. It had occurred to me, in fact, that the story of how Norma Jean's mother, Gladys, had traveled to Kentucky and then turned her back on her children was like a perfect reprise of that great Hollywood tearjerker, *Stella Dallas.* Fleetingly the thought crossed my mind: was it possible that Mrs. Baker, the woman steeped in the fantasies of Hollywood, had simply taken that script and grafted it onto her own life?

Maybe, I thought, the real story of her marriage to Baker and what happened subsequently to her two children was somewhat more prosaic than the version she gave Norma Jean. Maybe, just maybe, she had told a story to Norma Jean—herself a real child of Hollywood—that in terms of the silver screen, was much more exciting and heartrending than the grubby little drama her life represented.

I didn't spend much time thinking about it, for I tended to be preoccupied with Norma Jean. In those days, for people in love, Hollywood was a wonderful place. Aside from the nightlife, there were all those wonderful beaches—then largely uncrowded. There were plenty of beautiful stretches of sand and surf in which two lovers could be practically alone. And on a deserted stretch of beach, with the gorgeous weather, gentle breezes and sound of surf, you could forget you ever had a care in the world.

Norma Jean was not much of a swimmer (in fact, she hardly went into the water), but spent her time at the beach discussing her life, her hopes for the future, and citing passages of poetry to uncaring gulls. At such moments she would forget that she was married to a merchant seaman away at war, that she was pursued by the terrible ghosts of her past, and that her dream of becoming an actress was very far away. Time was suspended; we floated in some sort of soft cocoon into which the outside world hardly ever intruded.

But sometimes it did. And when that happened, I was reminded, again, that this bewitching child-woman still had more secrets to reveal.

"Eddie, you know I've been promiscuous," she suddenly said one afternoon while we were at the beach.

That was a heavy word in those days, the kind of word people nearly whispered, like *cancer* is today.

"What does that mean?" I answered, not quite certain what she was referring to.

"You know, other men."

"So?" Given her sexual maturity, I assumed she had slept with other men before me. It did not especially bother me.

"Eddie, you know I don't have much money," she said, the little nervous twitches beginning. "You can't make it without money, you know that. You know what acting lessons cost, what modeling lessons run. And you know, I have to pay my Aunt Grace room and board."

"She's not your goddamn aunt," I said irritably. "She's your goddamn foster parent." I was beginning to understand.

"Don't get mad, Eddie," she said, in a little-girl voice. "I'm just trying to tell you about me. You remember when I said that if you found out about me, maybe you wouldn't want me? Okay, now I'm telling you everything."

I was staring at her. "What does 'everything' mean?"

"I want you to try and understand this, Eddie. You know, there have been times when I didn't even have enough money for makeup; do you know how expensive that stuff is? And then there's clothes. How am I supposed to be a model if I don't have the right clothes? Then there are the lessons. Eddie, I can't make it on a government allotment check, believe me." She gazed for a few moments out toward the ocean.

"Sometimes," she said, after what seemed to be a long time, "men help me out. You know, a little money to get things I need, Eddie: some makeup, new shoes, a dress. The stuff I can't really afford. Are you listening, Eddie?"

"Yes." It seemed as though everything had suddenly gotten very still.

"I've been lonely, Eddie," she said. "You don't know how lonely. At least until I met you. But before then, you know, I was just another wife of a man away in the service. I wanted so desperately to be around people. So I would go out at night, to all the places around Hollywood. Just to have a drink and talk to people. Men liked to talk to me. They wanted to help me, Eddie. So I've gone to bed with a lot of them. I've always been careful, Eddie. I always make them put on a condom. I never let a guy fuck me without one. Gee, they're so grateful. They get so excited, Eddie, when I just take my dress off. They're nice men; they always compliment me and treat me nice. And they help out."

For a while I said nothing. "Norma Jean," I said after a while, "you can't live like that. I don't want you to live like that."

And in my mind, a great romantic idea began to take hold. I would marry Norma Jean, this troubled young woman. I would make everything better. I would support her in lavish style when my acting career blossomed. Somehow I would get her anything she wanted—especially that little white piano she mentioned often when discussing her mother. It had been in an apartment they both shared when Mrs. Baker was feeling well. Norma Jean remembered that piano; she dreamed of finding it again and making it the centerpiece of the home she never really had.

I held Norma Jean close. "It'll all be all right," I told her. "Just stay with me. Don't worry about anything, Norma Jean. I'll find that piano, guarantee you. And then everything will be fine. I'll be yours forever. My family will be your family. It will all work out."

At that moment I believed that love conquered all, even the mess that was Norma Jean's life. What a fool I was.

Chapter four

★

END OF THE GOLDEN TIME

It seems hard to believe today, but the Hollywood (and California) of those war years had a lot of the atmosphere you'd find in a typical small American town.

In retrospect the time seems almost hushed. With the exception of the areas immediately around the nightspots, Hollywood itself had a sort of languorous quiet about it. Many people strolled around the streets at night, taking in the wonderful smell of those jasmine blossoms and the slightly cool breezes that began just after the sun went down. In those presmog days, the air, especially at night, had a distinct smell about it, something like what you smell in the less-populated areas of Hawaii today.

For a boy and girl in love, the atmosphere made everything seem like a fairy tale. In those days there was very little traffic around Hollywood, and if you did have a car, you simply pulled over to park on any street. There were no parking meters. Even on Hollywood Boulevard, I would park right near any club I wanted, at any time of the day or night. Also, there were no freeways: if you had enough gas despite the rationing (or used a form of kerosene, like

I did), you could tool around all over California and see its natural beauty before parking lots, highways, and shopping centers paved over all of it.

Traffic jams were virtually unknown. Trips that today take forty-five minutes in the smog back then took less than five minutes. For a modest expenditure of gas, a boy and girl could head for an uncrowded beach someplace—or even head over to then-underpopulated Palm Springs. Like the other couples in love, Norma Jean and I often would drive out toward the ocean, pull the car up to the beach, and just walk down toward the water.

Life then had a wonderful simplicity about it. Living in this magic kingdom seemed a universe unto itself, and we paid hardly any attention to the bigger world out there someplace. Nor was the fact that we didn't have a lot of money of much consequence: a day at the beach cost nothing, and a meal in an unfancy restaurant was only a few dollars. It cost a quarter to see a movie.

We did not wonder then why that whole section of California was slowly being invaded by people. Most of them were soldiers and sailors who passed through on their way to war and were astounded by what they saw in a land of beautiful weather, no pressure, quiet, and apparently unbounded opportunity. We saw them coming, snatching up the homes that in those days, even in Beverly Hills, sold for eight thousand dollars.

We had no idea, of course, that this early invasion would someday lead to a horde that would transform all of California forever. For the aspiring actors and actresses, our concerns were more narrowly focused: how and when would we get our big break, the coveted studio contract that would open the gates to the careers of fame and riches we were sure beckoned just beyond the next horizon.

In our idylls around southern California, Norma Jean and I spent much of our time discussing our future in the movies. She talked almost nonstop about her ambition to become an actress and often recited verbatim entire monologues she had remembered from all those movies she had seen.

I cannot say I was much impressed, for even my limited training thus far in acting school convinced me that this girl had no real chance of ever becoming an actress. It was not simply all those nervous mannerisms she had. She also had, it seemed, no real sense of how to act, in the technical sense of the term. Then, too, there was that breathy, little-girl voice that could hardly be heard unless you were quite close to her.

Of course, I didn't tell her any of that. Madly in love, I was not about to tell the most captivating creature in the world that she had no hope of achieving the ambition that seemed to dominate her thinking. I admired her little speeches, showed the proper adoration when she demonstrated how she would move in a particular scene, and generally abetted what I thought was her harmless little fantasy. Everybody knew about the small armies of girls who came to Hollywood with stars in their eyes, eventually found out they had no real talent, and later went back to whatever small town had spawned them, there to nurse for many years the bitter pain of failure.

I assumed that Norma Jean would eventually forget her little dream. She would discover, I was certain, that she simply did not have the stuff of an actress. Then this beautiful creature would settle down with me. She would become my wife in the traditional sense of the term, lovingly waiting at home for me as I pursued my own acting career. Each day I would head for the studio, putting in my hours on whatever picture was in production, then return home to some sort of rose-covered cottage, where I would spend hours with her, passing on the latest studio gossip and relating the adventures of moviemaking.

Most important, I thought, she would give up her night crawling, the hours she spent in the clubs and bars, picking up various men, the guys who gave her a few bucks to help her pay for the acting and modeling lessons. She would also give up the string of jobs she occasionally took, the kind girls with eighth-grade educations were stuck with: waitress, sales clerk, and even one in an aircraft factory.

It was a youth's fantasy, of course, and although Norma Jean liked what I was saying, she was noticeably reticent whenever I mentioned the word *marriage*. She had already announced her intention of divorcing Jim Dougherty, so that was not the problem. What was it, then?

"That's something that has to be talked about—a lot," she said one day as we relaxed atop a cliff overlooking one of the beaches north of Los Angeles. We were discussing the future, and I had just finished fantasizing to her on how we would spend the first $100,000 (an incredible sum then) I earned.

"Okay, so we're talking about it," I replied, with what I took to be irrefutable logic.

"Well, it has to be thought about a lot, too," she said. She began making those little nervous movements with her mouth.

I tried to pursue the subject, but she kept changing it, making it clear that she did not want to talk about marriage any further. Not that day, in any event.

I assumed that her aversion to marriage might be related to the horrible example set in her own family. I couldn't really blame her, but another of those odd inspirations struck me: why not show her what a *real* family looked like? Why not prove to her that not all families were as screwed up as hers?

"Listen," I told her, "how about if we take a little trip? I haven't seen my folks for a while. We'll go out to Ohio, spend some time there, and I'll show you where I grew up. You'll really like it there. Wait'll you meet my mother." (My father, having finished his work in California, had returned to Ohio.)

Norma Jean was initially hesitant, which had to do, at least partially, with the fact that the farthest she had ever been from Hollywood was a childhood trip to Catalina Island. To her, the rest of the world was some huge, forbidding unknown out there. But the more I told her about my hometown and my family, the more she seemed to like the idea. On a cool day in October 1944, we set out on a two-week trip east.

When I picked her up, she had only a hatbox and an old pillow case stuffed with clothes, a pretty good indication of just how poor she was: she didn't even have a suitcase to her name. But I was hardly wealthy either, and after throwing her stuff in the rumble seat of my old Ford, we set off on Route 66, the car wheezing and puffing like an old athlete out of breath.

Laughing and giggling, we headed across the desert. Armed with a large waterbag—in those days, you could drive 150 miles or more without seeing a service station—we drove with the top down, the night air of the desert blowing our hair. The car held up fine until Gallup, New Mexico, where a broken fan belt and blown head gasket held us up for a day and a half pending repairs.

With my already small treasury now further depleted by the costs of repair, we set off again, spending most of the driving time talking about my family and hometown. Norma Jean seemed increasingly fascinated, for as I talked about my parents, my brother, and assorted other family members—all of them part of a very normal extended family that shared each other's joys and sorrows—I realized that I was discussing an alien world. Norma Jean had never heard of such a thing as a normal family and was astonished to hear about such things as family reunions. Each night, as we prepared to sleep in parks along the way—we did not have enough money for such things as motels—she pestered me with dozens of questions about my family and for details about how it had been growing up. Each detail, perfectly ordinary-seeming to me, left her in astonishment that anyone could have such a normal upbringing.

She was further astonished when, after reaching my parents' home in Dayton, my mother immediately welcomed Norma Jean into the family, just as though she had been there all along. While Norma Jean sat in the kitchen, positively bowled over by all this, my mother whipped up a huge batch of homemade spaghetti as she talked of her life. To Norma Jean's delight, my mother related how she had been brought up in foster homes, how she never felt truly a part of any family with which she had lived, and the way she had felt as a little girl—all of it very familiar to the Hollywood waif, who now hung on her every word.

My father was not nearly so outgoing. He not only disapproved of my life-style ("the wandering chicken," he called me), he also made it clear he did not think it was quite proper for Norma Jean and me to be traveling together. Fortunately, he did not know that it was much worse: Norma Jean just happened to be legally married to someone else at the time.

We spent the night at my parents' home, carefully occupying separate bedrooms (I would sneak into hers at night), and the next day, set out for Lancaster, where the annual county fair was under way. I showed Norma Jean the house in which I grew up, just across the street from the fairgrounds, and related how, after nightfall, I and other youngsters would sneak into the fairgrounds, climb to the top of the highest tent, then slide all the way to the bottom. Then we would pick up pieces of dried and flattened cow dung and sail them as far as we could—the ancestor of the modern Frisbee.

Norma Jean was enchanted by the Lancaster Fair. One of the largest such events in the state, it had a fairground, a half-mile racetrack, and underneath the grandstands were displays by various businesses. Elsewhere on the grounds, church groups had food stands, including fish fries, one-foot-long hot dogs, homemade sauerkraut, and a local homemade specialty known as ice-cream candy.

"My mother used to make it for the fair," I told her, "and my brother and I would sell it, right here. We used to have quite a spiel going. Like this: 'Ice-cream candy, two for a nickel, five a dime, and twelve a quarter! It cleans your teeth, it curls your hair, it makes you feel like a millionaire! Step right up, folks, and get your ice-cream candy!' "

"Jesus," she said, giggling, "you really were a ham then, weren't you?"

She giggled some more, and it struck me that she had never looked so happy. All the nervous mannerisms were gone, as well as the occasional self-consciousness. She was totally relaxed now, acting like the eighteen-year-old teenager she really was. She continued to giggle, her face shining with glee, as we ate popcorn and fish sandwiches, went on all the rides, watched the sulky races, gazed in wonder at the horse-pulling contest, saw the livestock judging contests, snickered at the seriousness of the tasters trying to decide who had made the best homemade jelly, and generally had a rip-roaring time in what was just about the most perfect example of pure Americana around.

By the end of the day she was carrying around two dolls, a teddy bear, two canes, and a knife with a deerfoot handle—all won in various little games of chance. Happy but exhausted, we fell asleep in each other's arms that night. Before going to sleep, I whispered to her, "There's one thing more I want you to see here, Norma Jean. I want you to see my mountain."

"A mountain?" she asked in some alarm, imagining something out of the High Sierras she would have to scale.

"Well, it's not really a *high* mountain, you know, like they have in China, or something," I reassured her. "It's more like a high hill."

"Okay," she said, groggily. "But not *too* high."

*   *   *

Early the next morning, confronting the mountain, she seemed newly energized. "Let's go," she said, pointing to a path that led to the top. Huffing and puffing, it took about a half hour to reach the top. There, as she stopped and turned to see what was below, she let out a cry of delight.

"Oh, God, Eddie," she cried, gasping, "it's so beautiful!"

Below us stretched the Ohio River valley; the fair could be seen in miniature, with occasional sounds of screams from terrified riders on the cyclone ride reaching the summit. There was not a cloud in the sky. The weather, unusually warm for that time of year, was clean and crisp. The leaves were changing, and all around us there was a riot of colors—including Ohio's native buckeye tree, which Norma Jean had never seen. I made her a necklace of buckeyes, and we stood, arms around each other, as we gazed all around.

"Let me show you something special," I said, leading her down several ledges on the mountain, to one of the special places of my childhood. It was a deep crevice known as the Indian Kitchen, so-called because many years before, the local Indians lived there during the summer. On the crevice walls generations of Indians had chipped pictures of deer, raccoon, fish, and other animals they hunted.

"Wow," she said, as we entered the large crevice and sat where Indians had rested for who knew how many thousands of years. "Eddie, it's like a church."

Perhaps so, but we carried out a distinctly nonreligious ritual there: we made love, the sounds of passion echoing around the walls.

"Has anybody else, do you think, ever experienced the joy we now have?" she asked in that breathy voice. The words, of course, were somewhat pretentious, but even the fanciest language tended to turn out fresh and innocent when filtered through her little-girl way of speaking.

"Sure as heck no," I replied. She made a face; she was, I suddenly realized, in one of her poetry moods, those moments of greatest intimacy when her mind would soar up into the clouds someplace. In many ways she was a true romantic.

"How about a poem?" she asked. Both of us were very fond of poetry, and as the relationship grew, we had taken to reciting parts of favorite poems. To my surprise, she had memorized a fairly wide repertoire.

"Which one?" I replied, aware that she liked particular poems, depending on the subtlety of her mood of the moment.

For a while she sat silently, thinking. "The one about the Indians," she said finally. "You know, we're here, in the Indian hunting grounds. We might as well recite some poetry in their honor."

The poem, an old Indian one, was known to me only by its majestic words:

> *Oh Father, Whose voice I hear in the winds*
> *and Whose breath gives life to all the world,*
> *hear me!*
> *Hear me now*
> *I am a man before You, one of Your many, many*
> *children*
> *I am small, and at times very weak.*
> *I need your strength and your wisdom.*
> *Let me walk in beauty,*
> *let my eyes ever behold the red and purple sunsets.*

Norma Jean was lying on the ground, very still, as

I recited the lines. She seemed to be hardly breathing. I continued reciting:

Make me ever ready to come to You with clean hands,
a pure heart, and a straight eye,
so that when life fades as the setting sun,
my spirit may come to You without shame.

At the end we both sat silently for a while. "It's such a beautiful thing," she said. "What's it about?"

"It's an Indian chief, and he's dying. Those are the words he addresses to the Great Spirit."

"Well, that's really something," she said in a near-whisper. "Okay, now it's my turn. You know, my two favorite poets are Robert Service and Carl Sandburg. You know their stuff?"

"Sure, they're great."

She frowned. "Well, they're not really appropriate right now. We need something else. A love poem, a real love poem. Oh, I know. Listen, do you know the one about the Indian lovers? I don't remember the title, but it starts out *'Whether I drifted your way . . .'* "

"Jesus!" I yelled, startling her. "Listen, Norma Jean, that's my all-time-favorite poem! It's called 'The Teak Forest,' and it's from ancient India."

"Who wrote it?"

"Nobody knows; it's been around for a thousand years. Let's recite it together."

And so, as the autumn wind rustled the trees around us, we begin reciting that ancient poem. To anyone walking by at that moment, we must have sounded mad as March hares: two teenage lovers, oblivious of everything around them, reciting in unison on that mountain deep in the American heartland:

> Whether I drifted down your way
> In the endless River of Chance and Change,
> And you woke the strange,
> Unknown longings that have no names,
> But burn us all in their hidden flames,
>   Who shall say?

We went on, reciting all its stanzas, including the one that made her weep; her favorite of all of them, she would remember it for many years to come:

> You are wise; you take what the Gods have sent.
> You ask no question, but rest content
> So I am with you to take your kiss,
> And perhaps I value you more for this.
> For this is Wisdom; to love, to live,
> To take what Fate, or the Gods, may give,
> To ask no question, to make no prayer,
> To kiss the lips and caress the hair,
> Speed passion's ebb as you greet its flow—
> To have—to hold—and—in time,—let go!

Twilight had fallen now. Below us, we could hear the faint sounds of the carousel in the fairgrounds.

"I think we have to go back," I said.

"Not yet," she said, almost as if she were in a dream. She lifted her arms toward the sky, red with the setting sun. "You see, you can almost touch it. You can almost touch the face of God."

The wind had increased; her hair was blowing behind her. "We have to leave our mark," she said. "Let's carve our initials."

With my pocket knife, I carved "E. F." on a tree. She took the knife and carved "N. J." right below them.

"See?" she said, her voice still almost all breath. "Now we're immortalized." She looked toward the sky again. "Eddie, wouldn't it be wonderful if there is life after death? How simply beautiful it would be to spend forever—an eternity—here? Forever and ever."

I suddenly felt a terrible chill run through my body. Once again, more talk of death, the one central theme that seemed to dominate her most intimate thoughts.

"Norma Jean," I said, "it's getting real cold. Let's leave now. I led her back down the mountain. All the while, I could not remove the terrible sensation that up there I had heard the whisper of the wings of death move very close to her.

On the drive back toward Hollywood, I sensed her mood changing. She sat deep within herself. The closer we drew to home, the more her personality seemed to change. The nervous habits were back: the twitching, the little, quick movements of tongue around her lips. It was almost as if I was seeing the second half of her divided personality emerge.

"Things are gonna be great," I said brightly, trying to cheer her up. "Things will work out for us, I just know it. You know, Norma Jean, there's a good possibility I'll get my [Screen Actors] Guild card real soon. Then I'll get a contract. Think of it: years from now, you'll say, 'Hey, I knew Eddie Friedman when he was just a lifeguard at the pool, trying to break in.' " I intended it as a joke, but Norma Jean wasn't smiling.

"Fuck your card," she said.

"What?" I was so startled, I almost drove off the road.

"I said fuck your card, fuck you, fuck everybody!"

It was not so much what she was saying, but how she said it. The little-girl, breathy voice was gone; now she was speaking in something like a low growl. It was a totally different Norma Jean, almost as though there was a second person inside her. And the person speaking now was not the carefree, soul-troubled teenage girl, but a hardheaded bitch.

"Let me tell you something," she said in that growl. "I don't have a card, I don't have a contract, but I know there's only one way to get them. I'm going to be in the goddamn movies if I have to fuck Bela Lugosi to get there, you understand that?"

"Norma Jean, why are you talking like this?" I was alarmed; she was talking like a wild woman, consumed by ambition.

"Don't give me that shit," she snarled. "Listen, I know how things work: you either play, or there's no pay. I'll fuck anybody that can help me get what I want. I'm tired of being broke. I've got a body and I'm gonna use it! What's the big deal? Hell, I fucked plenty of those bastards that hang around the Ambassador. Most of the time when they gave me a little money, it was just enough to buy a little bit of makeup or take myself alone to a movie, or maybe buy a couple of cheap print dresses. I don't feel guilty about it; why should I? I told you once, Eddie: when you're broke, you're a joke. And if I'm lyin', I hope I'm dyin'."

"Norma Jean, you got it wrong, and—"

"Oh, bullshit!" She was in full stride now. "I'm gonna go all out, you understand? Why in hell couldn't I just as easily give myself to a producer or a director, or some bigshot agent who can do me some real good? That's the way girls get into pictures, be-lieve me. What do you think, girls get movie con-tracts because somebody respects their talent? Come on, Eddie, where have you been? I'll tell you how they get contracts: they fuck the right people. That's what I'm gonna do. You think I want to depend on little modeling jobs the rest of my life? Forget it!"

We hardly spoke to each other after that, and the next few days passed in virtual silence as the Ford chugged its way across the desert and into Califor-nia. We arrived in Los Angeles completely exhausted. Hardly bidding her goodbye, I dropped her off at her aunt's place, then headed for my own bed to sleep. "I'll call you later," I said, hardly meaning it.

I was just settling down when the phone rang. At the other end was a tearful Norma Jean. "I can't live like this anymore, Eddie," she said, weeping. "You have to understand that. Do you?"

"Yeah, sure," I said groggily.

"No, you don't really, Eddie. You don't really under-stand how I have to be near somebody, somebody I really care for and love, mentally and physically. Come over now, Eddie. Be near me."

"Jesus, Norma Jean, I have to get some sleep. I'm completely bushed."

"Eddie, I'm so upset, I can't sleep now. When you left me tonight, I felt you were mad at me. I said something that really upset you, didn't I?"

"Look, Norma Jean, let's talk about this tomorrow. You go to bed now, get some rest, and we'll both feel better tomorrow, guarantee it."

She began weeping loudly. "Oh, Jesus, I really screwed it all up, didn't I? I really upset you."

"Norma Jean, let's just get some rest, okay? I'm

not really upset. It's just ... well, maybe we should be away from each other for a few days."

On the other end there was silence. At last she said, "Okay, Eddie. Just don't abandon me now, okay?"

"I won't," I said, adding, in spite of my anger at her, "I love you very much." I heard her sigh as I hung up the phone.

While I drifted off to sleep, the strange double image of Norma Jean dominated my mind. One minute the laughing, beautiful teenager; the next, the cold and ambitious bitch.

Which one was the real Norma Jean Baker?

Chapter five

TIJUANA

Like all lovers' quarrels, the sudden estrangement between myself and Norma Jean did not last long. A few days after the phone call, we were back together, swearing undying love.

When we had the time, we liked to head over to Palm Springs, then a sleepy little desert town where the assorted denizens of Hollywood went to unwind. One morning Norma Jean called me and announced she had gotten a modeling assignment in Palm Springs. It would last a week. "Why don't you come over," she said, "and we can spend some time together? Just hop into that puddle-jumper of yours"—then came that distinctive giggle—"and get your ass over there."

I told her I had gotten a bit part in a movie—*Circumstantial Evidence,* a prison drama—and was appearing in a play at the Bard Theater during the evening, so it wouldn't be until the weekend that I could get away. "You have to come," she said, a sudden note of urgency in her voice. "There's something important I've got to tell you." She began to cry. "I don't know what's wrong, Eddie. I just feel funny. I feel light-headed and nauseated all the time.

You know what I'm scared of, Eddie: maybe I'm going nuts, like my mother."

"You're not going nuts," I soothed her. "You're just coming down with something, that's all. Don't assume you're going off your rocker every time you don't feel well, for Christ's sake."

"No, listen, Eddie," she said, "I feel like I'm coming unglued. I feel all foggy inside. You know, yesterday I fainted right beside the pool while they were taking some pictures. You have to come as soon as you can, Eddie; if you don't, I think I'll throw in the towel."

By now thoroughly alarmed at what I was hearing, I begged her to keep calm. "I'll be there bright and early Saturday morning," I told her. "Just relax and keep calm. Probably you're getting the flu or something." Meanwhile I was thinking: what the hell is wrong with her? She sounds like she's about to commit suicide.

After arriving in Palm Springs Saturday, I immediately called Norma Jean at the hotel room she was sharing with another model. "Oh, thank God you're here," she said, as though I was the Messiah. Within five minutes she was at my own hotel room.

She looked somewhat bedraggled, as though she hadn't slept for days. Her eyes were red-rimmed from crying. "Tell me what's the matter with you," I told her.

"I don't know," she replied, slumping into a chair. "All I know is that I miss you and I need to be near you. I need to talk to you. I'm so confused. I've been sick ever since I got down here and I can't seem to keep anything in my stomach."

"Don't worry," I said, soothingly, although a sudden thought crossed my mind: she sounds as though she has the early symptoms of pregnancy. The thought ignited a twinge of panic: we had never taken any real precautions. I quickly dismissed it, not even daring to think of the possibility.

After drinks and dinner we went back to my room, where I tried to calm her down. I had little luck, for she was a nervous wreck. Around 4:00 A.M., unable to sleep—she had recurring bouts of insomnia—Norma Jean became violently ill and began vomiting. I put warm towels on her forehead and the back of her neck, and she slowly began to come out of it. Somewhere around dawn she fell asleep, assuming, as I did, that her trouble stemmed from bad food or too many drinks.

Some hours later, in the brightness of a Palm Springs morning, she appeared to have recovered. I sat by the swimming pool as she and another unknown model named Anita Ekberg posed in bathing suits. While Ekberg had that same stunning voluptuousness, it was Norma Jean whom the men around the place ogled. Again, I was struck by her amazing power to captivate men.

Later that night, to my delight, everything seemed back to normal. We made love, swam in the pool, and later lay under the stars, reciting poetry. But it was getting late, and I had to return to work the next morning. I had no sooner mentioned the word *leaving* than she began to cry. "Don't worry about anything," I soothed her. "Everything's going to be fine." At that moment I actually believed it, for I had chosen to forget what Norma Jean had told me on the ride back to Hollywood and to forget the dangerous direction in which she was heading her life. I preferred to believe that nothing had really changed. When she returned to Los Angeles on Wednesday following the end of her modeling assignment, we would be back together again, just a pair of typical lovesick teenagers flitting around the Hollywood fairy-land like carefree butterflies.

Or so I thought. I turned out to be quite wrong.

A few days later I was working (in a bit part) on a film at Twentieth Century-Fox. During lunch in the studio commissary, I heard my name being paged for a telephone call. It was Norma Jean at the other end. This time she was hysterical, sobbing uncontrol-lably. I could hardly make out what she was saying, but did catch the word *baby*. Occasionally she used the phrase as an affectionate nickname for me, but this time, it gradually dawned on me, she was refer-ring to the real thing. She was calling to tell me she was pregnant.

Any man who's been in a similar situation knows exactly what I did: at first nothing; I simply stood there in shock, unable to grasp what she was saying to me. Then, the effort to think through the prob-lem rationally. What could be done? (Keep in mind this was now 1945, and in those days a single wom-an's pregnancy was no small matter.)

"Take it easy. Don't get excited," I said in what I hoped was my most rational and calm voice. "It's not the end of the world. We'll figure this thing out together. We'll meet tonight at the Haig, and we'll just talk the whole thing out. How's that?"

"Look, Eddie," she said, that low voice coming to the fore again, "I'm pregnant and we've got to do something about it. We've got to do something *fast*."

"All right, all right, Norma Jean," I said, trying to calm her down. "Just don't go haywire on this."

Great, I thought, hanging up the phone; stupid

moron Eddie Friedman does it again. He gets so carried away by this beautiful girl, he forgets all about such little details as birth control. Now all that sickness in Palm Springs makes sense. The question is, what do I do about it?

I thought of an answer as my puddle jumper chug-chugged toward the Haig that night. The pregnancy would provide the final connecting link in my great plan, the one that Norma Jean had never seemed too enthusiastic about: marriage. Surely, faced now with the prospect of having a child, she would agree that it was time to get married.

Not a bad plan—except that Norma Jean wanted no part of it. "No," she said firmly. "I've been through enough hell myself, why in the name of God should I bring more unhappiness into the world? Every woman wants to give birth to a *healthy* child and rightfully so, but in my case, Eddie, it's too much of a gamble. Don't you understand? You want me to give birth to a child who'll be mentally unbalanced! Ask anything of me, Eddie, but not that!"

She began weeping. I was weeping, too, and as we sat there at the Haig bar, the place of so many happy memories, we must have sounded like a soap opera. For hours we argued back and forth. I felt as though my guts were being laid out.

"Norma Jean," I insisted, "forget all this crazy talk about having a retarded child. Where the hell did you come up with such a crazy idea? Just because your mother has a mental problem, you think that guarantees her grandchild will be born mentally re-tarded? That's wrong."

I tried every argument I could think of, but noth-ing worked. "Our child," I said—laying the stress on *our*—"will be my pride and joy, but it will never stand in the way of our love for each other. Do you understand that, Norma Jean?"

"Sure, but—"

"I want us to have this baby. There's nothing to stop us from getting married. Let me tell you something: if you have an abortion, I would lose all self-respect, and in the end, so would you. You can't do that, Norma Jean. If you have an abortion, I'm telling you, the hurt that I would feel would turn me against you. Do you want that to happen?"

"Oh, Eddie, no," she replied, weeping. "I would never want that to happen. But don't you see, I can't have this baby!"

The gut-wrenching argument went on like this for what seemed to be hours. We were oblivious of our surroundings, of whoever might be listening, of what anyone thought of us. Finally the owner of the place came over to us and quietly asked us to leave because we were making a scene. We sure were, but I didn't care. I was determined that Norma Jean marry me and have that baby.

Outside we continued arguing. I grabbed her by the shoulders and, shaking her like a rag doll, begged her to have the baby.

"No!" she nearly screamed. "I won't give birth to an insane child!"

Finally we were out of tears. There was nothing else to be said; we had argued and reargued the same issue dozens of times, to no avail. She was going to have an abortion, and that was that. Without either of us saying a word to each other, I took her home.

If I had been thinking more clearly that night, I would have realized that Norma Jean's explanation of why she wanted to abort her baby was not completely true. The clue was right in front of me as we arrived at her home—not her aunt's house but the place to which she had moved after returning to Hollywood from our trip to Ohio.

It was called the Studio Club, a glorified rooming house that rented only to young women. Predominantly, they were aspiring actresses, beautiful young women living there because of its cheap rents and easy access to the Hollywood industry. They spent most of their time in the grind of acting school, part-time jobs, and studio auditions. Needless to say, they were all dominated by a consuming ambition to become movie stars. It was the perfect place for Norma Jean, perhaps the most ambition-consumed of all.

The Studio Club guarded its tenants from the depredations of Hollywood wolves by strict rules: men weren't allowed beyond the lobby. There, a "den mother" presided behind a large desk. If you were dating one of the girls, she would take your name, then call upstairs. Your date would come downstairs.

Privately, among Hollywood actors, the Studio Club was called the "Pussy Palace," because of the astonishing range of pulchritude that lived there. The tenants included Kim Novak, Shelly Winters, Denise Darcel, and Virginia Mayo, among others, and there was a steady parade of men into the lobby.

More important, the palace was a monument to ambition, packed with tough little cookies who quickly learned all the angles. They were single-minded, and in that atmosphere, I realized, Norma Jean's own full-fledged ambition was really flowering.

It was not until some years later that I learned the

real reason for Norma Jean's reluctance to have our baby. The answer was in the all-consuming ambition that covered the Studio Club like a coat of paint. A number of its tenants, I discovered, had decided to counsel Norma Jean on her pregnancy. Simply put, their advice was: don't do it. Your career, they told her, will be at an end the minute you have that baby. Studios, with their pick of the vast ocean of gorgeous female flesh in Hollywood, want nothing to do with starlets who are mothers. It wouldn't fit the starlet image the studios like to present. As Norma Jean later admitted to me, one of her friends at the Studio Club told her, "Shit, honey, there's nothing to it. I've had two abortions myself, and I'm telling you, you don't even know it's happening."

I did not know the real reason for Norma Jean's decision not to have our baby and took at face value her fear about giving birth to a mentally retarded child. Thus I was vulnerable, despite my anger at her (I had determined never to see her again), when she began to call me and tearfully ask me to help her get an abortion. She had no doctor, very little money, and didn't even know how to go about finding somebody who would do the actual abortion. In those days, of course, abortion was strictly illegal. Only rich people with the right contacts seemed to know where to go.

Thanks to a recent succession of bit-part jobs in the movies, I had some extra money and agreed to underwrite the one act that was against every fiber in my being: killing my own child. But, as had happened so often before, the powerful emotion that was my love for Norma Jean overrode everything else. The sight of her crying her eyes out, begging me to help her, was enough to move mountains.

Actually I had no idea of how to go about finding an abortionist, save to search out a friend of mine who worked as a lifeguard at State Beach. He always seemed to know the right buttons to push.

His place of work was quite a beach in those days. The State Beach was a local hangout for all the beach bums, would-be actors, starving models, and volleyball players. They just hung around, passing time by ogling the girls and working on their tans, preening themselves in the hope they might be noticed. The other half of the beach, on the south side, toward Catalina Island, was known as Closet Corral, the place where all the Hollywood homosexuals—including several big-name actors—would gather on weekends. They sunned themselves in little groups, like families of seals snuggled together.

"I got a girl pregnant," I told my friend, getting right to the point. "I need some advice. She doesn't want the baby. What can I do?"

He thought a moment. "I think I got just the guy you're looking for. In fact, he's right across the street." He pointed to a large pharmacy on the other side of the avenue that bordered the beach.

"You must be kidding," I said. "I need a doctor, not a druggist."

"Don't kid yourself," my friend said. "You stay right there; I'm going to go across the street and talk to him, and then I'll be right back."

Some minutes later he returned. "It's all set. He says he can help you. But you'd better keep your mouth shut: he doesn't want this all over State Beach. He has to uphold his image, and he's got a license he doesn't want to lose."

The pharmacist turned out to be a somewhat legendary figure in those parts, known only as "Doc

Law." He had come west, looking for gold, long before the motion picture industry got started, and when he didn't strike the mother lode, wound up running a drugstore that was something of an "in" place for the Hollywood *cognoscenti*. He looked very much like Colonel Sanders with the smell of Listerine about him. But behind that image of local character and friend to a galaxy of old Hollywood stars was a man who was quietly dispensing various illegal drugs and potions to his friends—at a very healthy profit.

Doc took me behind two draped curtains that separated his pharmacy from the rear end of the store. We sat down on a small divan, and he flourished a small bottle. "Look, son," he said, "you take this home tonight and give it to your girlfriend. Tell her to take it on an empty stomach. It might make her sick, but if that happens and she throws up, it's only natural. Don't get scared. Repeat the tonic for about three days and then come on back. Don't call me on the phone, though. That'll be twenty-five dollars."

In the stunning ignorance of biology that marked my generation during that era, I honestly thought I had been given some kind of magic elixir. So did Norma Jean. She studied the bottle of dark liquid thoughtfully. "Oh, Eddie," she said, "I'm awfully sorry I'm not going to have the baby, really I am."

"I know that," I said. "Look, Norma Jean, I don't think I can ever live this down. You know I want that child."

"Eddie, we've discussed all that," she said, tears welling up in her eyes. "Let's not talk about it anymore."

The following day she called me to announce that she had been sick all night and still felt lousy.

"Don't stop taking it," I told her. "The guy I got it

from says that's only natural." The next day it was the same story, and the same for days afterward. She began to get panicky: she was sick as a dog, but she was still pregnant.

"The stuff doesn't work," I told Doc Law. "All it did was make her sick and nothing happened. What am I gonna do? I need help *now!*"

"Lower your voice," Doc Law hissed, grabbing my hand and leading me into the back room. "Look, kid, I'm going to give you the name of a guy to see. It'll cost you two hundred fifty dollars—fifty for me and two hundred for the guy. He's across the border, in Tijuana. His name is Gomez. But first you've got to come up with the money; he doesn't take anything on credit, and neither do I. Just get the money and don't ask questions."

The sum of $250 in that year of 1945 represented a small fortune to me. But I scraped it together, and the next day Norma Jean waited in the car as I met Doc Law in the back of his pharmacy. I gave him the $50, and he handed over Gomez's address and phone number in Tijuana.

Those days, Tijuana was the center of a thriving illegal abortion racket, and more than one Hollywood starlet had availed herself of its services. Now it was Norma Jean's turn. We headed south and then across the border and down the main street of the city and into one of its filthier sections. I found Gomez's house. A knock on the door brought a fat, dirty man carrying a cat under one arm.

"Doc Law sent me," I said, repeating the previously agreed password. Gomez stared at me and then at Norma Jean. "Where's the money?" he said. I handed him the $200.

"Come in, *pronto*," he said, beginning a patter of

broken English. His house was a pigsty, a dark and dirty place with cats all over the place. The floor was littered with cat feces.

In the rear of what passed for a living room, there were two lights hanging from the ceiling, illuminating a tray with boiling water, some medical equipment, and an old barber's chair with stirrups.

I felt nauseous and prepared to leave, but Norma Jean looked at me. "It's okay, Eddie," she said. "Don't worry. Let's just get this over with."

"You go outside," Gomez ordered me. I went out the front door and sat down on a broken small couch on the porch. About a half hour later, I heard a groan and a sharp scream. I was about to rush back inside when Gomez appeared.

"Don't worry, *amigo,*" he said, "she is all right." Nearly an hour later, Norma Jean, looking deathly ill, slowly walked out. Gomez handed me a little container with some pills.

"Give her one of these every hour for the next two days," he instructed. "She's got some packing inside of her. Don't take that out for at least three days. And do me one favor, *amigo.* When you leave the premises here, just forget you ever knew me. Forget the name of Gomez. Do I make myself clear, *compadre*? Do you understand what I am telling you?"

I nodded and, as quickly as I could, got Norma Jean out of there. She was moaning softly and holding on to me tightly as we drove northward toward Los Angeles. "The dirty animal bastard!" she snarled in that alter-ego low voice of hers. "The goddamn filthy pig! Eddie, you know what he did? After you left the room, he put me in that barber chair and stuck my legs in those stirrups. Then he brings this old kerosene lamp over, sticks it on the table, and goes to work on me. I thought I was going to die, Eddie; sometimes the pain was just so bad! 'Please go easy,' I told him, 'it's very painful.' But he paid no attention, the butcher. Eddie, I'll never forget that face of his as long as I live. He kept looking up me from between my legs, saying to me, 'Be quiet, miss, and don't worry.' He had four black teeth in his mouth. He looked like something between Frankenstein and the Werewolf."

I felt sick to my stomach, more sick than I had ever felt in my life. I also felt a terrible emptiness and was too empty to talk. All the way home I listened as Norma Jean, snuggled against me and holding on tightly for dear life, carried on a nonstop monologue.

"You know something?" she said at one point. "I talked to quite a few girls who were in this kind of situation, and they tell me that most of the guys that got them this way deserted them. To tell you the truth, Eddie, I never thought you would stand by me to the end. I'll never forget this, Eddie.

"You know something else, Eddie? I want to go right on seeing you, no matter what happens, Eddie, because you proved yourself to me. You're not like the rest of those Hollywood jerks. You didn't run away when the chips were down."

I made no reply, for in addition to the terrible empty feeling inside me, my head was becoming confused. My God, I thought, what have you gotten yourself into with this girl? She's probably nutty as a bedbug, her life has been a mess, she's just gotten an abortion, she's done some hooking on the side, she hasn't got the talent to fulfill her ambition to become a movie star, and she seems about as totally lost as the fabled orphan of the storm.

But no matter how much I thought about her, I always came back to the one thing I could not shake loose: I loved her, more than I had ever loved anything in my life. I could no sooner stop seeing her than I could stop breathing.

After we reached the Studio Club in Los Angeles, we sat quietly in the car for a while, just holding each other. She began to cry again.

"I hope this doesn't mean you'll stop loving me," she said. "Just because we lost a baby doesn't mean we have to lose each other."

"No, it doesn't," I replied, without too much conviction. The truth was that I wasn't sure anymore. Above all, I wasn't sure I could hold on to her; she was torn by so many conflicting passions, who could? And now between us loomed the memory of a dead baby. I could not remove from my mind the thought that I had killed it, just as surely as if I had held a gun to the baby's head and pulled the trigger.

"Well, there's always tomorrow," she said, with a deep sigh as we unclinched and she prepared to go inside the Studio Club.

Somewhere nearby a mockingbird trilled in the cool night.

Chapter six

UNCLE TED

Wounds heal quickly in youth, and only a few weeks after the abortion, Norma Jean and I were again two happy youngsters deeply in love. And, like all youths in love, we tended not to think very clearly or deeply about some of the curious aspects of our relationship.

Most of all, I didn't devote much further thought to the distinctly odd person known as Norma Jean Baker. It was no longer Dougherty, for she had divorced her merchant seaman husband. I was momentarily shocked when she casually announced that she had made this move by simply writing him a letter. But, as had happened so often before, the momentary shock passed. Again, I was so totally captivated, little she did or said affected the depth of what I felt for her.

The war was now over, and I was making nearly $250 a week—I considered that a major fortune—in bit parts on various pictures. I could support a moderately frivolous life-style, and we spent every spare minute we could (mostly weekends) together. We were like frolicking children, flitting around wherever the mood took us: a day at the beach, a jaunt over to Palm Springs, a quick trip across the border to Mexico. Occasionally we even had a mansion to ourselves. It was called the Ocean House, a seashore palace built by William Randolph Hearst for his girlfriend, Marion Davies, in Santa Monica. Later she converted it into a fancy restaurant and private swimming club. Thanks to another lifeguard friend of mine who worked there, Norma Jean and I had free run of the place when no one was around. It was a palace for lovers, with Davies's own huge canopied bed available for use, spectacular views of the ocean, a gargantuan swimming pool in black marble, walk-in fireplaces, and a well-stocked supply of champagne.

In this mood, free of any thought of the past or future, almost nothing of the real world impacted on me, not even the little bombshells Norma Jean occasionally dropped in my lap: more insights into her bizarre past. There was the night, for example, that she insisted that I accompany her to Van Nuys.

"What for?" I asked.

"A revival meeting," she replied. "You'll love it."

"A revival meeting? What are you, some kind of religious fanatic?"

"Hardly, Eddie. But a lot of my mother's relatives are; when I was little, they used to take me to those things all the time. It was quite a trip, let me tell you."

The revival meeting that night was, in fact, quite a show, with all the Bible-thumping shouts of "hallelujah!" and general carryings-on you'd expect at such things. As a mere observer, I found the whole thing ridiculous, although, as Norma Jean pointed out to me, several of her real aunts who were there seemed to be undergoing some sort of deep religious experience. As for Norma Jean, I wasn't quite sure how she was reacting, although when I asked her what she thought of it all, she said, "Oh, great stuff, Eddie. Didn't you know? I'm a Holy Roller!"

She giggled, and I couldn't be sure if she was serious or not. Her aunts sure as heck were: formidable-looking ladies, they had the aura of true fanatics.

There was one lady in particular who stood out. She moved with the grim determination of a Sherman tank, although she seemed to soften when she spoke to Norma Jean. "I wouldn't want to cross her," I whispered to Norma Jean, who frowned.

"Actually, she's not my real aunt," she said. "She was one of my foster mothers. One of the real interesting ones, too."

I sensed I was about to hear still another revelation from Norma Jean's past, and sure enough, it was a shocker. It turned out that the foster mother was a lesbian. When Norma Jean was six years old, the woman seduced her and, over the next eight years, introduced her to the pleasures of lesbian lovemaking. "At first," Norma Jean said in that casual air she had when discussing sex, "I was, you know, a little scared. But I grew to really like it. She'd come into my room all the time and play with my clitoris. It sure felt good."

I did not know it at the time, but the experience was partly responsible for an extraordinary aspect of Norma Jean's personality: she was in fact omnisexual. In other words she enjoyed sex in every possible dimension and combination, including with other women. Indeed, she had sex anytime she felt like it, with just about anybody who asked her, women included. At the Studio Club, where I picked her up for our dates, she was involved in an intense relationship with an aspiring actress who later became quite famous. (She is still alive, so I cannot mention her name.) And years later, when she became very famous, a few people around Hollywood were aware of the fact that Norma Jean also had intense sexual relationships with women. Elizabeth Taylor, among others, knew the secret and one day, while discussing Norma Jean, suddenly blurted out, "That goddamn dyke!" Studio officials also knew the secret and lived in constant dread that it would get out somehow. The effect those days could hardly be imagined: the greatest sex goddess of all time, revealed to be a lesbian!

The only cloud hanging over the relationship between Norma Jean and me was our professional careers. I should say *career* singular, for while I was just beginning to break into the movies, Norma Jean was going nowhere. She was still modeling, but despite her best efforts, she was no nearer toward getting her foot in the studio door than she had ever been. On the other hand, I not only had (at last!) a Guild card but I was getting bit parts in quite a few movies. Clearly I was on the way up, and there was talk I would soon be offered a studio contract.

Despite her best efforts to hide it, I detected a clear resentment when she learned that I had gotten a Guild card. She was properly congratulatory, but there was an edge to her words, almost as if she was jealous. As I realized, the fact that I had gotten the card sharpened her own ambition to an even keener edge. She was now more determined than ever to "make it."

"Here's the way I figure it," she said. "If I'm supposed to be that beautiful, why can't I be an actress?

If all these men admire me, why can't they let the public admire me, too?"

I found myself the target of endless pumping by her: how had I gotten the Guild card? Who did I know? What contacts did I use? What strings did I pull? How could she do the same thing? Through all these interrogations, of course, ran not only the thread of her overweening ambition but one of her most prominent character traits: she was lazy and did not want to hear any lectures from me (or anybody else) about the necessity of acting school, constant practice, and a long apprenticeship. She remained firmly convinced that all actresses got their contracts by the simple expedient of screwing the casting director or the head of the studio.

She was right only to a very limited extent. True, there were actresses who had won contracts via the casting couch—even some pretty famous ones—but in the aggregate, there was no substitute for hard work. Norma Jean did not like hard work.

I made every effort to help her, including rehearsing lines and scenes, along with suggestions on how I thought she might be able to break in. I even volunteered to take some of her first real "portfolio" photographs—the sheaf of glamor pictures required of all aspiring actresses as they made their rounds of studios and acting schools. The pictures weren't that good by professional standards, but I was pretty proud of them. Norma Jean, however, was nearly beside herself.

"Oh, I look so *ugly!*" she wailed as she leafed through the photos. She began a recitation of the faults she now thought so glaringly exposed: a noticeable bump on the end of her nose, a weak jawline, a seed mole on her face, mousy hair. She was even more upset when she got her first look at several nude photographs I had taken of her.

"Awful, awful!" she complained. "My God, will you just look at that ass! Oh, Eddie, my ass is much too big!" She threw the pictures aside. "Christ, I'll never make it; I'm so goddamn ugly, it's not even funny. No wonder I can't get a studio contract."

I was astounded. Convinced that she was one of the most beautiful women who had ever lived, I could not understand why she thought herself ugly. Ugly? With that face? With that body? No matter how much I tried to reassure her, she remained convinced that she was practically a hag.

That conviction, combined with her innate laziness, induced in her a dangerous way of thinking. Increasingly she became certain that the only route to her dream of becoming a movie actress was through what she called "the right button." In other words, she would need a key contact, a powerful patron, to smooth the way.

Norma Jean was perfectly aware that my uncle, Ted Lewis, had helped me out. I might have gotten my Screen Actors Guild card on my own eventually, but I had to admit that his phone call to a friend, the writer and producer Damon Runyon, certainly helped. And with Runyon behind me, obtaining a Guild card was that much easier.

Still, I felt I had paid my dues to get to that point, considering all those hours of acting school and bit-part work. Norma Jean, however, saw the process as one-dimensional: Uncle Ted had picked up a telephone, and that was that. We had seen Ted's show a few times, but she never realized the clout he had in the entertainment industry, including the movie business. And it was the kind of clout Norma Jean wanted for herself. I began to feel strong pressure from her: she wanted to see Ted's show again, the next time he was in town—and this time, she wanted to go backstage and meet him personally.

Enraptured, as usual, I failed to detect a new, urgent edge to that demand. I had even less idea that the encounter between my uncle and the bewitching creature named Norma Jean Baker would have astonishing consequences.

To succeeding generations, the name of Ted Lewis has faded into obscurity. But in the 1940s, he was "Mr. Entertainment," probably the most famous figure in all of show business. Born of Hungarian-Jewish immigrants just before the beginning of this century, Ted grew up in Ohio, where he had many black boys as friends. Those friendships were important, for Ted, a clarinetist, began to pick up the new music played by black musicians among themselves. It was called jazz, and Ted formed a band to play the new music for white audiences.

It was during this period that he acquired several distinctive trademarks. One was the line, "Is *everybody* happy?" Another was his battered black top hat, acquired one night in a crap game with a taxi driver in Harlem. He also became known for his "Me and My Shadow" routine, performed with a black entertainer. The act caused some problems, for there were many white audiences who didn't want to see black performers. Often, white people in the audience would throw knives (or anything else handy) and drive them off the stage.

But by the late 1930s Ted Lewis, with his clarinet and distinctive style of old favorites, was among the hottest acts in show business. He dominated the supper-club circuit, and the years of work on his act resulted in a performance that was a minor masterpiece, with all the right touches of humor, nostalgia, and pacing. He had long ago abandoned his real name of Friedman ("Lewis" was picked up from another jazz musician with whom he once played).

Ted, of course, was the star of my family, and that represented something of a problem to me. I had always determined to make it on my own and resolved never to approach Ted for any kind of handout or special favor. When I first started working in Hollywood, I once went to see him backstage at a theater where he was appearing. The encounter was pleasant enough—he had a particular fondness for me—but I became aware that he had ostentatiously put a fat wad of cash on the dressing table. As a struggling actor, uncertain whether I might make it through the month, I couldn't avoid staring at that pile of money. But I was also aware that Ted wanted me to make a move, to ask him for a handout. To underscore it, he began hinting of how tough it was in the beginning of any show business career. Then he glanced at the money, but I didn't rise to the bait.

Ted was funny about money. He liked to spread money around, as generously as possible. Partly he did it because he was generous, but he also liked the subtle form of control it represented. Any recipient of a handout—especially a large one—knows what eternal gratitude means. (Ted could also be stupid about money, though: a lifelong gambling addict, he dropped $80,000 one night in Las Vegas, moving his wife Adah to put him on an allowance of $350 a week.)

Ted was determined to help my career, and I had to fend off his efforts delicately. Still, at the time when I was desperately trying to get my Guild card, I didn't resist too strongly when he called his friend Damon Runyon and told him I was something just short of Clark Gable. Runyon dutifully put me in a picture called *A Wing and a Prayer* at Fox, and I was off and running.

However thrilled I was, Norma Jean displayed something less than total joy, as though she was jealous. That thought crossed my mind, but then was immediately dismissed; I was so happy about finally getting my foot in the studio door, I wasn't paying too much attention to her reaction at the news.

Ted Lewis was scheduled back in town, and Norma Jean made it clear that we would go and that I would take her backstage to meet him. At the time I couldn't quite understand why she was so eager to meet the master entertainer, since her star worship seemed to be concentrated on movie stars.

We sat through both shows one night at Slapsy Maxie's as Ted played to a packed house. Afterward I took her backstage.

"Oh, Mr. Lewis, I've been just dying to meet you," Norma Jean said as I introduced her.

Ted, who had a well-practiced eye for nice female flesh, smiled broadly as he gave her the once-over. "Well, how are *you*," he said, nearly melting as Norma Jean flashed her best smile at him. He stared boldly at the tight white sweater she was wearing. Her breasts, without brassiere, jutted out like two magnificent pieces of sculpture.

I might just as well have been a piece of furniture there, for neither one of them paid much attention to me after that. Norma Jean concentrated her considerable powers on Ted, who seemed to act as though he were mesmerized. Later, he introduced Norma

Jean to two of his friends who were in attendance, Runyon and the powerful columnist Walter Winchell. Both men also seemed to be totally captivated, and I was reduced to the role of spectator in still another Norma Jean conquest.

From that perspective, it was interesting to watch Norma Jean in action. Aside from the physical attributes that turned any man's head, she also had the knack of projecting a little-girl routine, complete with that breathy, sugary voice. The effect on men was devastating, for the combination of luscious sexuality and vulnerable little girl was a killer.

Sometime later, on the way back home, I listened as she gushed about Uncle Ted, an exposition I found somewhat odd, since Ted, while the master showman, was no matinee idol. Indeed, he was at best a plain-looking man; why, then, all this talk about how "sexy" she found him?

The answer did not come until much, much later. It was then I learned that at one point in their little backstage meeting, Ted had slipped Norma Jean a piece of paper with his telephone number on it. Soon they were meeting in hotel rooms whenever Ted was in town. For Uncle Ted, who had enjoyed the favors of many a showgirl in his time, the experience apparently was unprecedented. Soon he was pulling strings for Norma Jean, trying to hook her up with an agent who would do her the most good.

That was why Uncle Ted was so "sexy." Above all, he was powerful, with the right contacts in the right places. As Norma Jean had vowed to me, whoever she had to fuck, she was prepared to do it. And, for good measure, she did the same to Walter Winchell. He also was "sexy," largely because of the considerable strings he could pull on her behalf.

Norma Jean, the beautiful Hollywood orphan, had taken the first big step on her way to the top.

At the time, I knew nothing of all this. Norma Jean and I saw each other mostly on weekends, since I devoted most of my time to my budding movie career. Runyon had ordered a change of name for me: Ted Jordan, the new name a combination of tribute to my uncle, whom Runyon greatly admired, and the name of a character he was writing into a script (it later became the movie *Here Comes Mr. Jordan*).

I had been working for about seven weeks when Norma Jean began to pester me: when would I take her to the studio? I explained that studios didn't exactly roll out the welcome mat for guests of bit players, the lowest rung in the Hollywood pecking order. She was undeterred, and the sheer force of her considerable power of persuasion—I always found it impossible to resist her when she really wanted something—finally made me give in.

One morning my old Ford chugged through the front gate of the Twentieth Century-Fox lot. In the closed rumble seat was Norma Jean, scrunched up into a ball. "Don't pop your head up until I give you the signal," I warned her.

At Stage Eight, where I was working, I stopped the car, knocked once on the closed seat, and, like Venus rising from the waters, Norma Jean emerged as the seat opened. "Wow, look at *this*," she said, almost beside herself with excitement as she looked around at the sprawling lot. It was a beehive of activity, with several different movies being shot at once. People in costumes representing every possible period of human history were scurrying to and fro.

She was wearing that tight, white angora sweater. It was slightly chilly, and I noticed her nipples stood out, like large fingers. My God, I thought, this girl is going to cause a riot.

She wandered around like a starstruck tourist, absorbing everything. When it was time for lunch, I announced that we would eat in the studio commissary. She nearly squealed with delight. "The commissary! Do all the stars eat there?" she gushed, sounding almost out of breath.

"Yeah, sure," I said, with a deliberate air of nonchalance, as though I was an old hand at the studio.

The commissary had a strict social code, pegged to the pecking order. One section of it, called the Green Room, was reserved for the really important people involved with production of the picture—producers, directors, and so on. The peons (in those days of the studio system, all the actors were virtual indentured servants) sat elsewhere.

I could almost hear dozens of sets of men's eyeballs click as Norma Jean walked into the place. As a low-ranking bit player, I was not on intimate terms with most of the people working on the picture. But this day an extraordinary transformation took place: as I sat down at one table to eat with Norma Jean, just about everybody suddenly became my friend and felt compelled to stop by and inquire about my health. Even Dana Andrews, the star of the picture and a man who hardly ever looked my way, mysteriously developed an interest in my opinions on the course of the shooting. I might have been impressed by all this sudden interest, except that none of these people appeared to look at me when they were speaking; instead, they fastened intense gazes on Norma Jean and her sweater.

In response, Norma Jean really turned it on. She brought every ounce of charm to bear on everyone who stopped by, and there were moments when I thought some of these guys would actually melt right before my eyes. And when she left the table at one point, there was not a man in the room who did not follow every move of what would later become the world's most famous walk. Like two gazelles in heat, I thought, as I watched that incredible rear end of hers perform a symphony of movement as she undulated across the room. I distinctly heard at least two men sigh, as if they were in some sort of reverie.

Of course, as I realized, Norma Jean was putting on quite a show. Having achieved the undivided attention of every man in the room, she really turned herself on to full power. In many ways it was among her greatest performances; every little movement was a carefully studied one by her, each little-girl giggle was precisely timed, each dazzling smile was properly targeted, each movement of her body was measured to create the maximum possible visibility to her breasts. It was a preview of things to come, only I didn't know it yet; so far as I was concerned, it was just the voluptuous Norma Jean showing off.

She did not go unnoticed at the top roost in the Green Room. I heard Damon Runyon calling me, and as I approached him, I saw him staring at Norma Jean with a slight half-smile. Runyon politely inquired how I was doing, then murmured, "By the way, Ted, I must say you have very good taste in women. Who is that girl? She looks vaguely familiar."

I reminded him that he had seen her not too long before, backstage at Uncle Ted's show. He looked at me kind of funny. "Ah, yes, Uncle Ted," he said, almost absently. "Well, be sure to convey my regards to her."

There was an odd note in Runyon's conversation, but I couldn't quite put my finger on it. Later, when work was finished for the day, I chugged back out of the studio, with Norma Jean again hidden in the rumble seat. Outside the studio I retrieved her and we began heading for the Studio Club.

"What a place!" she gushed, and went on gushing about the fantastic things she had seen, the stars she had spotted, how everybody was so nice to her (except, I noted to myself, the women there, who just glared at her while the men made fools of themselves). While she was gushing on and on—"Oh, Eddie, that's where I want to be, that's what I want to do!"—I sat silent, thinking. Finally I asked her.

"Norma Jean, have you been seeing my uncle Ted?"

She bit her lip. "Sure, I have. What's wrong with that?"

"Look, he's already married, and to my aunt."

"So what? I didn't force him into anything."

"Norma Jean, he could be your father, for Christ's sake. I mean, what the hell's going through your head to get mixed up with him? Guys like him, they go after the young girls all the time; that's the way it is in show business. You know what he wants from you."

She bit her lip again. "You're making a big deal of this, Eddie, and it isn't. He's a real nice guy, and he wants to help me."

"Oh, now I get it. He's the shortcut, in other words."

"Don't be so goddamn jealous," she said, her voice dropping low. "Look, I told you before, if somebody can help me, I'm not going to pass up the opportunity. What should I say to him? Gee, no thanks, Mr. Lewis, for trying to help me. No, I'll just stay in my nothing little modeling job, and maybe if I wait long enough, I'll get to be a movie actress by the time I'm eighty years old. Sure."

"Okay, forget it." I was mad now, and she sought to dampen it by reverting to the old Norma Jean.

"Oh, come on, Eddie," she cooed, "you know we'll always be in love, no matter what happens, right? So let's make an agreement right now, right here: what I have to do for my career has nothing to do with us. I could give a fuck less for your uncle, but if he wants to help me out, I'm not going to say no. And if all he wants in return is for me to see him and be nice to him, I'm not about to say no. So we're agreed, right? Whatever you have to do to advance your career is perfectly okay with me, and whatever I have to do is perfectly okay with you. Deal?"

I looked at her; she was giving me that bright smile, those stunning blue eyes boring into me. "I guess so," I said, weakly.

Chapter seven

★

THE
LADY IN THE
CHAMPAGNE
GLASS

When I first started working in movies, Norma Jean would endlessly bombard me with questions about people at the studio. However, they weren't the kind of questions you'd expect from a starstruck model.

She was learning the ropes fast, and it showed in her questions. If I mentioned a particular star, she immediately wanted to know which agent represented him or her. What kind of deal had the agent managed to win for the star? What were the details of the star's contract? How much maneuvering and backbiting went on between stars and supporting actors? How did the stars get on the right side of producers? How did actors and actresses win the favor of cameramen and lighting technicians, whose extra effort might mean the difference between a shot that showed its subject to best advantage and one that didn't?

And on and on it went. To her disappointment, I didn't know the answers to a lot of the questions. She would pout when I told her I really didn't know the intimate details, say, of Dana Andrews's contract—

and didn't particularly care, either. Nor did I care much about which agent was representing some of the reigning queens of the silver screen. I was having my own troubles, trying to make a splash in a very large pond filled with many struggling actors trying to achieve the same thing, and I just didn't have the time or energy to gather intelligence on all the Hollywood intricacies.

Most intriguingly, I was pressed by Norma Jean for details about Betty Grable. Then the reigning sex queen in American movies, Grable was famous for her legs, the focus of the famous pinup distributed by the millions for GIs during the war. She worked at Twentieth Century-Fox, which was churning out a series of forgettable movies designed to highlight her beauty and sex appeal.

"How's she getting along with the studio bosses?" Norma Jean asked me.

"All right, I guess," I replied, not quite sure what she was driving at.

"What does that mean, 'all right'?"

"Jesus, Norma Jean, I don't know for sure. As far as I can see, she's big over there, so they treat her pretty well. She's a nice lady."

Norma Jean gave a little snort. "Sure she is. What I want to know is, who's she fucking?"

"Now how the hell am I supposed to know that? As far as I know, she fucks her husband, Harry James, and that's it. What difference does it make?"

"Well, let me tell you something, Mr. Ted Jordan. Mademoiselle Grable didn't get to be such a big star because they like the color of her eyes, let me guarantee you. Bet you a lot she's going down on some fat-assed producer."

In essence, this was the new Norma Jean: cynical,

burning with more ambition than ever, much more sharp-edged than at any time I could remember. Most of our dates during the year 1946 seemed to be dominated by her conversations about the political and sexual intricacies of studio politics. The more I heard, the more I became convinced that she had fallen under the influence of somebody well-connected in the film colony. Much of what I was hearing she seemed to be parroting. I had no idea of who it was, and she shrugged off my attempts to find out.

Quite by chance, I found out—and I didn't like what I saw.

In the summer of 1946 I was working on the new Betty Grable picture, a nineteenth-century costume musical called *Mother Wore Tights*. The chief camera-man for the picture was the delightful and gentle Leon Shamroy, noted not only for his skill with a camera lens but also for his wry sense of humor. He was also noted for his collection of expensive pipes; often, he seemed wreathed in smoke as he puffed away, contemplating a shot.

"You got a little time, Ted?" Shamroy asked me one day. "I've got some footage of this girl I want you to look at."

"Sure," I answered. "Which girl?"

"Oh, I don't recall her name; just one of the girls around here. But she's really something. You're quite a skirt-chaser; you'd really appreciate her."

Up in a projection room Shamroy began running some rushes of *Mother Wore Tights*. "I put this other girl on some leftover film," Shamroy explained. "Take a look; tell me what you think."

It was a standard nonsound screen test. As it flashed up on the screen, I saw this woman standing with her back to the camera. Then she turned around, smiled, and walked toward the camera. She mouthed, "Hi," toward the camera, then walked off, out of camera range.

I almost fell out of my chair. It was Norma Jean.

"Well, what do you think, Ted?" Shamroy asked, a twinkle in his eye. Too stunned to reply, I said nothing.

"I believe you know her," he added, smiling. "Not bad, Ted, I must say. I remember the day you brought her in here. You still seeing her?"

"Sure," I said. "Tell me, Leon, how did this test come about?"

Shamroy smiled. "Well, I don't know for sure, Ted," he said, "but from the looks of it, I'd say she had a friend in high places."

Things were beginning to make sense: whoever that "friend" was, he (or maybe she) was the one filling her head with all that how-things-really-work stuff. And more importantly, the friend had arranged for the screen test. (It was no easy matter to get a screen test then for a total unknown.)

Very quickly I learned the identity of her very powerful friend.

"How'd you like to go to a party?" my Uncle Ted asked me one afternoon on the phone.

"Sure," I replied, eager for some diversion from a grinding studio work schedule. "Whose is it?"

"A guy named Siegel." He gave me the address. I immediately called Norma Jean, inviting her to accompany me.

She sounded uncomfortable when I asked her. "Uh, listen, Eddie," she said, "I've already been invited to the party, and I'm going with somebody else.

And, uh, listen, Eddie, if I see you there, I might not be able to talk to you."

"What do you mean, you might not be able to talk to me? Do I have some kind of disease or something?"

"Oh, don't get mad, Eddie; try to understand. I'll be with some, uh, people who are trying to help me, you know, and, uh, it might not be a good idea if I—"

"So don't talk to me!" I shouted at her, and hung up.

The party was at a stunning Beverly Hills mansion. Its owner, described to me only as "Mr. Siegel," was in fact Benjamin "Bugsy" Siegel, the infamous gangster then moving in the highest Hollywood circles. As founder-owner of the new Flamingo in the equally new Las Vegas resort city, Siegel had a lot of money to spend, and he lavished it on top-name entertainment for his place, the better to attract high rollers. Nothing talks like money in Hollywood, and Siegel bought himself a fancy house there, then set in motion a frenetic social whirl.

Technically, the social affair that day at Siegel's was a pool party. His guests—among them Ted Lewis and Sophie Tucker, big-name entertainers who performed at the Flamingo for equivalently big fees— were seated around the house's huge pool when I arrived. I quickly spotted Norma Jean in a blue bathing suit. She was seated beside her escort, Johnny Hyde.

Now everything made sense. Hyde, a diminutive man just over five feet tall who wore monstrous-looking elevator shoes, was the biggest agent in Hollywood. Not so coincidentally, he was Ted Lewis's personal manager, who was just one of the super-stars he represented. He was best known for his close friendship with the big studio moguls and over lunch could seal major deals with a handshake.

There he was, seated next to Norma Jean, who was lavishing every watt of her considerable appeal on him. In turn he seemed to be totally smitten. They looked like Mutt and Jeff together, and at that moment I could have killed them both. Especially Norma Jean, who acted as though I didn't exist. Clearly she was not about to complicate her new relationship with Hyde—and all that it promised her—by admitting that she had a boyfriend.

Furious, I dived into the pool—and immediately encountered the infamous actress Lupe Velez, a notorious man-hunter whose appetites were legendary. She obviously wanted to know me better, and I played along, for I was intent on making Norma Jean as jealous as possible. Two can play your little game, I thought to myself, as I noticed Norma Jean stroking Hyde's leg.

In short order I left the party and went with Lupe to her home. There I discovered she was not called the Mexican Spitfire for nothing; she was ravenously sexual, and about the only place she didn't leave footprints was on the ceiling.

The following morning I began to feel twinges of guilt, but I was still sufficiently angry at Norma Jean not to call her. Two days later she called me, sounding somewhat contrite. We made a date for the following evening. "We need to talk a few things out," she said.

"Well, I guess things didn't work out too well," she half-whispered as we sat in my car near one of the beaches. In the cool night we heard the crash of surf nearby. Overhead a full moon shone. A perfect setting for lovers, but neither of us felt very loving.

"Speak for yourself," I said. "Things worked out for me, believe me." I was determined to hurt her, to punish her.

"Lots of luck with Lupe, the Mexican whore," she snapped bitterly.

"Oh, come on, Norma Jean," I said, "let's cut out all this crap. Let's be honest with each other: I was pretty pissed off when I saw you there with Johnny, and I admit it, I was trying to hurt you. I could care less about Lupe; I was just another body to her."

"I thought we made a deal," she said, staring at me. "I thought that what I had to do for my career would have nothing to do with us. What we have is something apart."

"There's a limit."

"What are you talking about?" She was angry now. "Look, Johnny Hyde is going to be the best thing that ever happened to me in this town. I told you, I have to have somebody who can open doors for me. And believe me, there's nobody who can open doors like he can. What does that have to do with us?"

"You don't get it." I was starting to feel pretty angry myself now. "First, there's my Uncle Ted. You use him to get Johnny Hyde. When you get what you want out of him, then what? Are you going to pull this little number on everybody in Hollywood? Come on."

"*You* don't get it," she said. "Who are you to talk? You mean to tell me you didn't use your uncle to help you?"

"Yeah, but I didn't fuck him."

"Okay, so I did. So what?" She had worked herself up into a fine lather. "And I'll tell you something else, smart guy. I still fuck him. And you know who else I fucked? I fucked Winchell. And I fucked

Runyon, too! Yeah, right, Mr. Integrity; I fucked him, because he asked me to. And you want to know what I did after that party at Siegel's house? He and some of his friends decided to fly off to Vegas that night. I went with him, and I fucked Siegel there. And do you know why? Because Johnny said it was a good idea! That's right; Siegel is a good man to know in this town, and I fucked him. And you think Johnny carries on the way you do? Of course not. He understands how things work. Don't you see? Johnny set me up with Siegel. It was business."

"Terrific," I said when she appeared, finally, to pause in the outburst. "What have you got, an agent or a pimp?"

This last sally apparently struck deep, for she suddenly fell silent. She began to cry.

"Oh, Eddie, why are we fighting like this? How can I make you understand? You just have to accept me the way I am. You know what I want and what I'm doing. Please don't think any less of me. You know, I still love you, and only you."

My anger was dissipating fast. I looked at this bewildering woman, this maddening creature who would probably drive me crazy someday. You're completely hooked, son, I told myself; it doesn't much matter what she does, you'll always be drawn to her, like a moth to a flame.

We slept together that night. Or, rather, I should say *I* slept, for Norma Jean seemed to have serious trouble falling asleep. She had always had bouts of insomnia, but this was the worst I had seen with her. At 4:00 A.M., I awoke from a sound sleep to see her polishing her nails.

"You have to get some sleep," I told her.

"I can't," she said, the nervous mannerisms beginning again. "I don't know what it is, Eddie, I just can't sleep anymore. I always need something to help me now." She pulled out an unmarked bottle of pills and took several of them.

"What are you taking?" I asked, noticing several similarly unmarked bottles in her purse.

"Nembutals," she replied. "I also take Seconals. One to go up, one to go down; it's the only way I can get to sleep."

"That stuff's dangerous to play with," I warned her. "I hope your doctor knows what he's doing."

"I don't have a doctor; your uncle helps me get these."

By now thoroughly alarmed, I asked her how many pills she was taking. "Oh, I don't know," she shrugged. "Enough to get me through."

"Are you crazy?" I shouted at her, grabbing her by both shoulders and spinning her around. I wasn't sure whether I was more mad at her for blithely using such drugs or at my uncle, for providing them to her. The old sonofabitch, I thought. He wants to keep the relationship going with her and he's found out the perfect method: get her hooked and become her sole source. No way she could ever get the drug supply I saw in her purse through a prescription.

As if reading my mind, she hastened to a defense of Uncle Ted. "He's just trying to help me," she said. "He saw how I couldn't sleep, so he said he'd get me the stuff. I get it in the mail. I guess he's got friends in the medical profession."

"For Christ's sake, Norma Jean," I said, near tears in frustration, "what the hell's the matter with you? Are you trying to commit suicide? What are you doing with your life?"

"Just trying to make my way, Eddie," she replied,

her jaw set stubbornly. "Norma Jean the little orphan girl is finally going to get what she's always wanted."

"We're back to that again. So my uncle and Johnny Hyde are going to give you everything, and they don't want anything in return, is that it?"

"Johnny's a whole separate problem," she said, biting her lip, the sure sign she was tense. "I hate to tell you this, Eddie, but he's fallen very deeply in love with me. Even his wife knows all about it. What can I do? I tell him I don't love him, but I don't think he's listening. He thinks he hasn't got much longer to live anyway. You know, he's got this really bad heart condition. Sometimes he looks as though he'll die any minute."

Recalling her customary sexual acrobatics, I asked her, "What are you doing, for God's sake? You want to kill this guy?"

"Oh, don't worry," she replied breezily. "I take it real easy, believe me; none of the heavy stuff."

"Norma Jean, a man of his age and physical condition is in no shape to handle somebody like you."

"That's right." She began giggling. "But there's nothing wrong with his tongue."

Almost without thinking, I slapped her across the face. She looked shocked and hurt. Then she began to cry.

"Hey, I'm sorry," I said, mortified that I had actually done such a thing. She twisted away from me.

"You think I'm a whore, don't you?" she asked.

"No, but I get so angry when you talk like that, the casual way you talk about using people. Jesus, Norma Jean, Hyde's got a wife and kids, and you're just playing with him. When you're finished with him, you'll just throw him aside, like an old rag. And you know what else I resent? I'll tell you: sometimes, I get the feeling you used me. You know, I was the guy through whom you could get Ted Lewis. I don't want to believe it, but—"

"Oh, no, never!" she said, gripping me tightly in her arms. "No, no, you have to believe that what we have is real, Eddie. Please believe me."

I did believe her—perhaps only because I wanted to—and by dawn she finally went to sleep. Exhausted by the emotional drain of another gut-wrenching encounter with Norma Jean, I also collapsed into a deep sleep.

What was evolving between us, as I understood it, was something of a new relationship, a relationship very much on her terms. It was more in the nature of an understanding: we could see each other occasionally, enjoy each other, but she was no longer giving all of herself to me. In fact, very little, for the mind (and body) of Norma Jean Baker was now devoted to her total obsession: becoming a movie star. She was going to do whatever she had to do, and if I didn't like it, that was just too bad.

Reluctantly I accepted the terms. I really had no choice, for my only option was to break off with her. And that I could not do. However appalled I was with the way she was running her life, she was still Norma Jean, and I was still hopelessly in love with her. Clearly, whatever there was between us would not last much longer, given that overwhelming ambition of hers, but I was determined to hang on to her for as long as possible.

She was becoming somewhat notorious around Hollywood. Hyde was getting her name into the columns occasionally, trying to puff her up, and he was often seen with her in various nightspots. They made a ridiculous pair: Hyde often danced with her, and on the floor, with his face at the level of her breasts, they looked like some kind of burlesque skit. The whole industry was snickering at Hyde behind his back, but he didn't care: totally smitten with Norma Jean, nothing seemed to faze him anymore.

None of this seemed to faze Norma Jean, either. The whispers around Hollywood were that she was some sort of brazen hustler, sharing her body with anybody she thought might help her. Friends of mine, aware of my relationship with her, often asked me if what they had heard was true: was she really breaking into the studios via the bedroom? Trying to be as protective as I could of her reputation, I would vaguely ascribe it all to "rumors," the inevitable result of her friendship with people like Johnny Hyde.

Frenetically involved in her assault on the studios by this time, Norma Jean got in touch with me only on an erratic basis. She would call me when she wasn't too busy, and we would go out on a date, acting as though nothing had happened. Often she would talk about her encounters in Hollywood's corridors of power, notably her run-in with Harry Cohn, head of Columbia Pictures.

Cohn had very few redeeming qualities. An uncouth slob, he liked women, money, and movies in that order. One of the handful of studio moguls who ran Hollywood and the studios like feudal barons, Cohn kept a riding crop at his desk; often he would slam it down with great force to emphasize a point.

Hyde had sent Norma Jean to be interviewed by him for a possible role in a new production. "It wasn't much of an interview," she told me. "He looked at me for a little while without saying a word. Then he said, 'Take your clothes off.' So I did. Then he made me pose in every possible position, like a whore. Meanwhile, I noticed he took his cock out while he was sitting there at his desk. Ugh! Eddie, he reminded me of an old monkey at the zoo I saw once, showing everybody its penis. I was getting pretty sick to my stomach by this time. He made me bend over in front of him, with my ass spread open. I suddenly realized he was about to screw me in the ass. I don't know why, but I suddenly got really upset. I just completely lost my temper. I started screaming at him, and I scratched his face as hard as I could with my nails. I didn't care if I didn't get the part, but there was no way I was going to let him do that, the ugly old bastard."

Given that kind of account—she often regaled me with many others like it—many of our dates were none too pleasant. Still, there was enough of the old Norma Jean, with that giggle, delightful way of looking at things, and sheer life force, for compensation. Then, too, she would often come up with interesting places for us to visit.

One night she came up with an idea that was to have momentous impact on her career—and my life.

"Let's go to a striptease show," she said, with characteristic directness.

"Why?"

"Because there's somebody I really want to see. I saw her picture in the paper: Lili St. Cyr."

I was puzzled. Lili St. Cyr was the reigning striptease queen of that generation, an incredibly beautiful blond woman famous for her elaborate routines. These included an act that featured a ballet in which she made love to a parrot, and her most famous, an exquisite skit in which she appeared in a giant champagne glass. By today's standards it was pretty tame stuff—there was no nudity, even partial—but St. Cyr was a headliner at some of the best supper clubs in the country. A former ballet dancer, she elevated striptease to something of an art form. In the process she became the adolescent fantasy of millions of American teenage boys. That being the case, why was Norma Jean so interested in seeing her?

"I'll explain when we get there," she said.

St. Cyr was appearing at a theater in Los Angeles, situated in one of the city's seedier sections. They sold popcorn at the theater, and Norma Jean and I sat munching a box of the stuff as several burlesque acts did their stuff. Then it was time for St. Cyr's appearance.

Norma Jean stopped munching. Totally enraptured, she watched as St. Cyr went through her routine. It was just about the sexiest thing I had ever seen. St. Cyr never took her clothes off, but in a skimpy costume that highlighted the best features of her statuesque body, she moved with unbelievable grace through a series of balletlike sketches. There was the parrot sketch, featuring the bird making love to her in time with the music, and the famous champagne glass. Not once did St. Cyr ever touch any part of her body, yet the effect was electric.

"My God, Eddie, do you see that?" Norma Jean whispered to me during the show. "Look at the way she moves, look at how she carries herself! Isn't she just the most beautiful thing you've ever seen?" She squeezed my arm, and throughout the entire performance I felt constant squeezes; clearly Norma Jean was excited by what she was seeing.

"Let's see the second show," Norma Jean announced

when it was over. (St. Cyr did two shows at the theater, a standard nightclub schedule.)

"Gee, Norma Jean," I protested, "we haven't eaten yet. I'm starving. We've already seen the show, why see it again?"

"Please, Eddie," she said in that breathless voice that was so irresistible. "Take me to the second show. I've just got to see her again."

To prevent collapse from hunger, we bought some cheap fried chicken up the street. Washed down with soda pop, it was enough to stave off hunger pangs. Reluctantly I took her back to see the second show.

"Notice how she works on every single little move," said Norma Jean, who couldn't seem to stop talking about Lili St. Cyr. "See, Eddie, she has *presence*. Everything is sex, and yet there's nothing dirty about it. And nobody takes their eyes off her. I'll tell you something, Eddie: that's what I want to be."

"A striptease artist?"

"No, to have that kind of presence, to have that kind of sex appeal. That's the way I have to look."

She whispered into my ear almost nonstop during the second show, and I realized that Norma Jean had found her role model. I was skeptical: Norma Jean was sexy, all right, but sex in the movies was pretty understated and staid then; there was no way I could see that kind of direct sex appeal getting onto celluloid.

After the second show was over, Norma Jean hectored me to meet St. Cyr. We left the theater and headed for the stage door. The way was through a very narrow alley, which was reeking of urine from the local winos. The stage door was a battered old metal one, lit by a single light bulb.

Like starstruck autograph seekers, we stood, waiting outside the door. Finally Lili St. Cyr came out.

"Hi, Miss St. Cyr," Norma Jean said in a rush, "we just saw your show and we thought it was absolutely great. I'm an actress just starting out, and this is my friend. He's an actor."

"Well, thank you very much," St. Cyr said. She was stunningly beautiful. "Good luck in your acting careers." She swept past us.

"God, she is *it!*" Norma Jean gushed. "That's who I'll be!"

"Sure," I replied, unconvinced. I was wrong again.

Chapter eight

THE
STARLET

"I got a contract!"

I had never seen Norma Jean so happy. She was positively beside herself with joy, waving around that piece of paper like a gold miner who had just struck the mother lode.

To celebrate, she took me out to one of the fanciest restaurants in Hollywood, where she chattered gaily for what seemed to be hours about how she had achieved the threshold at last. "From now on, Eddie," she bubbled, "nobody can stop me!"

I hardly had the heart to tell her that a studio contract was not what she thought it was. To be sure, it was highly prized, the sure guarantee of movie work. Still, in its standard form, it had six-month options for the first two years. In other words, the studios held the whip hand: at the end of six months they could just dump you. That would be it.

Additionally, the contracts bound the actors and actresses in a form of slavery. They became totally the studio's chattels, to be used (or abused) as it wished. When the contract players weren't working on a picture, they were assigned to go to a studio acting school or used in other productions. You might be a bit player in a movie in the morning, then shifted to be an extra in still another movie that afternoon.

All in all, a contract bound its signatories to a life of very hard work. And Norma Jean, as I was aware, was not very enamored of hard work. I didn't say anything, but I couldn't imagine her lasting out the first option period. Her lazy work habits—she simply showed up whenever she felt like it—would be fatal to her. Those days, the studios didn't fool around: there was an endless supply of new talent, and unless you made a good impression in the first six months of a contract, it was a virtual certainty you would not be around for the second.

I was convinced she wouldn't make it, even though she had a powerful patron: Johnny Hyde, the man who had arranged for that screen test and her entrée into Twentieth Century-Fox. By coincidence, that was where I was working, under my own contract.

"Oh, don't worry about anything," she said, shrugging off my subtle reminders that she would have to work very hard. She did not seem to pick up the hint, assuming, as she hinted to me, she really had nothing to worry about—considering certain powerful friends she had.

Among them, I discovered later, was none other than Joseph M. Schenck (pronounced "skank," as in *skunk*). One of the founders of Twentieth Century-Fox, he was regarded virtually as a god. Occasionally I'd see him imperiously strutting through his domain, followed by lesser lights: Darryl F. Zanuck, dressed in riding boots, cracking a whip against the boots like a plantation owner out inspecting the field slaves; and producer William Perlberg, respectfully keeping a few paces behind his master, hardly daring to look at the god who walked in front of him. As they walked, crowds coming from the commissary would part, like herds of cattle, to let them through. It was extraordinary, like a scene out of some epic of ancient Rome, and demonstrated the unbelievable power these people had. One word from a mogul like Schenck meant you were through in the movie business, or on your way to incredible riches and fame.

Behind his back Schenck was known as "Kid Varicose" because of the horrible-looking veins that protruded from his legs. He was generally a physically repulsive man and had a business style to match. A virtual thug, he had the habit of trying to shout down anyone who dared to disagree with him.

It was Hyde, Norma Jean later admitted to me, who made the introduction. Like virtually all men with whom she came in contact, Schenck was bowled over. And as did the other moguls, Schenck had his pick of the battalions of beautiful female flesh trying to get jobs in his studio (Zanuck owned an especially notorious "casting couch"), but Norma Jean was quite something else again.

"Christ, he's ugly," she complained to me about Schenck one night shortly after she had won her contract. It was the summer of 1946, and we sat beside the Pacific Ocean, relaxing in the balmy breeze. "I think he's probably the ugliest man I've even seen—or touched."

"So why do you have anything to do with him?"

"Are you kidding, Eddie? You work over there; you know how much power he's got. Johnny told me, 'Listen, you want anything at Fox, Schenck is the man to deal with.' " She shrugged, her characteristic motion whenever she was confronted by a situation in which she was the helpless victim.

"You think I *want* to have anything to do with him?" she asked, in that low voice, her "business voice," as I had come to call it. "But Johnny was right: the minute he took a shine to me, I had no trouble getting a contract."

"I saw your silent test," I said, trying to change the subject.

"I bet I looked terrible."

"No, no, you looked teriffic, I thought. A little self-concious, maybe."

"Maybe that's because I had my clothes on." She giggled.

"Look, Norma Jean, don't think that because Joe Schenck likes you, you have some kind of permanent status there. Unless you show some talent, they'll boot your ass out of there. You know, Schenck doesn't need to keep his, uh, friends on contract. He's a businessman, above all. He's only got a certain number of contracts he can let out. Anyone who doesn't produce doesn't get renewed."

She giggled again. "Oh, I know that. But, Eddie, Johnny says I can really go places. Hey, this is just a start for me. Johnny says he's going to get my nose fixed up and my chin and have me really made over, like a real glamor queen. Mr. Schenck says I have unlimited possibilities."

"I can just imagine what he means," I murmured.

"Come on, Eddie," she whined, "don't start that jealousy stuff again. I knew what I was getting into with him, but it's just something I have to do, you understand. It's not forever. Besides, the guy is practically impotent. Most of the time he can't even get a hard-on. When he does, all he wants me to do is take my clothes off and go down on him. You can't believe how ugly this man is when he takes his clothes off. I always have to close my eyes. He's got this really ugly cock, you know, but like I learned from the other girls, all I have to do is pretend in my mind that it's an ice-cream cone."

"An ice-cream cone," I repeated, snickering in spite of myself.

"See, Eddie? You're laughing, too. Hey, it isn't forever that I have to do these kinds of things. You know how many actresses I've met who tell me that when they were starting out, all the cock they had to suck? See, all these big wheels, that's the big thing with them. They always want the girls to go down on them; it gives them a sense of power, I guess."

"Maybe so, but he's got power over you."

Her face broke out in a dazzling smile. "Oh, but that's where you're wrong, Mr. Ted Jordan, or whatever your name is now. What you don't know is that someday people like Mr. Schenck and Mr. Hyde are going to come on their knees to me, and in order to get what they want, they're gonna have to kiss Miss Norma Jean's big, fat ass!"

I hope you're right, I thought to myself.

Actually Norma Jean's relationship with me was becoming somewhat secretive. Terrified that Johnny Hyde would find out about us (although many people in Hollywood already knew), she kept me at arm's length. When we met, it almost seemed like two spies carrying out a secret rendezvous.

There were other changes I noticed. One was physical: some fast surgery had removed that bump on her nose and slightly rearranged her chin. Moreover, she had apparently been put into the hands of a professional makeup artist, and that fresh youth in her face was gone. It was replaced by a look I would describe as "professional model," with exaggerated eyebrows and lips. She looked gorgeous, but I much preferred the old Norma Jean, the innocent, yet uninhibited teenager who used little makeup.

I was finding it increasingly difficult to see her, and a fast glance at the trades told me why. Judging by the items planted by Hyde, Norma Jean was everywhere. She was at this club. She was at that club. She was carrying on an affair with Howard Hughes (not true). She was seen at a dance, dancing with this or that leading man.

All of them discussed a girl named "Jean Norman," Hyde's inspiration for a new Hollywood name, the idea being that "Norma Jean Baker" was too flat and suggested middle America. What Hyde wanted was *glamor*, and strategically placed gossip-column items about the "new blond bombshell named Jean Norman" were designed to create the proper atmosphere for the buildup of a superstar.

But she was very far at that point from being a superstar, and she still felt compelled to continue a relationship with Schenck. She bitterly complained to me about Schenck, who had made it clear what her primary function was: sex. Often she stayed with Schenck at his place in Arrowhead Lakes, about eighty miles outside of Los Angeles, a somewhat nerve-wracking experience.

"I never know what's going to happen there," she told me. "He's got this black guy who works as his butler and general assistant. Sometimes it'll be about four o'clock in the morning, and this black guy will come running into the bedroom where I'm staying. 'It's up! It's up!' he'll yell at me. Then I have to jump up, run into Schenck's room. A miracle has occurred: Joe's got an erection! No time to waste; I have to do fellatio on him right away, before he loses it."

That kind of service got Norma Jean into Schenck's studio, but no amount of devotion to his sexual needs was about to make her a movie star. To achieve that, she would need a lot of work—and it was work she was not about to do.

That infuriated a woman named Helena Sorell. Helena was the drama coach at Fox, a no-nonsense former actress who was trying to make movie actors and actresses out of the young contract players assigned to her. We took the classes seriously, for Helena graded us all on how well we were doing. Anyone graded poorly stood in danger of not being renewed when option time arrived.

"What is with this woman?" Helena complained to me one day, aware that I knew Norma Jean very well. Among other nervous mannerisms, Helena discovered that Norma Jean, when particularly nervous, tended to chew her nails.

"Damn it," she yelled at Norma Jean one day, "if you don't stop biting your nails, young lady, we are going to put that stuff they use for babies on your fingers. You know, the terrible-tasting stuff they use to break babies from the thumb-sucking habit?"

Helena, who often argued about the necessity of "presence" for actresses, also was angered by Norma Jean's habit of picking at her skin. Ever since I knew her, Norma Jean had very dry skin, and she was cursed by little scales of it that would crop up; she would pick at these absentmindedly, a horrendous habit for an actress.

Worst of all, Norma Jean did not take Helena's classes seriously. The only female student who appeared there in an expensive set of false eyelashes—part of her equally expensive make-over—she started coming less and less. I'd try to warn her that it was not a smart move to antagonize Helena Sorell, but Norma Jean casually waved it off. "I was too busy," she would say, laughing.

Neither Helena nor anyone else in the class failed to put two and two together: obviously the liaison with Joe Schenck and the powerful agent Johnny Hyde put her above ordinary mortals. As she was perfectly aware, there wasn't a damn thing Helena—or anybody else—could do about a girlfriend of the man who ran the entire studio. Not unnaturally, Helena and some of the students resented it.

In a way, I did, too, although I realized that Norma Jean had given me fair warning: this was the way she had chosen to go to the top, and she didn't much care what anybody thought. She was moving, obviously, in a very fast lane: I'd get phone calls from her in New York or San Francisco or Chicago. Who she was with and what they were doing I never bothered to ask. We were no longer, clearly, boyfriend and girlfriend, and with whom she was spending her time was now her own business. I assumed these jaunts—taken when she should have been trying to perfect her acting skills—were part of her now well-established habit of forging important links with those who could help her.

The links, of course, were being forged sexually, and the whole town was soon abuzz with gossip about how the ex-model and bit player was plowing her way through the Hollywood establishment. I was not exactly thrilled to hear all the talk.

By now the persona of Norma Jean was gone. Even the old name disappeared, replaced by "Marilyn Monroe." Many actors and actresses those days changed their names, sometimes for good and sufficient reason (for example, Tony Curtis's career certainly would have gone no place without changing his real name of Bernard Schwartz). In fact, contract players often spent their leisure time sitting and talking with each other, with a prime topic of conversation the question of stage names. Frequently various stage names were batted around, until a consensus emerged that a particular name would suit somebody the best.

Contrary to later claims, Norma Jean's new name did not come from the studio chiefs at Fox. Actually, it arose one day when several contract players, including Norma Jean, were sitting around. Norma Jean wanted a new name—she despised "Jean Norman," Hyde's inspiration—and tried out a number of possibilities. None seemed to work. Then one of the players, Laurette Luez (who later left the movie business), began playing around with the name "Monroe," Norma Jean's mother's maiden name. Laurette, who considered herself something of a psychic, ran through alliterative first names for "Monroe." When she hit "Marilyn," she suddenly stopped. "That's it!" she cried. "You're Marilyn Monroe, a name that will be great."

The "Marilyn Monroe" Twentieth Century-Fox now had was a problem. As Schenck's girlfriend, the bosses couldn't get rid of her. On the other hand, she had such little talent, there wasn't anything in which they could use her. Indeed, much of her first contract year was spent as an extra and posing for cheesecake shots, the kind the studios used to produce in gargantuan amounts to publicize their starlets under contract.

Norma Jean—I insisted on calling her that—was becoming restive. She was given a bit part in one movie, with only one line ("Hi!") to say, but it was cut. Finally it was agreed to give her a screen test with sound. I rehearsed with her for days, all the while telling myself this woman, as much as I still loved her, had no real hope of making it. She couldn't act worth a damn, and here she was, facing a three-and-a-half-minute screen test with Richard Conte, a talented actor, playing the male lead. She was so nervous, she could hardly think straight, and I spent most of the rehearsal time trying to calm her down.

"Jesus, I'll never get this right," she wailed, as we went over her few short lines for what seemed to be the thousandth time.

"You'll be all right," I constantly reassured her, while in my heart I knew better. If only I could calm her down and at the same time get her to stop taking those damn pills. She was becoming a junkie.

The test itself was okay. She remembered her lines and did the best she could. But the lack of technical training showed. She sounded like a high school thespian suddenly thrust into the world of the big boys. That breathy, little-girl voice barely carried.

There was something else on that screen, but very few people then recognized it. The effect was hard to describe. "Luminescence" is maybe the right word. There was something almost ethereal about her that shone right through. It was "presence" in a way the acting teachers never could impart. In other words, she riveted a viewer's attention, no matter what she was doing. Quite unconsciously, she projected herself out of the screen and to the audience, a rare quality that blesses maybe one in a million.

Leon Shamroy, the cameraman, recognized it, although he couldn't quite articulate the effect she created. Neither could I, but I had the feeling it had something to do with sex. She projected an innocent sexuality that was so strong, the screen literally could not hold it. However, it was not the normally strong sexual projection I remembered from Norma Jean; this was quite something else. Where had she picked it up?

I should have recognized it: the new "Marilyn Monroe" was almost a precise imitation of Lili St. Cyr. Curious, the next time I saw Norma Jean, I asked her about it.

"Oh, but of course, *ma chérie*," she said in a perfect imitation of Lili's French-Canadian accent (Norma Jean was a gifted mimic). "Eddie, she's been *incredibly* helpful to me, really. I got a nice introduction to her through Johnny, and you know what, Eddie? She remembered us from that night when we waited outside the stage door for her. You remember that?"

"Sure, but I'm not sure I understand how she could help you. After all, you're not a striptease artist. Besides, I thought your new look came from your"—I laid heavy sarcasm on the next word—"*mentor.*"

"Silly," she said, ignoring my little thrust, "only women really know anything about how to make another woman sexy. I was a mouse, Eddie, no matter what you think; a dull, little gray mouse. You know what I found out? It's really simple, just a few little tricks that work. She told me how to fix my eyebrows, how to accentuate my mouth more. Here's a neat little trick: when you have your picture taken, make sure your mouth is slightly open. That conveys sex and makes you look a thousand times sexier than you are. And always look in a picture like you're half asleep. Men go crazy over that, because it makes you look like you've just had your brains fucked out. She's also been teachng me a lot about how to move; you know, how to accentuate your best parts, how to make sure every man is watching you, no matter what you're doing."

Lili's biggest contribution, it seemed, was putting Norma Jean in touch with the biggest glamor photographer in Hollywood, Bruno Bernard, known as "Bernard of Hollywood." A master at the glamor shots all actresses used, Bernard was a genius in his craft. In his hands, Norma Jean was transformed into a sultry sex bombshell. The pictures he took of her practically smoldered. Compared with the amateur shots people like me had taken of her earlier, it looked as if two totally different people had posed.

"That's all very nice of Lili," I noted, "but are you telling me she's doing all this just because she took a liking to you, or because Hyde asked her?"

"Not exactly," Norma Jean said, giggling. "I think Lili's in love with me."

"What?"

"Oh, yeah, I think she's pretty wild about me, actually." She paused, almost as if for effect. "At least she acts that way in bed."

I could hardly believe what I was hearing. "What are you telling me, that you're fucking Lili St. Cyr?"

"Sure, why not?" she answered, with that disarming innocence. "She really knows how to please a woman, let me tell you."

I was not nearly as shocked as I might have been some years before, but my long intimacy with Norma Jean had taught me to expect just about anything. I was getting to the point where nothing surprised me anymore, but this was a bit much.

"Every time I turn around," I said, shaking my head, "it's something else I never expected. Is there any limit?"

The giggling began again. "Hey, can I help it if everybody loves me?"

I had barely recovered from that episode when my world collapsed. I got a mysterious phone call one night: a man who did not identify himself warned me to stay away from Marilyn Monroe. The call was more puzzling than ominous, and I promptly forgot about it.

Two days later I was called into the casting director's office and informed curtly that my option would not be renewed. The director, Ben Lyon, seemed uncomfortable, and did not deign to look me in the eye. The thought flashed across my mind: Joe Schenck was behind this. The seventy-two-year-old ugly boss, trying to make sure the lady he was most smitten with would not be tempted to dally on the set with a fellow contract player and boyfriend named Ted Jordan.

I felt crushed; I wept like a baby. On some level I blamed Norma Jean: if I had not been involved with her, there never would have been a problem with Schenck. I'd still be working at the studio, gradually moving ahead, getting bigger and bigger parts until someday—who knew?—they might regard me as a *star*.

Whatever resentment I felt toward Norma Jean evaporated the next night, when she sat with me on the beach, commiserating with me about being bounced. She admitted that Schenck had mentioned me to her—"Why are you seeing that asshole?"—but did not know if that was the direct cause of my dismissal. She was astounded to hear of the telephone call.

"Don't worry, Eddie," she said, reversing roles: now she was the one doing all the soothing. "You'll get something else, I just know it." Said that way, with the breathlessness and smile, I believed it.

The shock was all the greater, then, when she called me a week later and tearfully announced that she also had been dropped by Fox. No explanation, no nothing. Schenck wouldn't even speak to her.

"I wish to hell I knew why," she said, as we sat at our favorite spot on the beach, again mulling over a disaster. "Johnny's pissed, but what the hell can he do? Schenck doesn't want me around, and that's that." (Schenck, I discovered later, became insanely jealous over the men that she seemed to attract so effortlessly and solved the problem by getting rid of her.)

"Well," she said, "here we are, Miss Marilyn Monroe and Mr. Ted Jordan, unemployed actors. Now what do we do?"

Chapter nine

★
THE
DREAM
FACTORY

Oddly, I was more concerned for Norma Jean than myself at the nadir (to that point) of my career in Hollywood. I was convinced I would make it, somehow: I'd get a part here, a part there, and gradually I would work myself back up to contract status at a studio.

But Norma Jean, I was convinced, had now hit the proverbial blank wall. Notorious all over town as a bedroom tigress who was trying to screw her way to the top, she had no discernible acting talent to peddle. Further, everybody was aware that she had been booted out of Fox after Schenck got tired of her. At the studio she was noted for almost total lack of any discipline or willingness to work. What kind of a reputation was that to sell elsewhere?

However, I again seriously underestimated Norma Jean. (It wouldn't be the first time, nor the last.) I wasn't alone in that underestimation, for even the people who liked her felt she was washed up. No way, the general consensus ran, could this sexy but talentless hustler make any kind of breakthrough.

Johnny Hyde sure was trying. I don't think there

was an issue of *Variety* or *Hollywood Reporter* (the Bibles of the movie industry) in the year 1948 that didn't contain at least one item about "Marilyn Monroe, Hollywood's sexiest starlet." She was everlastingly linked in the gossip columns to assorted male stars, and there was an endless series of pictures showing her dancing at a nightclub or attending some party. Many showed her with Hyde, and apparently they went nowhere without a press agent being notified beforehand.

I began to see Hyde as some sort of Svengali. "Johnny says" or "Johnny feels" or "Johnny believes" were the prologues to just about every sentence she said to me when we had our infrequent dates. She was busy, very busy, she would tell me, apologizing for our not being together often enough. There was more to it than that, of course, for I noticed that she never wanted us to appear in public places—fearing that if Johnny found out, he would drop her. Johnny kept her on a very tight leash.

"You know, his wife is divorcing him over me," she said, sounding somewhat distressed. "Jesus, Eddie, I never wanted that to happen; she's a nice lady. But you know, he's just gone crazy over me. He wants me to marry him."

"What a great couple," I said sardonically. "I always thought the two of you look like Mutt and Jeff walking around. Who wants to marry a dwarf?"

"Well, *I* don't, that's for sure," she said emphatically. "I just wanted him to help me. Now he follows me around all the time, like a little dog. I think he's suffocating me."

"Look, Norma Jean, what did I tell you once? You can't play around with this stuff. You know, you want to use people, then if they really get to like you, you get all upset. What's he supposed to do? Here's a guy, forty-six or forty-seven years old, or whatever, with a bad heart, who looks like the hunchback of Notre Dame, and this gorgeous woman throws herself at him. What do you think he's going to do, shake your hand and say, 'Oh, yes, Miss Baker, I'll do everything in my power to help you, and of course, Miss Baker, we'll have a totally platonic relationship while I'm doing it, because, as you know, Miss Baker, I'm just a total eunuch and therefore your sexy body doesn't interest me in the slightest'? Come on, Norma Jean, use your head."

"Well, I didn't throw myself at him."

"You didn't? Please, don't insult my intelligence, Norma Jean. You know goddamn well you went after him hammer and tongs because he was the guy who could write your ticket. You made your bed, and now you're going to have to lie in it."

For a while she said nothing. Then she started those nervous mannerisms with her mouth. "Why does every conversation we have get back to what I'm doing?" she asked, a note of hurt in her voice. "Baby, don't you remember the agreement we made? We said we would let nothing stand in our way when 'career' was involved. I love you, Eddie. But I also have to love myself, or my ship doesn't sail. So why do you keep throwing it in my face? I don't know what else to say. I always want to see you when possible and hope you feel the same way toward me. I never want to lose track of you, and if you ever need help and I'm in a position to help you, I'll be there. Please, please try to understand: I'm not in love with Johnny. I've even told him so many times.

See, Eddie, when he touches me on my arm, there's no buzz. You know what I mean? It's like there's no electricity at all between us."

"That's not the point," I snapped. "What I'm trying to figure is who's using who. I get the feeling you don't take a piss anymore unless that little creep tells you to. Let me tell you something honestly, Norma Jean: the kind of reputation you're getting around this town you don't need. Everybody knows it. You're Johnny Hyde's big bimbo. How obvious can you be? People see this ugly little guy traipsing around with this big, beautiful blonde, and they can read the whole story right there: hey, little miss tart has got Johnny's pecker in her pocket; he'll do anything for her. The next time somebody sees you on the screen, what do you think they're going to say? Hey, there's that Monroe broad. Looks like she fucked old Johnny real good, because here's another part for her."

"You're really cruel, sometimes," she said quietly.

"Norma Jean, I'm not trying to be cruel. I'm trying to make you see something. I mean, for Christ's sake, all I ever hear about you is who you're fucking this week."

"Everybody gossips."

"Maybe so, but the point is, sweetheart, you're making yourself awfully notorious."

She considered this for a moment. "Funny, whenever I go out with somebody, or have a good time, right away I'm a whore. A man does the same thing, and nobody bats an eye."

"It's different for men."

"Yeah, sure, so I'm beginning to find out. So it's okay for————and————[naming two famous Hollywood stars, still living] to fuck each other, right in the goddamn studio dressing room! And nobody says anything about it, right? And how about———— and————[two world-famous directors, still living]? Everybody knows they're queer as a fucking three-dollar bill. And everybody knows if a man wants to get a good part in their movies, the way he gets it is by screwing these two fags in the ass. Nobody says anything about that. Nobody calls these guys whores, nobody says they're trying to fuck their way to the top. But if a girl does the same thing, she's a whore. You're like all the other men, Eddie. You're so wrapped up in your little world, you have no idea what it's like for a woman in this business. If you're a woman, believe me, you're just a goddamn piece of meat to the guys who make decisions. They just snap their little fingers and, baby, you better spread your legs. Some of them are clever about it, you know, just dropping little hints. But most of them are direct. They just come right out and make it clear: honey, you want a job, here's what'll it cost you. And the price is always what's between your legs."

Our discussions then tended to end like that, in a blazing burst of cynicism. Maybe, I thought, we had been around too long on the Hollywood merry-go-round, the carousel of sex and indentured servitude where flesh was the chief commodity. Back then sex was the chief diversion in Hollywood, much the way cocaine is today. Sometimes, I got the idea that the entire place was like some overcrowded brothel.

"Norma Jean," I said to her one day, "can you remember the way it was, just a few years ago? How totally innocent we were?"

"Speak for yourself, friend," she replied, giggling. "I didn't think what we were doing was so innocent."

"You know what I mean: you know, when we were first starting, how little we knew about what really goes on inside those studios? Why the hell were we so eager to get inside those gates? Would you have been so eager if you knew then what you know now?"

"Bet your sweet ass," she said firmly. "I'm not disillusioned. I just know more how things really work. Eddie, don't ever forget this: the movies is where I want to be. That's it. So what if the business isn't what I thought it was? I know what my destiny is, and it's to be in the movies."

"Okay," I said resignedly. When she started talking about her "destiny" in the movies, it was time to end the conversation. In that mood she'd forgive the world of Hollywood just about any crime, even if they demanded two pints of blood each day before she'd be allowed to work. Clearly she'd do *anything* to be in the movies, and my attempts to dampen that maniacal drive to get onto the screen were doomed to failure. At that point, Norma Jean didn't much give a damn what anybody thought of her, so long as she was in the movies.

We were sitting, our backs to a wall, alongside the volleyball courts at the State Beach. It was one of our favorite hangouts when we got together. We'd swim a little bit, talk a lot, and sometimes sit along the courts, watching the games. Once in a while I would play.

By one of those odd coincidences that became important only much later on, the de facto presider over these games was one of the more notable beach bums, a young actor named Peter Lawford. The scion of what he insisted (falsely) was a blueblood English family distantly related to royalty (he always referred to his mother by the title "Lady"), Lawford then was a charming young rogue with an eye for quality female flesh. Naturally he noticed Norma Jean right away, and they struck up an acquaintance-ship that was later to blossom into something much more significant.

For the moment, however, Lawford was just an-other handsome Hollywood actor on the way up. Norma Jean, of course, lavished her charm on him, although I detected that at least initially, he was not flattened by her. The reason, I suspected, was that Lawford, himself a charmer of the first order, imme-diately recognized a fellow charmer on the make. You can't bullshit a bullshitter, as the old saying goes.

"Well, I must say I'm a little surprised," I teased her after Lawford had gone for the day. "For some odd reason he's not been reduced to a puddle at your feet. You must be losing your touch, Norma Jean Baker."

"Not my type," she said. "He's all stuck up, like some kind of snob. I suspect he could be a lot of fun, though."

"Yeah, absolutely. Imagine the fun you could have at his place, while he shows you his genealogy charts."

"Oh, stop, Eddie," she said, grimacing. "Listen, don't give me any of that crap. I know you've been out with other girls."

That was true: with the cooling of my relationship

with Norma Jean, I had been dating other women. One of them, Norma Jean knew, was the wife of a producer. The relationship had ended badly after the woman decided to end the affair and get back together with her estranged husband.

"Well, we did agree that would be all right," I said, a little defensively. "It's not like any of them is very serious. You know, I just go out to have a good time." I wanted to say that none of them were anything like Norma Jean—who was?—and that no matter how many dates I was on, my heart still belonged to her. But I thought it would sound trite and decided to say nothing else.

"Oh, I'm not jealous," she said. "Hell, I'm a fine one to talk, with the men I know. Of course, with me, it's business, mostly. Yours isn't business?" She cocked her head at me, while giving a searching look.

"No, no," I answered laughing. "Jesus, Norma Jean, you think I know some studio head's wife or something? I don't. What would I do, hire myself out as a stud? Then, at the right moment, tell her, 'Listen, honey, I want that contract!' "

She was giggling again. "Hey, that's a great idea, Eddie. Did you ever see some of these ugly old broads these big studio heads are married to? No wonder they chase after the young girls all the time. Tell me something honestly, Eddie: you mean to tell me that if you could fuck somebody and it would mean a studio contract, you wouldn't do it?"

"I don't think so," I answered, perhaps not entirely truthfully.

"Bullshit," Norma Jean said. "At least I'm honest with myself. I never told you I was madly in love with Johnny Hyde or Joe Schenck, and that's why I slept with them. Now you tell me you only fuck for love? Crap, Eddie, and you know it. You just haven't been offered the opportunity."

At some level maybe she had a point. Without a contract, I was free-lancing all over Hollywood, scraping together a string of bit parts in various movies to keep my head above water. Part-time I worked at the Hollywood Roosevelt Hotel.

Nothing seemed to work, and I fell into something of a deep depression. I never admitted the depth of it to Norma Jean; whenever we talked, I was upbeat, rattling off the string of movies I was working in, with my big breakthrough right around the corner.

As for Norma Jean, she was studiously vague about what she was doing. I continued to read the items planted in the trade papers about her and then suddenly heard she had wound up at Columbia Pictures. Since that was the domain of Harry Cohn—the studio boss whose face Norma Jean raked some time before—I was puzzled how she had wound up there.

The grapevine soon provided the answer. Hyde had prevailed upon Schenck, still unraveled by his own experience with Norma Jean, to perform one small favor. It amounted to a phone call to his close friend Harry Cohn of Columbia, asking Cohn to put Norma Jean into a picture. The picture was *Ladies of the Chorus*, in which she would have a small speaking part and sing at least one song.

Sing? I had heard Norma Jean sing once, and that tiny voice, with hardly any timber to it, had no hope of ever carrying a tune, much less a movie big-production musical number. Politely I asked her how she proposed to sing in this movie.

"Oh, I have a coach who's going to teach me," she said, mentioning the name of Fred Karger, a musician who was retained by Columbia as a singing coach.

I was skeptical, but again I had underestimated Norma Jean. The next thing I knew, Norma Jean had moved into Fred's house, which he shared with his wife and two children. Like she did everywhere else, Norma Jean's effervescence soon transformed the house and its occupants into planets that revolved around her own personality. She was completely captivating, and even some of her habits—sleeplessness and tendency to walk around casually in the nude—were soon forgiven.

What Mrs. Karger did not realize until much later was that Karger had become totally smitten by Norma Jean. Like a man with a drug habit he could not shake, Karger underwent something of a personality transformation, walking around the studio in some kind of narcotic state. At the same time he was trying to fight it, for he did not want to jeopardize his family.

The movie that finally emerged was thoroughly forgettable, but there was one distinctly eerie aftereffect from it. I had gone to see the movie when it was first released at a movie theater in Hollywood. The audience seemed to be made up mostly of men. They sat quietly through the picture—until Norma Jean/Marilyn Monroe first appeared on the screen.

The effect was extraordinary, one of the most incredible things I've ever seen in a movie audience. There was a noticeable stir among the men in that audience. I distinctly heard a few low whistles, and several men actually sighed, as though they had just glimpsed paradise. Perhaps they had: Norma Jean, with her stunning figure and new platinum-blond hairstyle (she had borrowed that beauty idea from Lili St. Cyr, along with all the others), looked positively ravishing. More to the point, she seemed to reach out from the screen and touch every man in the audience. Although I was watching a screen image, I had the distinct feeling she was right in the room with me.

To my surprise, she did fine in the music portion of the picture. She sang two songs—"Anybody Can Tell I Love You" and "Every Baby Needs a Da Da Daddy"—and there did not seem to be a man in the audience who was not hanging on every word of what were otherwise-forgettable songs. What they were concentrating, on, of course, was not the silly songs themselves but the lady singing them, this starlet listed in the credits as Marilyn Monroe.

Some nights later, Norma Jean accompanied me as we watched the movie together. She was terrified of what she would see: hunched down in the seat, as if about to confront the sight of a Frankenstein monster, she covered her face with her hands.

"There you are!" I whispered loudly in her ear the first time she appeared on the screen. Slowly she opened the fingers of the hand covering one eye. She stared, transfixed, at the sight of herself, ten times normal life size, on the big screen.

"Oh, Jesus, don't look at me, Eddie," she whispered. "God, I'm awful. Shit, I look fat as hell; don't laugh, please!"

She went on like that, almost for the entire time

she was on screen. Somehow she was convinced she was awful up there. In that mood she failed to notice the murmur of the men in the audience, that distinct hum of approval I had heard the last time I saw the movie.

"Okay, how bad was I?" she asked as we strolled along the street afterward.

"You were terrific!" I said with perfect honesty. True, she obviously needed some acting lessons—she spoke in a near-strained voice—but her presence and the surprising quality of her musical numbers (an obvious result of Karger's work) more than made up for any acting deficiency. As the reaction of the men in the audience attested, clearly none of them cared very much about the quality of her acting. What they wanted to see was *her*.

"You're just saying that," she said, pouting. A Norma Jean characteristic: she needed constant infusions of love and reassurance.

"Listen to me, Norma Jean, you were fine. I mean that." It was true. The girl I once believed had no hope of ever becoming a movie actress now turned out to be something very special indeed.

"Well, maybe you're prejudiced, in my favor," she said brightly. "We'll see what everybody else has to say."

Oddly, nobody else had much to say at all. The simple fact was that however much a small circle of people realized that in Norma Jean they had an authentic phenomenon who could project her unique persona outward from the screen, Columbia Pictures saw no future in her. After *Ladies of the Chorus* was released, Norma Jean was dropped.

"I can't take much more of this, Eddie," she sobbed

to me one night. "Jesus, I work my ass off, I think I look pretty good, and what do I get? Another kick in the ass!"

I tried to comfort her as best I could, but I was puzzled myself: it made no sense. Norma Jean's appearance in the movie had caused a minor ripple in Hollywood, just the right debut for an up-and-coming starlet. Surely she had demonstrated potential. Why not cast her in another movie, perhaps with a slightly enlarged part?

Most likely the reason lay within Harry Cohn's own resentful psyche. He had never forgotten Norma Jean's rejection of him and, after *Ladies of the Chorus* was made, refused to even watch a rough cut. As far as he was concerned, he had paid the debt of his favor to Joe Schenck and Johnny Hyde; now, with the books balanced, he wanted no further part of her.

"You're probably right," Norma Jean said when I mentioned the possibility of Cohn's personal motive. "I'll tell you something: the sonofabitch never really gave up. Halfway through the damn picture, you know what he did? He comes up to me—and up to that point, all I got out of him was a drop-dead look—and says that when the movie's finished, I'm invited to a big party on his yacht. For a minute I figured he was trying to make up to me, you know, by having me to this big party. When I tell him thank you for inviting me to his party, he says, 'Oh, it's just a small party, honey; just me and you and the sailors.' Boy, was I pissed off at him! So I said thanks but no thanks. He didn't look too happy about it, so maybe that's why I won't be at Columbia anymore."

She was probably right, but I wondered to myself why, if she was willing to give herself to Schenck in the name of career advancement, she held herself out from the less ugly Cohn. She never did explain, but I remembered the incident of her encounter with Cohn in the studio chief's office. The real trigger for her anger, I recalled, was Cohn's brutal attempt at anal intercourse with her. That was a real flash point for her because, as she had often told me, men who liked to demonstrate their dominance over women sometimes compelled her to assume a doggielike position, then penetrate her anally. Often they hurt her deliberately, taking satisfaction in the sight of her in that helpless position, complaining about discomfort and pain. Thus it was a real sensitive issue for Norma Jean; to her, that form of intercourse symbolized, usually, a man's attempt to dominate and hurt her. Norma Jean liked men more than any woman I ever knew, but she also retained contempt for most of them and decided that the largest portion of men were power-mad pipsqueaks who often used sex to humiliate a woman.

Possibly it was this conviction that caused her occasional withdrawals from all forms of sex with men. She was not celibate during these brief periods: she would begin liaisons with various women. One such occurred during the making of *Ladies of the Chorus*, when Norma Jean was assigned to a drama coach named Natasha Lytess.

Natasha looked like something out of a Gorky drama; Russian born, she had the tragic appearance of someone who has seen it all. Thin, nearly emaciated-looking, she dressed in dark clothes and regarded everything unsmilingly with large eyes under a mop of gray hair.

For reasons I never really understood—and which Norma Jean could not explain—Natasha took an immediate shine to her. Very quickly they became very close friends. When the affair with Karger went sour, Norma Jean moved into Natasha's place. Soon, Norma Jean told me, they were sleeping together.

As usual, Norma Jean was casual about the whole thing. "Why not?" she said. "Sex is something to do with people you like. What could be wrong with a natural act?"

She had a point, but not everybody saw it that way.

Chapter ten

THE
GODDESS

Under the curious unwritten code of Hollywood, vaunting ambition was no sin. Even using sex to get to the top was not frowned on, but the trick was not to be too obvious about it. It was considered somewhat gauche to become notorious for using sex to get ahead (although an awful lot of people did it).

Norma Jean never quite understood that unwritten code, and it caused her a lot of problems. She was quite right when she would complain to me about the film colony's hypocrisy: some looked down their noses at her because she was considered a tramp for having sex with anybody she thought might be able to advance her career.

But, as I often argued with her, that really wasn't the question. Hollywood, like the rest of American society, was very much the epitome of the sexual double standard. Anything went—so long as you didn't make it obvious. Norma Jean, with that astonishing openness and let-it-all-hang-out attitude about sex, didn't realize that as a culture, we liked to keep sex covert. And sex connected with ambition was something to be kept even more covert.

There wasn't an aspiring actress in Hollywood those

days who hadn't heard the famous story about Joan Crawford. A lady of voracious sexual appetites, Crawford had starred in an early stag film, during which she demonstrated a range of sexual talents that made the *Kama Sutra* look like a Sunday school lesson. When she was trying to break into the studios, she got nowhere until several studio executives were given a private screening of her stag film. They sat open-mouthed as they watched the woman with the slim figure wear out a group of men. The movie became the hottest item on the underground screening-room circuit around Hollywood, and in short order Miss Crawford won a studio contract.

Norma Jean knew all about this episode and wondered why it had not prevented Crawford from becoming one of the reigning queens of the screen. "I don't hear the whispers about her like I hear about me," she complained. "Hell, I didn't fuck six guys in a stag movie like she did. So why is everybody snickering about me?"

"Because Joan wasn't obvious about it," I tried to explain. "Look, the point is you have to understand how the game is played. You know what 'discretion' is, Norma Jean? Okay, discretion is when a big star like Edward G. Robinson plays around with other men. Everybody knows about it, but he keeps it quiet, you know? Or when a guy like Randolph Scott, this real manly Westerns star, fools around with little boys. He's as queer as you can get. Everybody knows about his little vice, but Scott hides it all well, so he's not *obvious*. Get it?"

"I still don't see what that has to do with me," she said. "I don't understand what's wrong with fucking people you like, or fucking for any reason. I mean, who am I hurting?"

Norma Jean at sixteen, during a family gathering. Beside Norma Jean are three of her formidable-looking aunts, religious fanatics who were fond of storming into bookstores and ripping up what they considered "offensive" books. *The George Zeno Collection*

Norma Jean's formal wedding picture in June 1942, when she married James Dougherty. She was sixteen years old. She later described the wedding as a "marriage of convenience" to avoid being sent back to the orphanage. *The George Zeno Collection*

LEFT: Clearly bored with being a housewife, Norma Jean chafed during the early years of her marriage to Jim Dougherty. When he joined the Merchant Marine and went overseas in 1944, Norma Jean began actively to pursue a modeling career and her dream of becoming a movie star. This snapshot, of Norma Jean posing with two neighbors, was taken during a trip to Catalina Island just before her husband left for overseas. RIGHT: Norma Jean, dressed in her Sunday best, with a neighbor and infant son during a Sunday stroll in Van Nuys, sometime in 1944. Neighbors of the young wife of a merchant seaman were friendly to Norma Jean— unaware of the double life she was leading. *The George Zeno Collection*

This rare snapshot, taken at a dinner to celebrate Norma Jean's first modeling job, is one of the few to show Norma Jean and her mother together. Mrs. Baker is at center, turning to face the camera. Norma Jean is second from right, between two of her aunts. © *Ted Jordan*

Following Marilyn's first big contract with 20th Century Fox in 1950, the studio's flacks began a furious publicity offensive for its new starlet. The Fox flacks snapped publicity stills showing the starlet engaged in every aspect of the movie business—including this staged shot of her in the studio's makeup department. *The Bettman Archive*

Another picture from Norma Jean's early modeling career, with her natural hairstyle of tight, curly light brown hair— a style she was urged to change to straight blond hair. *The George Zeno Collection*

A 1945 pose showing Norma Jean as an all-American farm girl. *The George Zeno Collection*

Ted Jordan performing a handstand on the diving board at the Lido club of the Ambassador Hotel in Los Angeles, where he worked as a lifeguard in 1943 and 1944. It was there that he met a young, nervous model named Norma Jean Dougherty. © *Ted Jordan*

Ted Jordan at a 1974 Hollywood party with his friend actor James Arness. Years before, as struggling young actors, they had shared a boardinghouse room. © *Ted Jordan*

Ted Lewis performing his famous "Me and My Shadow" routine at a Hollywood nightclub, sometime in 1949. Introduced to Norma Jean by his nephew, Ted Jordan, Lewis began an affair with the then-unknown model and introduced her to narcotics. © *Ted Jordan*

The stunning Lili St. Cyr, the glamorous striptease artist of the 1950s. St. Cyr played a pivotal role in the transformation of Norma Jean Baker to Marilyn Monroe.© *Ted Jordan*

Lili St. Cyr during her famed trapeze act at a Las Vegas nightclub sometime in the mid-1950s. Does the circled man in the audience look familiar? Hint: At the time a fading actor working in Las Vegas, he later went into politics and became president of the United States.© *Ted Jordan*

A nude study of Norma Jean, taken in 1945 by Ted Jordan. Norma Jean was appalled when she saw the picture, insisting that it made her rear end look too big. © *Ted Jordan*

Ted Jordan and Lili St. Cyr dining in Las Vegas. © *"Flash" McAdams*

Another nude study by Jordan, shot around the same time, Norma Jean thought she looked ugly in the picture. © *Ted Jordan*

"That's not the point; the point is that you're too obvious about it. People around here don't like that. See, you have to be two people at all times: your public personality and who you are in real life. In real life you can do whatever you want in Hollywood— little boys, little girls, elephants, you name it—but you can't ever let it show. Sure, the place is a god-damn zoo; I know that. But in public, you have to be a whole other personality. It's like playing a role."

"So that's why so many people in this place are screwed up."

"Sure, but that's the way it is."

Norma Jean frowned. "Well, maybe that's *their* rule, but it isn't mine. Eddie, I told you many times, I have to be me. So fuck them if they don't like it."

In a way, of course, I was glad she didn't listen to me. She had changed a great deal since I first met her, but beneath her new hard cynicism and con-suming ambition still lurked that refreshingly natu-ral Norma Jean, a pure child of nature who simply said what was on her mind and acted on any impulse that struck her.

In retrospect I realized that she was actually far ahead of her time, and part of the problem she had in coping with life stemmed from that fact. In an era of double standard, she was completely open; at a time of caution, she was reckless; in a period of constraint and strict social mores, she was as natural as a sunrise. I loved her all the more for it.

This is not to say, however, that our relationship was blossoming. Far from it, for we were stuck in a rut. When we did get together, talk was almost totally dominated by her complaints about being unable to get a studio contract. She wailed about the strictures of the studio system, she wailed about how Johnny Hyde wasn't really doing enough for her, she wailed how important people just used her, she wailed about how people were snickering at her behind her back. She wailed about everything.

I was in little mood to hear it. My own situation was not very encouraging: I was getting bit parts here and there, but nothing really substantial. In fact, things were looking so bleak, I had been turning over in my mind a dramatic plan: I would go to New York, the Mecca of actors, and try to break through from that direction. The plan had a drawback, at least in my own mind: I would be separated from Norma Jean. But then, she was so consumed by her own ambition—I sometimes got the idea she'd commit suicide unless she got a studio contract soon—we weren't exactly hitting it off that well. Perhaps, I reasoned, a little time away from each other, and things might get back to normal.

"Well, if you have to go, you have to go," she said when I told her about it. "It's not forever, right? Just make sure you call me regularly from New York. Hey, imagine this, Eddie: while you're away in New York, making your big breakthrough, I'll be making mine here in Hollywood. And then we'll star together in some fantastic show. Think of it, Eddie! 'America's hottest new stars, Ted Jordan and Marilyn Monroe, in a way you've never seen them before! Yes, the team you've dreamed about, together, for the first time on the screen! Passion! Drama! Romance! It's the movie you've been waiting for! Soon at your neighborhood theaters! *Lust!* The movie they said couldn't be made!' "

She began giggling hysterically as she wound up her imitation of the typical Hollywood movie trailer bombast of the time. I began laughing, too, at the sheer improbability of it all.

New York was a cold place for actors in that spring of 1949. There were plenty of productions—but there were also battalions of struggling young actors. I made the rounds for two weeks and got noplace. The fact that I had been under contract briefly to Twentieth Century-Fox was of no consequence in that world.

In my phone calls to Norma Jean I tried to hide the true dimension of the disaster. I was getting along fine, I reassured her; I had tried out for this or that role; I was virtually guaranteed of getting one of them; things were really looking up. In fact, I was worrying where my next meal was coming from. I worked as a bartender to eat, and just when I despaired of ever getting anything, a chance meeting with a producer led to a role as an extra in the movie *Gladys Glover,* which was shooting on location in New York City.

What a job: I was to work as a double for Jack Lemmon, who at one point in the script was to dress up in a gorilla suit and swing around a large zoo cage. (I can't remember how exactly this rather odd script development came about.) At any rate, I found myself in a cage in the Central Park Zoo, making King Kong—like noises as a crowd of extras threw bananas and other fruit at me.

It earned me the princely sum of three hundred dollars. Not bad in those days, but I felt humiliated. All that work, all those acting lessons, to swing around in a monkey cage? This wasn't going to work.

During the shooting I decided to visit my uncle, Ted Lewis. I knocked on the door of his apartment on Central Park West and was greeted by Aunt Adah, peeking through a chain on a half-opened door. Clearly she was not delighted to see me, although I had always been considered her favorite nephew.

"What do you want?" she asked, as though I were a salesman.

"I'm in town, working, Aunt Adah," I said. "Can I come in for a few seconds?"

"I'm not dressed; it's early," she snapped. It was 1:00 P.M. "If you want to see Uncle Ted, go to the Friars' Club. He's down there, I think." Seeing the look of hurt and shock on my face, she sought to explain.

"Is that girl with you?" She tried to look past me, into the hall.

"No," I said, suddenly getting it. Adah knew about Norma Jean and Uncle Ted, and there had been hell to pay. (As I was to discover later, Ted had made a complete fool of himself over Norma Jean. Totally infatuated, he called her constantly and on every opportunity tried to see her. Meanwhile he controlled her drug supply, the lifeline that connected him to her.)

I didn't bother tracking down Uncle Ted at the Friars Club. I was infuriated, both at him for his pursuit of Norma Jean and at Norma Jean herself, for coming on to an old man who should have known better.

I spent the rest of the day hiking around Central Park in the bright sunshine, trying to collect my thoughts. I couldn't stay in New York, I concluded. I simply could not get enough work in the city to support myself. My only hope was movie work, the kind of work I could get in Hollywood. Besides, Norma Jean was there. Try as I might, I could not stop thinking about her, and it was clear I would go crazy unless I could be near her again. Okay, I told myself, it's decided: head back to Hollywood.

That night I called Norma Jean to announce my decision. "Great," she bubbled. "Listen, Eddie, I think things are looking up for me again. Guess what? I got a new part! And you'll never guess with who. The Marx brothers!"

The Marx brothers? All the way back to the West Coast, I could not figure it out. The Marx brothers hadn't made a picture in four years. What was she doing in a picture with them?

I found out the answer as soon as I got back to Hollywood. Although nobody seemed to want Norma Jean in the movies, a producer named Lester Cowan was putting together a revival of the Marx brothers. Called *Love Happy,* the film was a United Artists production and designed to prove that Groucho and his brothers still had some box office dynamite.

Cowan had one problem: he had the stunningly beautiful Ilona Massey cast as head of a gang of smugglers, but Massey, despite her beauty, had all the charisma of a tablecloth. Cowan needed some kind of luscious blond bombshell with personality who, even in a bit part, could ignite some of Groucho's famed lecherousness. Hyde alertly proposed Norma Jean. Cowan, however, was skeptical.

"I had the feeling he [Cowan] didn't want me in the movie," Norma Jean told me later. "I had just about given up, when to my surprise, I find out

Groucho himself will make the final decision. Hey, I figured, 'If I can't get the attention of Groucho, who really likes the ladies, I'll never get the attention of *anybody!*' So I go onto the set, and Groucho looks at me, and just raises those big eyebrows a little bit. I said to myself, 'Okay, you're halfway there, honey; he's looking.' Next he explains to me that in the scene, Groucho is this private detective named Grunion. I'm supposed to go into his office and hire him to break up this gang of smugglers. Then I suddenly look afraid and say to him, 'Some men are following me.' I walk away, and Groucho looks at my ass and says, 'I can't imagine why.' First he tells me to walk, just a few steps walking away from him, so he can see how I do it. I was scared, Eddie. I did it and he never said a word. Not a word, Eddie! This guy, who never shuts up, doesn't say a goddamn word to me. I didn't know what to think, but then Cowan says to me, 'You're it.' "

Norma Jean's walk and Groucho's leering line became an immortal scene in film history, but nobody knew it at the time. What everybody knew was the the picture was a dog, an absolute disaster that is still known as the worst movie the Marx brothers ever made. Cowan ran out of money, United Artists backed out of the distribution deal, and before long Norma Jean was worried sick that her little scene would never be seen.

Cowan, however, had two little tricks up his sleeve to save things. First, he contacted his old friend, the powerful Hollywood columnist Louella Parsons—she was practically a god those days to the movie community —and filled her head with tales about this new star named Marilyn Monroe who was "a poor Hollywood orphan." Cowan embellished somewhat Norma Jean's childhood, a move shrewdly calculated to play on Parsons's well-known sympathy for the poor and misbegotten of this world. Soon Parsons's columns began to be sprinkled with tender little items about Norma Jean, "Hollywood orphan." Parsons's column was read by the right people, and the name Marilyn Monroe was thus seen in the right places. (Parsons remained a big booster of Norma Jean right to the end, often explaining away the accumulating collection of Monroe outrages by citing her background as an "orphan.")

Cowan's second move saved the picture. To raise money, he actually sold advertising time in the movie. Although such advertising is now common in movies—watch how certain products are prominently featured in today's films, the certain tip-off that the companies are paying for the privilege—back in 1949, it was considered somewhat daring. The high (or low) point of Cowan's shoehorning of subtle product commercials into the film came in one scene when Groucho is seen high atop a "Flying Horse" sign (then the symbol of Mobil gas), soaring into the sky out of the reach of the villains.

So, Cowan saved the picture, and it was duly distributed. I didn't think much of it (neither did Norma Jean), but there was another unforgettable reaction when a movie audience got a look at it.

It happened in a small Hollywood theater. As Norma Jean and I sat, watching the film, there was a pronounced change as she appeared on the screen. The audience, mostly men, suddenly erupted in wolf whistles. Norma Jean sunk her head and slipped lower into her seat, but from her increased breathing and tightened hold on my arm, I had the sense that she was greatly turned on by the reaction.

"Gee, didn't they ever see a woman walk before?" she asked later.

"Not like that walk," I said. She giggled.

That two-minute scene in the movie, combined with some clever promotion—much of it in Parsons's column—made Norma Jean the subject of much talk in Hollywood. Convinced that her big breakthrough was now imminent, she bought a used Pontiac convertible. Late one afternoon, she picked me up and took me for a ride around Los Angeles.

"Well, I can't afford a Cadillac, but this is pretty close enough!" she squealed, her hair blowing out behind her as she drove around. She was happier than I had seen her in a long time, and the reason was clear: she honestly believed that the publicity she was getting from *Love Happy* would lead to bigger and better parts.

Like everthing else in her life, she drove a car with a sort of reckless abandon. I tried not to engage her in too much conversation, fearing even the limited attention she was giving to the road and traffic might waver even further. Actually she was bubbling over with joy, and whatever conversation there was took the form of one of her typical stream-of-conciousness monologues. I don't think I ever saw anybody so energized by the prospect of appearing in a motion picture.

She had bought the car on time, I discovered, which caused me some disquiet. Norma Jean really had no sense of money and even less about things like budgets. In effect, the purchase of the car was a gamble: she hoped to get more parts now, and the money from them would pay off her car. But, I wondered, what if she didn't get any more parts? What if the Marx brothers movie was just a brief flash in the pan?

As usual, she just waved off my concern. Some way, somehow, it would all work out. "Eddie, you worry too much," she said, giggling. "You sit there like a goddamn old lady, wringing your hands. How many times do I have to tell you? Your friend Norma Jean is here to stay! Ain't nobody gonna stop me now!"

But, as I feared, the notoriety of the walk scene turned out to be just temporary. Hollywood has a limited attention span, and only a few months after *Love Happy*, she seemed to have been virtually forgotten again.

"What am I, invisible?" she complained to me two months after the picture had come out. "Same old crap, Eddie: round and round I go to the casting offices. 'Ah, yes, Miss Marilyn Monroe; very nice to see you. Um, what was the name of that picture you were in some time ago? Uh-huh. Um, well, we have nothing available for . . . what did you say your name was? Oh, yes, Monroe. We'll be sure to call you if anything comes up for you.' Jesus, what do I have to do, wear a sign?"

"So what is your friend, the great agent Johnny Hyde, doing for you?" I asked her, a little wickedly.

"Oh, Johnny's trying, just as hard as he can," she replied, missing the barb. "He says just be patient, things will happen. You know, he gets a little pissed sometimes with me, Eddie, the way I always want to go, go, go. But sometimes I tell him, 'Look, Johnny, things move too slow around here for me sometimes. If you push things a little bit, you'll be surprised what can happen.' I have to be careful not to push him too hard, because after all, he's a big-time agent, and I don't want to be in the position of telling him his business or anything like that."

"Well, you're the client," I said, choosing my words carefully. "You have the right to insist on things if you think he's not completely responsive to your interests."

"Yeah, well, it's not that simple," she said, biting her lip. "Although, I'll tell you something. He never thought that Lili St. Cyr would give me the time of day. But you know what? One night, we're in Ciro's, where Lili's appearing, and I said to him, 'Johnny, please call her over to our table. I just *have* to talk to her.' Well, Johnny was a little hesitant. He didn't want to waste his points, you know, by getting Lili to sit down and talk to this totally unknown starlet. But wouldn't you know, Lili came over and she couldn't be more helpful. Anything I wanted to ask, she was more than willing. We must have sat there for I don't know how long. Lili took this makeup pencil and right on the tablecloth she drew sketches of how she thought I should change my eyebrows, how I should do my lips, the right kind of makeup to work with, the whole thing. The next thing you know, Lili is telling me how she'll get me to see Bernard of Hollywood. Bernard of Hollywood! Eddie, you have to be royalty, practically, just to get inside his studio! Johnny just sat there with his mouth open. He just couldn't believe what was happening. He told me there's no way Bernard is going to bother with some unknown, and I told him, 'You want to bet?' Sure enough, Lili takes me to see Bernard, and the next thing you know, he's got me all fixed up, clicking away on all those beautiful pictures. Johnny just shook his head."

However impressive, none of that translated yet into what Norma Jean really wanted: more roles. The plain fact was that beautiful asses were a dime a dozen in Hollywood, and none of the supposed geniuses who ran the studios recognized yet the very unique talents Norma Jean represented. Studio moguls didn't bother to mingle with the peasants in the movie theaters; if they had, they would have heard some of those audience reactions to Norma Jean's first screen appearances. And those reactions would have told them a lot more than the balance sheets they spent their time reading.

While Hyde was trying his best, Norma Jean, attempting to survive on a few modeling assignments, was feeling real money pressure. I was in no position to help out, since I was barely surviving myself on some occasional bit parts.

Her worst fear was loss of her car, in which she spent much time tooling around Hollywood. She loved the sense of freedom it conveyed, the feel of wind on her face. But she couldn't make the payments and was soon confronted with a direct threat: the finance company told her it would repossess the car unless she came up with a fifty-dollar payment very quickly.

Another fortuitous encounter came to the rescue. This one was with a man I knew slightly, a Hollywood photographer named Tom Kelley. He had gotten to know her after she crashed into a car one day with her pride and joy, that Pontiac convertible. Kelley was among several male eyewitnesses to the accident who pushed her damaged car out of the way, then helped her into a taxi. Not surprisingly, Norma Jean's minor accident attracted a small horde of males eager to help; one would have thought a major disaster had occurred. (I understood the reason for all the sudden male interest in her welfare, but I was more surprised by the fact that she had had only one accident. The way she drove, I thought Hollywood would be littered with wrecks.)

Kelley remembered the woman with the startling figure, and he and his wife later became good friends with her. Hearing she was a model, Kelley took a daring step: would she pose in the nude for him? Norma Jean initially said no, for back then, modeling nude was considered extremely daring. She had no real objection to nudity per se, of course, but worried that word of her nude posing would somehow wreck her movie career.

By fortunate coincidence, at the very time Norma Jean faced loss of her beloved car, Kelley had an assignment to shoot a nude calendar—the typical kind that hung in the male-only barbershops and automobile repair shops in that era. He needed a nude model, and since the job paid fifty dollars for whoever wanted to pose, Norma Jean changed her mind and became his model.

Thus was born what is probably the most famous nude photograph of all time. No one at the time had any inkling what would happen; then it was simply another, typical "nudie cutie" shot that made barbershops such stimulating places for young men to get their hair cut.

"It might be a problem," I told Norma Jean when

she showed me the pictures. "You know how things are. If it gets out that you in fact posed for it, Christ knows what might happen."

The pictures Kelley took were stunning, but Norma Jean was frowning at the ones the photographer did not distribute to his client. "Look," she said, "my pussy hair is showing. Now everybody will know I'm not a natural blonde!"

"Who cares about that?" I said. I was wrong again.

Chapter eleven

★

THE WOO-WOO GIRL

Sometime during the spring of 1950 I picked up one of the local newspapers in Los Angeles and spotted, on an inside page, a large picture of a woman very familiar to me. She was sitting in a chair, provocatively posed, and holding three ice-cream cones.

"Marilyn Monroe, the hottest thing in Hollywood," the caption read, "cooling off. Miss Monroe stars in the new Marx brothers film *Love Happy*."

The picture represented the kind of silly journalism then very much in vogue for Hollywood starlets. They were endlessly set up in ridiculous poses, usually pegged to the prevailing weather conditions or with some sort of obvious phallic symbols (huge firecrackers around July Fourth were a favorite).

I studied this picture of Norma Jean carefully. It was taken in New York, where she had gone on a desperate gamble by United Artists to promote their hopelessly bad movie. She was stunning, all right, but I was also struck by another change in her. Now she seemed to take to the camera naturally, instinctively assuming the pose that showed her off to best advantage.

"Christ, what a nightmare!" she told me when she returned from her two-week tour. "Les [Cowan] gave me seventy-five bucks to get some clothes for my appearances in New York, and for some reason, I bought three woolen suits for twenty-five dollars each. I don't know what was running through my mind, to buy *woolen* suits. I guess I figured it must still be a little cold in New York. Cold! Jesus, they were having some sort of a heat wave there. The temperature was somewhere around ninety degrees. I thought I'd pass out from the heat. What a horror show! The only funny part was when some of these reporter guys decided to give me a nickname. You know what these meatheads decided on? 'The Woo-Woo Girl.' The *Woo-Woo Girl!* Can you beat it, Eddie?" She collapsed in giggles. Thereafter, if I wanted a laugh out of her, I simply had to say, "Hello, woo-woo girl," and she would immediately convulse in hysterical laughter.

However funny, the effort by the reporters to find a label for the stunning new beauty indicated that Norma Jean had attracted more attention than was usual for such publicity tours. The result convinced Hyde that it was time to turn up the juice a little bit. To Norma Jean's delight, he bought her a whole new wardrobe, then escorted her to just about every party within the Hollywood movie community. He introduced her to every single producer and director he could find.

At this point Hyde's entire life revolved around Norma Jean, the woman with whom he was so totally infatuated, he could seldom take his eyes off her. To his friends around Hollywood, he was clearly becoming unglued. Soon the whispers and gossip began: Hyde was nuts about her, but she wouldn't marry him. Why? "I love you, but I'm not *in* love with you," she supposedly told him enigmatically. No one except those who really knew her understood it—and the real point of it all. Norma Jean, as she had often told me, simply could not bring herself to love this man who had now devoted his entire life to her.

For his part, Hyde did not understand. No matter how hard he tried, no matter that he had given up his family, no matter that he reoriented his entire professional career to her, no matter that he wept like a baby while begging her to marry him, nothing seemed to move her to marry him. In his totally smitten state he chose to overlook the fact that it was Norma Jean who went after him first, in a completely calculated move to enhance her career. She never expected him to fall so deeply in love with her, but at the same time, she felt he held the key to her future career, so she could not break off with him completely.

Thus her enigmatic reply to his persistent attempts at marriage. It only made things worse, and Hyde's friends, concerned about his health, intervened. In a steady procession the friends came to Norma Jean, begging her to marry Hyde. (The supplicants included, incredibly enough, Joe Schenck himself, one of Hyde's closest friends, who used the occasion to try to convince Norma Jean to go to bed with him.)

The whole experience unhinged her. We went out together one night and wound up in a motel just north of Los Angeles. To my distress, she was jumpy as a nervous cat.

"How do I get myself into these things?" she complained. "I know you don't like Johnny, Eddie, but you have to believe that he really wants what's best for me. Now every minute it's 'Marilyn, when are you going to marry me? Marilyn, when are you going to marry me?' I tell him as nicely as I can, and it's like I'm talking to the wall. What am I going to do, Eddie? I don't really want to hurt him. How can I solve the problem?"

'There's no easy way," I replied, although there was another thought running through my mind. That thought was supremely cynical, but also correct: the minute Norma Jean made her big breakthrough, that would be the end of Johnny Hyde. And it would be the end because she would simply turn her back on him. At that point she would no longer need him.

We batted around the problem for what seemed to be hours, and just when I thought the topic of discussion was ended, she'd come back to it. All the while she complained how she couldn't sleep. Periodically she'd dip into the pills she carried in her handbag, the ones my Uncle Ted was providing. It seemed to me that she was gulping more pills than ever.

"Well, I *need* them, Eddie," she explained defensively. "You know I find it real hard to get to sleep. We've discussed this before."

"I know, but it's getting worse."

"So? My sleeping problem is getting worse."

End of discussion. There was really no point in going on. As a friend and lover (the latter role was becoming more and more occasional), I was not getting through to her. To my way of thinking, she was developing the dangerous habit of conducting increasingly self-centered monologues, then looking to see if the listener agreed with her. When the listener did not, she became very petulant. I had the feeling that Hyde (and perhaps others), in their eagerness to win the favor of Norma Jean, were feeding that bad habit by stroking her ego and agreeing with just about everything she said. I still loved her, but I never felt any compunction to agree with everything she said.

When Norma Jean's first big break came, nobody—least of all Norma Jean—was quite prepared for it. The break came because of the famed director John Huston's habit of living beyond his means.

In late 1949 Huston began to cast for a new movie called *The Asphalt Jungle*, a crime melodrama to be shot in the style the French cinemaphiles call *film noir*. There was one small part, that of the moll of the leading criminal in the movie. Huston already had an actress in mind for the part, but did not reckon on the formidable figure of Lucille Ryman.

A talent scout and vocal coach for Metro-Goldwyn-Mayer, Ryman was married to the actor-director John Carroll, who once met Norma Jean on a beach in Santa Monica. Not unnaturally, Carroll fell madly in love with Norma Jean, and even after the affair broke up, Norma Jean remained friends with both Carroll and his wife. (This was a consistent pattern with Norma Jean: her sheer life force tended to make even the most emotionally wounded forgive her just about anything.)

Ryman ran a ranch where Huston quartered his horses—a particular Huston passion. But he was dreadfully behind in the stabling bills, and Ryman used it as a wedge: Norma Jean was exactly right for the role, and Huston should cast her in it. If he did not, then, Ryman hinted, Huston might have a financial problem when she sued for payment of his stabling bills, seriously in arrears.

Huston got the point, and the next thing Norma

Jean knew, she was invited to test for the part. Largely the test was a sham: Norma Jean was going to get the part.

Norma Jean did not know of the setup and suffered an acute anxiety attack. "I can't do it!" she shrieked into the phone to me one morning. "Jesus, Eddie, he's such a famous goddamn director. He'll take one look at me and that'll be the end of it. He'll eat me alive!"

I tried to reassure her as best I could, but she was nearly beside herself. Finally, when she calmed down, she knew what to do. She headed over to see her old friend Natasha Lytess, the drama coach, and rehearsed her lines. She was as ready as she could be when she was ushered into the presence of the great director himself, who was rather startled when Norma Jean asked if she could read the part lying on the floor (in the script she would be lying on a couch).

Actually, as Huston later reported, Norma Jean did quite well. Apparently a lot of what Lytess had taught her took hold, and Norma Jean was in the cast. The movie, with its noted semidocumentary style, became a classic of the American cinema, and there was a considerable amount of critical attention focused on the stunning blonde with a whispery little-girl's voice who played the part of the criminal's girlfriend.

Before the movie was released, I told Norma Jean that she should prepare herself for the absolutely worst possibility: even after all that work, it was conceivable her part might be cut out of the picture.

"Forget it, Eddie," she said. "You see, the part represents such an integral part of the story line, there's no way it can be cut. That's why I worked so hard to make sure I got the part."

Well, well, I said to myself, you're really learning fast, Norma Jean.

The much-noticed small role in *The Asphalt Jungle* led directly to the one thing for which Norma Jean had dreamed and schemed for so long: a long-term studio contract. It resulted directly from Hyde's frantic efforts on her behalf. In an attempt to capitalize on the momentum built up by the role, Hyde opened negotiations with Fox, of all studios, the outfit that had thrown her out some years before, convinced she had no future.

Norma Jean was thrilled, but I noticed a slightly sharper (and more cynical) edge on her joy. "You remember that sonofabitch Zanuck?" she said to me in her low voice, referring to Fox producer Darryl F. Zanuck, who had openly belittled her potential when she was dropped from her first contract. "Well, you should have heard him, Eddie. I could see he was trying to explain himself out of how he dumped all over me when I was there the first time. So he hemmed and hawed for a little while, blah blah, and then he says, 'You know, Marilyn, you have a three-dimensional quality. That's what we're looking for now.' Three-dimensional quality? I just looked at him, you know, and just smiled nice, and all the while I'm thinking, 'Boy, are you full of shit, Mr. Big-shot Producer. You don't know what the hell you're talking about.' "

She was quite right, for Zanuck, like other producers, didn't quite know what to make of her. As far as they were concerned, she was first and foremost a dumb blonde who couldn't act worth a damn and had no talent. And yet she was a woman who obviously turned on movie audiences and attracted critical attention. To protect themselves, they signed her up to a contract—and immediately confronted a big problem: where to put her?

Since Fox conceived of her as a dimwit blonde, the first role for Norma Jean immediately suggested itself: in a new film to be called *All About Eve* there was a part for the empty-headed blond girlfriend of a drama critic, to be played by George Sanders. Norma Jean burst out laughing when she heard she would be working with Sanders.

"Oh, Christ," she said on the telephone, reporting to me on her new role, "do I remember *him!* One night, about a year or so ago, I was at this party and I almost stepped on him. He was sitting on the stairs, looking pretty drunk. He asked me, in that voice of his like a foghorn, 'Ah, my dear, come sit by me. And who might you be?' So I told him, 'I'm Marilyn Monroe.' He just looked at me for a second and then he said, 'How very interesting. Will you marry me?' Then he fell asleep."

I was almost flabbergasted by what I saw when I watched the movie for the first time. Clearly it was a great movie, but I was most struck with Norma Jean. She was perfect in the role, a real actress. I couldn't get over it: what had happened to the shy, nervous teenager who appeared to have no hope of ever becoming an actress?

"The secret was that I was just *myself*," she said as we sat on our favorite perch looking at the Pacific Ocean. "You know who gave that to me? Natasha. 'Look,' she said to me, 'consider the character. Nobody thinks she's very intelligent, but she's very perceptive. She has a great deal of naive insight. Don't you see? The character is *you*. All you have to do is just be yourself, and I guarantee you, you will be perfectly fine.' She was absolutely right, Eddie."

It was late evening, and in the silence that followed, the wind picked up. It began to get chilly. We had our arms around each other, and in that moment Norma Jean stepped back in a time capsule. Again she was the teenage voluptuary named Norma Jean Baker. In that little-girl voice, she began to recite our favorite poetry.

"I've got it set up so that I never forget our poems, Eddie," she said after a while. Reaching into her pocketbook, she drew forth a book that in the moonlit darkness I took to be some kind of red diary.

"It's all here," she said, "flipping the pages. All the poems that mean so much to me. Also it has all my important thoughts, all the important things that are happening to me. Funny, I never thought I'd keep a diary. When I was little, I used to hear about girls who kept diaries. But I never could figure out what I'd do with such a thing. I mean, so few good things happened to me, what would I write? You're only supposed to put good things in a diary, right?"

"Not necessarily," I said. "You can put anything you want in it. I mean, it's supposed to be something very private between yourself and it, so you can put all bad, or all good, or maybe both in there."

"I don't want to put bad in there," she said, her voice a near-whisper. To my astonishment, I was seeing still another of those remarkable personalities of this woman. Now she was in a time warp, moving backward in her life. I was hearing the ten-year-old Norma Jean. She had drawn her knees up to her chin and with her arms wrapped tightly around them she actually seemed to be rolling herself up into a protective ball.

"No, I just want happy things in there," she said. "I'm tired of bad things, Eddie. I'm on the road I want to be on now, and nobody is going to do anything bad to me ever again. Nobody. Every time something happy happens to me, every time I read a good poem, I'm going to put it in this diary. And many years from now, long after I'm dead, I want you to publish this diary, Eddie. I want everybody to read what's in there and have them say, 'That Norma Jean, what a great life she must have had! Look at all this beautiful poetry, look at all these beautiful experiences.' So whatever people say about me, everybody will really know that I was a nice person."

The tragedy of all this was that terms like "nice person" had no place in the Hollywood of 1950 (or any other year, for that matter). I never was much of a believer in astrology, but I couldn't help thinking that Norma Jean, a Gemini, exhibited all the classic symptoms of a split personality. Indeed, it was the real crux of her entire approach to life. On the one hand she was totally naive, a child-woman who craved love and affection, along with reassurance, in gargantuan amounts. But, as her single-minded drive to succeed demonstrated, she was also just as hard as nails, with a habit of using people that was almost breathtaking. She was soft and hard, and you never quite knew which Norma Jean you would be dealing with at any particular moment.

The case of Johnny Hyde demonstrated clearly both sides of her personality.

Whatever I thought of Hyde, I had to admit he had really knocked himself out for Norma Jean. As a matter of fact, he had done *too* much. Soon after his chief client won her Fox contract, the wear and tear on Hyde's already weak heart began to show. Those who saw him around town proclaimed him a walking dead man. He looked as though he was about to keel over any moment. (Indeed, he had suffered a heart seizure before the filming of *All About Eve* began. Advised to rest and take it easy, Hyde threw himself with even greater energy into the task of building up Norma Jean's career. It was a course of virtual suicide.)

Around this time Norma Jean began what would become her lifetime habit of late-night phone calls to friends, sharing her most intimate thoughts and fears. I got a lot of them, and in the winter of 1950 they were dominated by her concern for Hyde's health.

"God, he looks awful," she reported one night. "He's lost a lot of weight, and he can't even climb stairs anymore. His chauffeur has to carry him up the stairs and put him to bed. Eddie, to tell you the truth, I don't really want to be around him anymore, he looks so bad. But I can't leave him now. I get the feeling I'm the only thing keeping him alive now. I'm just about the only spark he's got left."

By mid-December Hyde was obviously slipping fast. On the sixteenth he had his last heart attack. Two days later he was dead.

Norma Jean fell apart. The burden of grief and guilt— there were whispers around town that the sole source of his heart failure was the pressure brought on by trying to keep up sexually with Hollywood's most noted sexual athlete—was just too much for her to bear. Despite the Hyde family's specific request not to do so, she attended the funeral services, during which she unsettled everybody by screaming out Hyde's name repeatedly; at one point she tried to throw herself into the open grave.

I received one phone call from her that was virtually unintelligible. I did sense she was badly unhinged and set about to find her.

She was not at Hyde's house, and nobody else seemed to have seen her since the funeral. By now thoroughly alarmed, I searched every place I thought she might be hiding out. My fear was that in her mental state, the possibility of suicide was very real. Certainly she had talked of death often enough, and I always regarded her as the classic suicidal personality.

I did not know it at the time of my search, but Norma Jean had in fact tried to commit suicide. She had returned to Natasha Lytess's house, locked herself in a room, then taped up a note on the door ordering that Hyde's children not be allowed to enter. The note was a cry of despair. Overwhelmed by guilt, she was convinced that Hyde's children held her personally responsible for their father's death.

Fortunately Natasha arrived at the house and immediately deduced that Norma Jean was in serious trouble. She burst into the room and found Norma Jean lying on the bed, a stream of purplish, thick liquid oozing from one side of her mouth. Natasha knew immediately what it was. She forced her fingers into Norma Jean's mouth and found it choked with several dozen Nembutal capsules, sufficient to induce a coma from which no one would ever awake.

It was not hard to reconstruct what had happened: Norma Jean had decided to commit suicide and began stuffing the capsules into her mouth. At some point, realizing what she was doing, she had second thoughts; her throat dried in terror. But she was already slipping away. It was only a matter of time before the capsules would melt and slowly leak into her digestive system. It would be a slow death, but with no one around to stop it, the death would be quite certain. Had Natasha not arrived in time, Norma Jean would have died.

"I'm not sure I understand," I said. Norma Jean sat beside me, her chin on her knees. Again, we were beside the Pacific, looking into the eternal waters.

"You don't know what the whole Johnny thing did to me," she said, in a hoarse whisper, the heritage of the damage done to her by the near-suicide. "Jesus Christ, Eddie, I've got guilt about the size of the Rock of Gibraltar. You don't know what it is to walk into Johnny's office and see all those people looking at you, saying with their eyes, 'Here's the whore, the whore who's killed Johnny.' Everybody says that."

"Everybody doesn't say that."

"Oh, come on, Eddie," she said, tears in her eyes. "What do you think, I'm dumb? You don't think I hear the whispers all over this fucking town? You don't think I can feel people pointing at me behind my back, saying what a bitch I am, the whore, the man-killer who just sucked this guy dry, who wouldn't even marry him, when that's all he wanted from me?" She wiped the tears from her eyes with her sleeve.

"I'm your friend, and I don't believe it. And I don't know any other friend of yours who believes it. So who gives a shit what anybody else thinks?"

"Are you sure you feel that way, Eddie?"

"Look, Norma Jean, we've discussed the Johnny Hyde thing to death, really we have. I just don't want to talk about Johnny Hyde anymore. He's dead, let's let him rest in peace. I want you to move past that, to stop thinking about it. You're driving yourself crazy."

"You're right, I am," she said, very quietly. She sighed deeply, as if collecting herself. After a while she suddenly said, "Eddie, hold me."

Wrapped in my arms, she seemed tiny and vulnerable—terribly vulnerable. "Eddie," she said, "I'll never forget that you've stuck by me, no matter what I've done. Whatever happens to me, I want you still to be my friend. I don't care what I'm doing, I don't care if I'm any kind of a big star. Whenever you want to see me, you just come, and no matter what I'm doing, I'll be there to talk to you. Promise?"

"Sure," I said. "I've always loved you, and I still love you. I'm always yours, you know that."

"I know that, but I just want to hear you say you'll never leave me. And even if I'm a big star someday, we'll always be close friends, always. All through the years, forever. Okay?"

"Okay," I replied automatically, but the thought crossed my mind: how many years did this confused lady have left?

Chapter twelve

★

"I JUST WANT TO BE WONDERFUL"

Hollywood has strange and subtle ways of showing power, and in the case of Norma Jean, there was a demonstration of just how the system worked—and how it could destroy.

Betty Grable saw it first. When Norma Jean was just another beautiful bit player, the studio heads at Fox arranged for an elaborate introduction between her and Grable in the reigning sex queen's dressing room. Still fairly innocent in the ways of Hollywood studio politics, Norma Jean was thrilled to meet a legend in person. But Grable was not so thrilled, for she knew what the "introduction" was all about: it was a warning from the studio chiefs. Don't get too uppity, Betty, the warning meant. If you get out of line, here's your voluptuous replacement.

By 1951, as her career began to skyrocket, Norma Jean gained understanding of these little games. She only had about one hour of film to her credit, but it had set off such a wave of publicity, there was a prevailing impression she was the biggest star on the

Fox lot. In fact, she was a mere bit player—and, reputedly, not a very talented one, at that.

However, Norma Jean was learning fast. That year Fox arranged a very fancy reception for studio executives, distributors, and the studio's stars. It was intended as a big public relations gimmick to promote the Fox stable and butter up the powerful distributors into booking Fox pictures. The glittering jewels of this exercise were the beautiful actresses Fox had under contract, especially Jeanne Crain and June Haver. They were lavishing their charm, beauty, and smiles on the moguls, when the entire show stopped dead in its tracks.

Making a late entrance was a bit player named Marilyn Monroe. Dressed in a skin-tight white gown that showed off her hourglass figure, she strolled into the room via that famous walk. The eyes of every man in the room immediately riveted on this gorgeous apparition.

"Hi," she said breathlessly, as men stumbled all over themselves for the honor of escorting to her table. The women, neatly upstaged, glared.

"No, over here!" a voice boomed out from table number one, the big table where the highest and mightiest of the moguls sat. The voice belonged to Spyros Skouras, and it was a voice that commanded attention. As head of the studio's distribution network, Skouras had the *real* power at the studio: money. He decided which films would be shown, and how. Based in New York, he demonstrated the truth of an old Hollywood truth: movies are made in Hollywood, but New York is where the money is. And New York, therefore, is where the important decisions were made.

To the astonishment of everyone in the room, Skouras ordered the bit player to be seated next to him, by his right hand. (A studio executive who had been occupying that seat was immediately banished to a lower-ranking table.)

The effect could only be described in terms of a medieval court: the king, to everyone's shock, had ordered an obscure lady-in-waiting to sit beside his throne. Skouras not only had Norma Jean sit beside him, he spent the rest of the evening devoting every attention to her. He treated her like a queen.

Skouras, a shrewd old pirate, knew exactly what he was doing. While the studio executives were telling him this bit player did not have much of a future, Skouras heard about the nearly four thousand fan letters a week that were arriving at Fox demanding to see more of the bewitching creature. And while the same executives insisted to him that they saw little future in the curvaceous blonde, Skouras's network of distributors were telling him that their male audiences couldn't get enough of her. In other words, male moviegoers were willing to pay their money to see her in anything, and they didn't seem to much care what she was doing on the screen. Singing a song, painting a house, whatever, she was, in Skouras's terms, *box office*.

It was Skouras who ordered Zanuck to find movies for her to act in. When Zanuck remonstrated, noting that her limited talents (or so he believed) made choice of a proper vehicle nearly impossible, Skouras snapped, "I don't give a shit what it is. Put her in *anything!* I want her up on that screen."

Zanuck dutifully complied, but his limited vision

saw Norma Jean as a dumb-blond character. The chosen vehicles for her, therefore, would be a succession of empty-headed movies that amounted to exploitation of the only asset Zanuck saw: her considerable physical attributes.

Norma Jean was not happy about this development— she wanted to be a "real actress"—but she had brought it on herself. Her performance at that Fox reception got the desired result and served as a warning shot to Fox executives that she was not to be trifled with. But Skouras was no mental giant and, as a businessman, saw Norma Jean in precisely the terms she hated: as a beautiful vision, to be fully exploited on the screen and every other way he could think of. She could not have it both ways.

But then, Norma Jean always wanted it both ways. She wanted to become a sex symbol in order to break through the studio gates but then wanted everybody to forget about all that at the moment she decided to become a "serious" actress. But movies are businesses, Twentieth Century-Fox prominently among them. What studio, having achieved box office success with a sex symbol, would jeopardize that profit by changing that image?

The simple fact was that Norma Jean had become a commodity of flesh. That is the way the studio saw her, and the way they would always see her. It was the same way they regarded her most famous predecessor, Jean Harlow. Norma Jean, despite the fact that part of her name came from the famous sex queen of the 1930s, never bothered to find out much about her. That was too bad, for if she had, Norma Jean might have learned some valuable lessons.

For one thing, the minute Norma Jean embarked on the road of actress-as-sex-symbol, there was no turning back. The role would impose a terrible burden that few human beings were able to carry: these women could never escape the onus of being a sex symbol—until, of course, their looks started to fade and they were tossed aside like old rag dolls. Harlow discovered that truth the hard way, and she became so enraged by the exploitation, she cut off all her platinum-blond hair once. That exploitation, she also discovered, extended to her private life. When she was divorcing her third husband, studio executives were appalled to discover that among the grounds she cited was her husband's habit of preferring to read in bed rather than have sex with his wife. The studio desperately tried to suppress this document on the grounds that it would severely injure their sex commodity: how sexy could she be, it was argued, if she couldn't even get this guy's mind off a book?

To their delight, studio executives at Fox had a new sex queen who had no trouble keeping men's minds focused on sex. Clearly Norma Jean regarded sex as one of nature's great gifts and seemed to have no inhibitions whatsoever (people who worked in the wardrobe and makeup sections of the studio were soon abuzz with tales about how Norma Jean often walked around in the nude, with no self-consciousness whatsoever). They began to exploit that naturalness by making it somewhat suggestive and smutty.

Norma Jean seemed to have no sense how the studio was beginning to warp her persona in the name of greater profit. To her bosses, she was a slightly bizarre, puzzling creature who seemed to be a mass of contradictions, unlike anyone they had ever dealt with before. The studio gossip circles began to hum with Norma Jean stories, including one from the contract department about what she said the day she signed her contract. One of the executives there was trying to explain the meaning of some of the provisions, including a stepped salary schedule that started her at a salary of five hundred dollars a week.

As he droned on, he got the sense that Norma Jean really wasn't paying attention, which he interpreted as a signal that she was unhappy with the contract provisions. "Well, Miss Monroe, what, then, do you want?" he asked her.

"Oh, I just want to be wonderful," she said, in that vague, airy tone she used when she didn't really care about something. It took a week for the man to get over his shock; he had never encountered an actress who did not care about her contract in minute detail.

Or there were the stories about the vague fog in which she seemed to move many hours of the day. I recognized it immediately, for Norma Jean tended to move only in response to the sound of her own drum. It was largely why you could never depend on her for punctuality. She would show up when she was ready to, and even when she finally arrived, hours late, her apparently guileless innocence and breathy charm would make all those forced to wait forgive her.

Studios run on tight schedules, and Norma Jean's chronic lateness and general ethereal air finally brought Darryl F. Zanuck himself on the set one day to crack the whip. Chomping on a cigar, Zanuck laid down the law: all this crap would cease immediately. She would get to work on time, and that was that.

"Oh, I'm not late, Mr. Zanuck," she said with perfect wide-eyed innocence. "Everybody else is too early." Zanuck was rendered absolutely speechless.

There was also much talk about Norma Jean's reading habits. Never an intellectual, she nevertheless had a deep hunger for learning and was always reading books—especially poetry—recommended to her by other actors or friends. (During the shooting of *All About Eve*, director Joseph L. Mankiewicz, who had heard that Norma Jean was an empty-headed bimbo, was astounded to see her devouring a volume of Rilke's poetry. As Mankiewicz noted, he doubted that hardly anyone else in Hollywood had ever heard of Rilke, much less read his poetry.)

No one knew quite what to make of the beautiful woman with the breathy voice who in conversation could often sound like a thirteen-year-old—and yet, minutes later, would be seen reading a difficult volume of poetry or literature. Nor could anyone make much sense of the incident one day when Norma Jean was deeply absorbed in a book of love poetry. When a crew member interrupted to tell her she would be needed shortly, she replied, without even looking up, "Go fuck yourself."

The answer, of course, was that this was Norma Jean, an often maddening and contradictory personality. All the stories about this distinctly nonconformist woman in a conformist era made perfect sense to me, for as I often told people, Norma Jean operated in an existence that made you accept her on her terms, and her terms only. You felt like either killing her or making love to her; there was seldom anything in between.

At the time, I had no real fear that the studio would eventually destroy the fragile personality that was Norma Jean. What I was concerned about was the extent of her awareness of the danger. Not much, I found out.

"Oh, I don't give a shit about them," she said, with that characteristic wave of the hand, as though she were shooing away a pesky fly. I found the answer alarming: as usual, she was quite convinced that no matter what happened, she would impose her own order on things. I was not prepared to argue the point, although I had the sense that she might have difficulty in dealing with the great fame that seemed to beckon on the horizon.

I had never known fame, but I knew plenty of people who did, so I had some sense of the terrible toll it can take. I tried to warn Norma Jean, the child-woman, about it, but she did not appear to be listening.

"Well, that's the last cock I'll ever have to suck," she announced to me just after she got her studio contract, and that was the extent of her analysis about the whole thing. She did not realize that her real struggles were just beginning.

"You know, I feel funny about this," I said one Saturday morning as we headed toward San Francisco together. We had decided to spend a weekend there.

"What for?" Norma Jean asked.

"Oh, you know, you're Marilyn Monroe now."

"No, I'm not; I'm Norma Jean. You remember me, don't you?" She giggled.

"Yeah, yeah, but you know what I mean. It's different now. I'm running around, trying to scrape up a few nickels, and here you are, the big starlet all of a sudden. According to the trades, you're going to be the biggest star in the history of the movies. So what are you doing with some broken-down actor?"

"Oh, bullshit," she said, giggling again. "Hey, Eddie, this is old Norma Jean. You think just because I have a big contract now, Norma Jean died or something?"

I did not answer, for that was precisely what I feared. As if to prove there was no possibility of it ever happening, Norma Jean was very much her old self during that weekend. It seemed like old times, and we acted like two teenagers, excitedly walking around the city and sampling its delights. That night we stopped in at Bimbo's 365 Club (then one of San Francisco's leading nightspots) to watch the chief act on the bill, good old Uncle Ted Lewis.

In a way, stopping in at the club to watch Ted's act was something of a mistake, for it reminded me of a few things I would rather have forgotten. After the show Norma Jean and I went backstage. Norma Jean greeted Uncle Ted by kissing him full on the lips, like a movie clinch.

"Oh, Teddy, it's so good to see you again!" she gushed. What a crock, I thought, acting like she hadn't seen him in a long time. I knew she was not only seeing him on the sneak but was also still getting her drugs from him.

I was still glowering as the three of us adjourned to Uncle Ted's favorite Italian restaurant for a huge dinner. I watched as Uncle Ted acted like a little puppy, hanging on every word she said, fawning over her as she discussed her adventures in the studio. Uncle Ted, like most people in show business, loved gossip, and Norma Jean regaled him with malicious little tidbits. "They call me the personification of sex," she said at one point. "Hell, I'm nothing compared to the biggest goddamn sexpot I've ever seen. You know who? You'll be surprised: Shirley Temple. That's right. She's the busiest little vamp I've ever seen. She goes after every man on the set. All that cute shit. Meanwhile she knows every second exactly what she's doing. You wouldn't believe some of the little stunts she pulls. You want to know how to use sex to attract a man? Watch Shirley." (Later Norma Jean, who had a habit of making catty remarks about any female she perceived as a rival, was to refer to Temple as "Lolita.")

All very entertaining, and I laughed along loudly with Uncle Ted as Norma Jean, a very gifted natural comedienne, told hysterical stories about the assorted peccadilloes of the Fox stars, along with a few devastating imitations. Yet, all the while, I felt irked. I tried hard to hide it from Norma Jean, but after the dinner was over, I took Uncle Ted aside.

"Listen, Uncle Ted," I said, "I really think this crap ought to stop."

"What are you talking about?" he replied, playing dumb.

"You know what I'm talking about: you and Norma Jean."

"Listen," he said, "she's over the age of consent, and so am I. If she wants to tell me something, she'll tell me. She doesn't need her boyfriend to send me a message."

"She's not talking through me. I'm talking to you. If you want to play around, Uncle Ted, that's your business. I tell you what bothers me: all those god-damn drugs you're getting for her."

He looked alarmed. "What drugs? I don't know anything about drugs."

"Don't give me that shit. What do you think, I'm blind? Besides, she told me about it. That's not right, Uncle Ted. Those goddamn drugs are addictive, and you know that just as well as I do. What are you trying to do, turn her into a junkie?"

"Eddie, you don't understand, you really don't. I'm just helping her get some prescriptions. What's wrong with that? Can I help it if she abuses the stuff? What am I supposed to do, stand over her twenty-four hours a day, making sure she doesn't take too many pills? For Christ's sake, you sound like your Aunt Adah."

I wasn't getting anywhere. "Okay, Uncle Ted, forget it," I said, turning away from him. "I'm just telling you, it's not right. If you think it's okay to get her that stuff, fine. What I'm telling you is that she can't handle it. Don't you know she tried to commit suicide once with some of those capsules you get for her?"

Uncle Ted seemed stricken. "Oh, Jesus, Eddie, I didn't know, I really didn't. I swear to God I didn't. She told me that she got very sick."

"Yeah, well, very few people know about it, but that's what happened. She came about this close to dying." I held two fingers close together.

Uncle Ted looked thoughtful for a moment and then, in a flash, reverted to his mask as the old master entertainer. "Hey, Eddie," he said, putting his arm around me, "we shouldn't be talking about this kind of stuff. We're here to have a good time, right? So let's have a good time! Tell you what we'll do: I'll start to cut her down on that, uh, stuff we talked about, all right? Pretty soon, it'll be down to zero."

"Fine, Uncle Ted, I'd appreciate that."

Now Uncle Ted felt fully expansive. He was playing his stage role. "Eddie, you know how I feel about you, always have. I felt so bad when I heard you were in New York and we didn't get together. Jesus, I had so much to talk to you about and a couple of nice places I wanted to show you."

He dropped his voice to a near-whisper. "Hey, Eddie, I know how it is. You know, a nice girl, a real nice city. Things can get expensive. You gotta have money to have a good time. I should know." He reached into his pocket and pulled out a large wad. Taking a big chunk from it, he pressed several one-hundred-dollar bills into my hand. A lifetime of pressing bills into the hands of fawning maitre d's and hatcheck girls made him very good at it; the money was in my hand before I knew it.

For a brief moment I considered handing the money back to him. But Uncle Ted had read me well; a struggling actor, very little money, determined to show Norma Jean a good time. I kept the money.

I realized I had made a mistake the moment I put the money in my pocket. Uncle Ted knew he had me, and he was now in full mettle. We returned to the table, and Uncle Ted, stretching his arms out wide, as if greeting an audience, roared, "Is *everybody* happy?"

Norma Jean squealed in delight.

He lied, of course. Uncle Ted had no intention of cutting off his drug supply to Norma Jean. There was no motive to, really. So long as he was her drug lifeline, the relationship she had with him was guaranteed to continue.

Had she used him? Absolutely. Did she ever have any feelings for him? Not really. He was, first and foremost, the link to Johnny Hyde, the superagent who became responsible, more than any one man, for the transformation of Norma Jean Baker into Marilyn Monroe. Normally she would have abandoned Uncle Ted at that point, having achieved her chief aim of the liaison in the first place. But she did not count on a trump card that Ted Lewis, a very shrewd man, kept up his sleeve. He spotted her vulnerability—the dependency on pills to get a night's rest.

It was that vulnerability that Uncle Ted fully exploited. It kept Norma Jean coming to him for years, as late as 1957, when Uncle Ted, sick and ailing (he was to die some years later of lung cancer), would meet her secretly at a park-bench rendezvous in New York City's Central Park. What a pathetic sight! The old vaudeville trouper, increasingly living in the past as the new show business passed his generation by, desperately trying to impress the love goddess. Somewhere in the city he would take her to a hotel room, trying to rejuvenate his dying body with the woman who represented the symbol of sex and youth. And all the time he tried not to tell himself that the only reason she was there was because of the bottles of pills he had obtained for her.

What did Norma Jean think of all this? I never did find out, because while she was always totally frank with me about her relationships, she was extremely careful when discussing Uncle Ted. Aware of the close relationship between the two of us, she trod very carefully in that area.

In San Francisco she was very curious about what Uncle Ted and I had talked about privately. "You guys both planning to dump me?" she asked, only half-kidding.

"No," I answered, "we're planning a new vaudeville act: Ted Lewis and his nephew, the schmuck."

"The schmuck?" She was giggling. "Hey, that's a real funny word. The Jews have a lot of real funny words. I keep forgetting, Eddie, you're half Jewish."

"You'd never know it from the size of my bank account," I joked.

There's an old saying to the effect that nothing is ever said entirely in jest, and my little joke about "schmuck" was more bitter than she supposed. The more I contemplated the course of my life to that point, the more disappointed I was. And yes, at some level I resented the sudden, cometlike success of Norma Jean. She couldn't sing, she couldn't dance, she couldn't act, paid no attention to the rules, did whatever the hell she wanted, broke every convention, and there she was, nearly a star. Where was I? Nowhere. A schmuck.

"Oh, don't start that self-pity crap again," Norma Jean said to me late that night in San Francisco. We were staying in a hotel high on a hill. Through the window the lights of that delightful city glittered.

Naked, she stretched languidly on the bed, unashamedly displaying her body to me. Tom Kelley the photographer is right, I thought: she really is a gorgeously beautiful panther.

"Hey, look at it this way," she purred, stroking her breasts. "How bad off can you be? Here you are, in bed with this great Hollywood sexpot who'll do absolutely *anything* a woman can do to a man. And you tell me you feel sorry for yourself? Hey, tell me another one!"

In spite of myself, I began to laugh uncontrollably. As usual, she had her own distinctive answer. In that mood I hardly noticed later as she began gulping pills.

Chapter thirteen

MARILYN

Although I didn't know it at the time, our little sojourn in San Francisco would be the last of such idylls. She was taking off like a skyrocket, and her time, increasingly, came to be dominated by her exploding career.

I felt the lack of actual physical contact acutely, although Norma Jean continued to call me on the phone. A telephone, I learned, is a poor substitute for the real person—especially if that person, like Norma Jean, possessed a unique physical presence that had to be experienced in person.

Combined with what I considered the dead end of my own acting career, I was not exactly in a jolly frame of mind. Those who knew me—especially my mother—became worried about my depressed state.

"What's wrong with you?" my mother asked one day when I visited her. I almost had to laugh at the question. Like many mothers, my own seldom asked a question for which she already did not have the answer. I mumbled a few vague generalities about life in Hollywood.

"You think I'm stupid?" she said after I had finished.

"No, but—"

"Look, Eddie, you can fool some of those people out there, but you can't fool me." She was knitting, and I was astounded how she could keep unerringly at the job, even while talking. The *click-clack* of the needles continued in a steady rhythm.

"I don't know what you mean," I said.

"Yes, you do. It's that girl."

"What girl?"

She sighed, the deep, patient sigh of a parent trying to deal with an especially thickheaded child. "What girl," she repeated. "You know perfectly well. Norma Jean Baker—oh, excuse me, Miss Marilyn Monroe. The one with the body."

"Oh, Norma Jean, that's who you meant."

"Eddie, stop playing me for a fool. She's your problem, and she's been your problem for a few years now. You think I don't notice things? You think I'm deaf, dumb, and blind? Eddie, I saw it the day she was in our house. I said to myself the first moment I laid eyes on her, 'This is trouble. This is big trouble.' You know what she was, Eddie? An angel and a devil all in one person, about the most dangerous combination of all. Now you can't pick up a newspaper without reading about her. She acts like a whore, Eddie. Beautiful, sure, but a whore."

"Mama, she's not a whore."

She smiled. "Oh, no? All right, have it your way: she's not a whore. But she *is* dangerous, Eddie, very dangerous. And do you know why? Because I saw it the first minute I met her: she loves herself too much, Eddie. She's so much in love with herself, she hardly has any time to love anybody else. Believe me, I know just how she ticks. And I also know what she does to men—fools, all of them, falling all over her.

She'll destroy every single one of them. She doesn't mean to; it's just the way she is."

I was silent a moment, considering. My mother, an Italian, had her people's wonderful native shrewdness. They are hard to fool. "I just can't help it," I suddenly blurted out.

"Of course, Eddie, I understand that. Don't you see? She'll say she loves you, but she never can, really, because she's so much in love with herself—or her career, which is the same thing. God help her, Eddie, she's doomed."

Odd, I thought, how much my mother had deduced just after a short while with Norma Jean. "Listen, it's a very complicated situation. I feel a certain way about her, and that's it. I can't help it. When I'm away from her, she's all I think about. Sometimes I think it's like a nightmare, only I never wake up."

My mother nodded, as though I was simply confirming what she already knew. "So tell me, Eddie, how did she get to where she is today? You know, when she came to our house, I thought she was quite beautiful, but she appears so different today. What happened?"

"It's a long story," I replied, and seeing she wanted to hear a long story, I recited to her the saga of Norma Jean's amazing rise. I left nothing out, including my own role. As I talked, my mother occasionally said, "tsk, tsk," and "Oh, my God," in disapproval. But never once did her knitting falter; the needles clicked away. She didn't falter even when I carefully addressed the question of Uncle Ted.

"You don't have to pussyfoot about Uncle Ted," she snapped. "I know all about that. It's all over the family. The damn fool!"

It was the only time I heard her talk sharply during my entire recitation. As I understood, my mother had a long history of tense relations with her husband's side of the family. They tended to look down on her because she wasn't Jewish, and she returned the animosity by making it clear she thought a lot of them were immoral lepers. She had a particular dislike of Uncle Ted for a variety of reasons, not the least of them her discovery that he had a bad habit of fooling around with women. His wife Adah caught him a couple of times, but he had always managed to win her forgiveness.

I felt the sting of her contempt, for I was aware that I had often been compared—unfavorably—to Uncle Ted. Like Ted, I was the wanderer, the rootless seeker of show business glory.

"I'm nothing but a bum," I confessed to her. "Eight years now, running around, acting like a damned teenager, and what have I got to show for it? Nothing."

"You're not a bum," she said. "You're young, that's the problem. You think you're the only man who went through something like this? Of course not. Eventually, Eddie, you'll find your niche, I know it. Meanwhile, I'll tell you what you must do. You must get this woman out of your system. Just stay away from her, Eddie. You'll see how quickly your feelings will change. Trust me on this."

Easier said than done, for there was no way I could stay away from Norma Jean. To a certain extent, events had already conspired to keep us apart most of the time, along with the constraint of simple economics.

The fact was that I was down and almost out. I

was making a living, to be sure, but it was just a living. I was in no financial position to take her out, certainly not in the style she was getting used to. Her liaison with Hyde had introduced her to the Hollywood social whirl of parties, expensive nightclubs, and all the rest of it. She liked that world. Like poor Cinderella entering the castle for the first time, she had really had no idea that people could live that way. And in Hollywood, I always thought, the phrase "conspicuous consumption" had been born.

Then, too, I felt a little ashamed of myself. To supplement my meager earnings in the movies, I had taken a job as a taxi driver. I carefully kept that fact from Norma Jean, for I could not bring myself to admit that I was a failure. In our phone conversations I was always upbeat: things were moving along nicely, I had the promise of this or that big part, I was just swamped with acting work, things were really going well for me, et cetera, et cetera.

I'm not sure whether she believed it all, but she acted like she did. "Oh, that's so terrific, Eddie," she would say, in what was almost a squeal of childish delight. "Great, just really great." Then she would talk about her own adventures at the studio, and these turned out to be somewhat incredible.

In a word, Fox was rushing pell-mell to turn her into some kind of sex bomb. The problem, as Norma Jean failed to perceive at that point, was that the studio saw her not as an actress but as a *personality*. That personality, Zanuck and his henchmen decided, would be an empty-headed blonde, innocent yet loaded with sex. Her roles in her early movies were always the same: voluptuous working blonde, innocently caught up in some sort of situation comedy involving a man and another woman. For these roles she somewhat exaggerated her breathy little-girl voice.

"Natasha [Lytess] is raising holy hell about these parts," Norma Jean told me one night. "Jesus, Eddie, she's making a big stink about it. I mean, you'd think I'd committed a crime or something. 'These parts are for shit!' she yelled at me the other day. What am I supposed to do? Hey, I just work here. I don't write the scripts, I don't cast the parts, I don't decide what I can act in and what I can't act in."

"Maybe she's got a point," I suggested. "Look, Norma Jean, what she's trying to say is this: you're going to get typecast. You know what that means? Don't you know how this place works? Once they get the idea you're some kind of dumb blonde, that's it; they'll cast you as a dumb blonde for the next fifty years if they can get away with it."

"Who said I'm going to be a dumb blonde forever?"

"The system does. Look, if they start making a lot of money out of you from that kind of casting, do you really think they're even going to listen to you the day you say, 'Well, folks, here I am, ready to do serious parts.' Come on, Norma Jean."

"You're forgetting something, Eddie. If I get to the point where they're making real money on me, my bargaining position is that much better. After that, you know, you're talking about script approval, and all that. And if they don't do what I want, I'll just say, 'Good-bye, fellows,' and head off to another studio."

"I wish that were true, but it isn't. You know, it's a big monopoly out here. All these guys are in on it together. I'll tell you what will really happen: you screw around with Fox and they'll blackball you all over this industry, believe me. Read your contract, Norma Jean. Your ass is theirs."

I might just as well have told her to go to MIT and

study nuclear physics. Norma Jean, I was quite certain, had never bothered to read that contract and had no real idea of what the "studio system," as it was called, really meant. She also had no real idea of what the studio's publicity machine was doing to her.

They had cranked up that machine to maximum power. Whether it was *Life* or *Look* or just about any other printed publication, there was always something about what Fox now modestly claimed was its own personal discovery. She was "hotter than Harlow." She was "America's sex goddess." Little cozy press interviews were arranged, where the interviewers, primed by the publicity department, asked questions about whether she wore any underwear and whether it was true she slept in the nude. Norma Jean played along, projecting precisely the personality the studio wanted: innocent sex, with a brain the size of a pea.

"What do you have on when you go to sleep?" she was asked by one interviewer. "The radio," she replied, deadpan. It was funny, admittedly, but how did that kind of publicity help her eventual goal of becoming a serious actress? It didn't, and that was precisely the problem. To a large extent, she was becoming a victim of her own publicity. Much later there was a great deal of nonsense written about how she was a "victim" of the studio. Perhaps so, but no more willing participant in the execution can be imagined than Norma Jean. During this critical period in the formulation of her career, she willingly participated in the making of an image she later tried desperately to shed.

"I've got to get away from her," she said to me on the phone one night. She was in tears. "Natasha's driving me nuts, Eddie. Christ, she's at me all the time. 'They're coarsening you! They're making you into a cheap tramp! Don't let them do this!' I just can't fight her anymore. That's it, I've got to go and get away from all this crap. I'm so tired of arguing about it."

Norma Jean was very upset—she later did move to a local hotel—but I had to admit that Natasha Lytess had a point. Her objection was not only to the image created by the Fox publicity machine, but also to Norma Jean acting like a puppet. Whatever the studio wanted, Norma Jean did. If they wanted her to pose for a publicity still wearing nothing but a potato sack, she did it. (Such a picture was actually made and distributed.) If they wanted her to give an interview to a leering radio interviewer who concentrated on her sex life, Norma Jean did it. If they wanted to write parts for her that made her sound like a moron, Norma Jean did it. When they snapped their fingers, Norma Jean jumped.

It was pointless to rehash that old argument, for I discovered that Norma Jean seemed to be on another planet. Occasionally I would visit her at the studio and, even more seldom, would have lunch with her in the commissary.

Several things struck me as I watched her in that context. The most striking was her pronounced self-absorption. I would sit in her dressing room, chatting, and notice that she hardly looked at me. She seemed to stare endlessly in the mirror at the image presented to her. She constantly touched her face and body, readjusting her hair and—in a larger sense—almost literally making love to that image.

"I'm not keeping you from anything, am I, Norma Jean?" I snapped at her sarcastically.

"Oh, no," she said, not looking away from the mirror. "I have some time. We can talk."

"Who am I talking to?"

"What are you talking about? Me, of course."

"No, what I mean is, do you ever stop looking at yourself?"

She turned to look at me. "Eddie, they're shooting in two hours. I have to make sure I'm ready."

"You've *been* ready. Why do you keep staring at yourself? You know, I came here to talk to you, not your goddamn reflection in the mirror."

She turned back to the mirror and said nothing for a while. "Well, folks, he's pissed off. He doesn't want me to look in the mirror. Gee, I hate to tell you this, Eddie, but what do you think actresses do in their dressing rooms, play basketball?"

"That's not the point. Jesus Christ, Norma Jean, that's all you ever do, look at yourself in the mirror."

"Don't be stupid. Look, I have to keep myself looking right, you know what I mean? Let's stop fighting about it."

"Okay." I lapsed into silence while Norma Jean, humming softly to herself, began working on her eyelashes for at least the tenth time since I had entered the room. Occasionally she interrupted that project to sip from a large champagne glass.

"What's that?" I asked.

"Dom Perignon champagne," she said, offering me the bottle.

I stared at the label. "Expensive stuff," I said, handing it back. "Too expensive for my tastes. Besides, I don't drink during the day. Very bad habit to get into."

She giggled. "You're such a goddamn Midwest square. Where is it written you can't drink cham-

pagne during the day? You can drink it any goddamn time you want, silly. Let me tell you, once I got
introduced to this stuff, I can't stay away. A hell of a
pick-me-up."

"Maybe," I said, noticing the little bottles of pills
on her dressing table. As if afraid of being over-
heard, I dropped my voice to a half-whisper. "Listen, let me give you a piece of advice, Norma Jean,
you have to stay away from the booze. You drink
booze and take pills, you could have yourself one
hell of a problem."

"It's not booze," she said firmly, "it's champagne."

"For Christ's sake, Norma Jean, wake up! You
cannot combine booze and pills. And champagne is
booze. Just because it has bubbles in it doesn't mean
it isn't booze."

"Oh, God help me," she said, sighing, "we're back
to the pills again. I don't want to talk about the
goddamn pills."

"Well, *I* want to talk about the pills. Norma Jean,
listen to me. You've got to stop with these pills.
They're going to kill you someday."

"Who made you a doctor?"

"I'm not a doctor, but my brother is. You know
that, right? Okay. You want to know what he says
about the pills you take?"

"No, but I'm sure I'm gonna hear it."

"Just listen. He says they prescribe them in small
amounts because anyone who takes them can very
easily become addicted if they're used too much. See,
here's why: gradually the body builds up a resistance
to them. So you have to take increasing amounts to
get the effect, such as falling asleep. You with me so
far? Okay, so what you wind up with is a dependency. The real problem is that if you use too much

of the stuff, you can suddenly go into a coma. And then—"

"Don't say it. I don't want to hear that kind of talk." She was glaring at my mirrored reflection, not even bothering to look at me directly.

"All right, then, I won't say it. But you understand what I'm trying to tell you."

"If you had the problem getting to sleep like I have, you wouldn't talk like that. I mean, you talk about me like I'm a junkie or something."

"Okay, let's forget the whole thing. I said it, I tried to help, that's it. Subject closed." Angry now, I refused to look at her—or her mirror image.

"Okay," she said, brightening. She moved her face closer to the mirror and began a minute inspection of her nose. "Hey, Eddie, you remember that seed wart I had on the side of my nose? Remember how ugly it made me look? Look, it's gone! Jesus, why did I carry that thing around for so long? One little twist of the doctor's scalpel, and poof! it's gone. See how much better it makes my nose look, Eddie?"

"Yeah, terrific," I replied, hardly looking.

"Uh-oh, he's mad again," she said in her little-girl voice. "Oooh, little Eddie's so-o-o-o mad."

"Cut it out, Norma Jean."

"Oh, come on, Eddie, what are you getting so angry about? Hey, everything's gonna be fine, guarantee it. Stop worrying."

I left her dressing room with my head spinning. I've got to get away from her, I vowed to myself. She's like some sort of powerful vortex. If you come anywhere near it, you get sucked in. I was convinced she was in the first stages of a process to destroy herself. How many people would she destroy in that process?

On the way out of the studio, I stopped in to see a number of people I knew who were working at the studio then, including Rory Calhoun. Nicknamed Smoky because of his smoldering handsomeness, Calhoun saw the look on my face and assumed I had just spoken to Norma Jean.

"Jesus Christ, can you believe it?" he asked, shaking his head. "Can you believe this blond idiot and all this publicity? I've never seen anything like it in my life. I know she's a friend of yours, Eddie, but for God's sake, how the hell did this blonde with the big tits get to this point? The whole goddamn studio is working to build her up."

Calhoun had a reputation for bluntness, but his criticism was not very much different from what a lot of people were saying around the studio. I heard it everywhere: "How the fuck did this bimbo wind up where she is now?" Or: "I remember her from acting school. For Christ's sake, she never even opened her mouth." Or: "She can't do anything, she's got no personality, she can't even walk straight, and you're telling me this is the 'star of tomorrow'?"

Nothing is so resented in Hollywood as success, and I'm sure some of this animosity was part of that phenomenon. But a lot of it wasn't, and an awful lot of people were both astounded and appalled at the rapid rise of Norma Jean's career. They simply could not believe that a woman they considered of little or no talent had advanced so far so fast.

To a certain extent, I wondered about that myself. Despite my intimate knowledge of Norma Jean, I was surprised that she had made such an early impact. I always thought she had an indefinable "something," but I assumed it would take a good number of years to develop—if Norma Jean ever cured herself of her laziness and settled down to work.

I should emphasize that Norma Jean really had no idea that she was anything special then. She tended to believe that her success was the result, first, of her beauty, allied with the important contacts she had made, polished off by the cosmetic surgery, and finally the invaluable advice she got from Lili St. Cyr.

Most of all, she concentrated on the little things. For example, one day she showed me how she was painting her lips now to make them more sexy. "This is a great trick I learned from Lili," she said. "See, you always try to keep them moist—not with spit, but with Vaseline. It lasts quite a while and always looks moist. Like Lili told me, what you want to create is a look that makes it appear as though your mouth is ready that very second for some guy to shove his cock in. It's very sexy for men."

Perhaps I got tired of hearing such talk. Perhaps I was getting tired of her. Perhaps I realized I would have to put some distance between us.

Whatever the reason, I began deliberately to lengthen the relationship between us. I still listened to her frequent phone calls—most of them, unfortunately, came in the wee hours, when she couldn't sleep—but I stopped visiting her at the studio. When she acted a little hurt about the end of those visits, I covered it up with excuses about how busy I was at the moment.

That was not true, of course. In fact, I was the very picture of the struggling actor, driving my taxicab when I wasn't snagging a few bit parts. It was while driving my cab one day that I stumbled into a very fortuitous change in my life.

I spotted a line of actors—including two I knew—standing outside a small building. Stopping, I asked what they were waiting for. It turned out that they were trying out for roles in a new play called *The Caine Mutiny Court-Martial.*

I went inside to put my name on the list of tryouts. The director, I noted to my satisfaction, was Dick Powell, whom I knew quite well. Just then a door opened and I saw Powell standing there.

"Ted Jordan, you old fart!" he yelled. "Come on in here!"

It helps to know a director, and Powell offered me the part of one of the judges in the play. To my delight, he told me that the play would be going on a national tour and would eventually play on Broadway. Henry Fonda would play the lead.

I turned in my taxicab and never went back. I was walking on air: Broadway! And better yet, it was far from Norma Jean.

Chapter fourteen

THE STAR

While I was drifting away from Norma Jean—or trying to—she was drifting away from me. The phone calls were becoming more infrequent and seemed to be made only when she experienced another crisis.

She always had crises in her life. Every time somebody yelled at her or she confronted a decision of some sort or got some reminder of her past, she began to go to pieces. Then the phone calls began, a series of them to just about everybody she knew. During the calls she'd pour her heart out, revealing the deep streak of self-doubt and insecurity that ran through her, and ask advice. Sometimes she even followed it.

She still had the capacity to make the right connections. One was Sidney Skolsky, the powerful Hollywood columnist, who became almost totally smitten by her (not an unusual experience among the men who came in contact with her). Nothing intimate went on between them, but Skolsky moved mountains to promote her career. He was close friends with a number of major producers, and one of them, the powerful Jerry Wald, was convinced by Skolsky to borrow Norma Jean from Fox to make a movie called *Clash by Night*. It was not a major part, but since it represented Norma Jean's first serious movie role, she worried to death about how well she did.

That question became obscured by what at the time was an even greater crisis. While Wald was busily cranking up the publicity machine for the movie—concentrating on Norma Jean—he got a call from Tom Kelley, the photographer. Kelley noted that the nude contained in the calendar hanging in God knows how many barbershops and garages was in fact Wald's new star, Marilyn Monroe.

At first Wald was aghast. In 1952, remember, the fact that a movie actress posed nude was big news and very devastating to a career. But Harry Brand, the publicity chief at Fox, was something of a genius at his craft and had an uncanny sense of the public pulse. What Brand knew about public opinion told him that times were changing. He decided on a dramatic ploy: through a series of press interviews Norma Jean freely admitted posing for the nude picture, citing the need for money as the reason. She implied that she was practically starving at the time, although the truth was that she used the money to get her car out of hock.

I was surprised at Brand's gambit and even more surprised that it worked. Brand was right: the public's attitude had changed on such things, and they were apparently sympathetic toward a young actress who seemed to be candid about her past. Clearly the old stigma about posing nude was eroding. (Further proven when Hugh M. Hefner, starting a new magazine called *Playboy*, used Norma Jean's picture as his first centerfold "Sweetheart of the Month." He paid all of five hundred dollars for rights to use the picture. Norma Jean never saw a cent of it.)

However breezily casual Norma Jean was in public about the episode, privately she was very angry. "That sonofabitch!" she fumed to me one night on the telephone, referring to Tom Kelley the photographer. "He never says a word to me. He just calls the studio and starts all this trouble. I'd like to kill him."

"Don't be so harsh," I told her. "Look, the guy is just trying to make a buck. He's got a nice nude picture of an unknown model. Later she becomes famous. Who can blame him for trying to capitalize on it? Look, the more publicity the picture gets, the more he'll make. It's business."

It took a while for Norma Jean to calm down, and when her anger was finally spent, she called Kelley to ask a big favor. Some of the photos he took of her, which were never distributed, clearly showed her pubic hair. This was a big no-no in those days, and Norma Jean feared he would release them to general circulation. Graciously, however, he gave her the pictures as a favor. (Somewhat later she gave them to Joe DiMaggio as a wedding gift.)

There was another crisis in Norma Jean's life occurring at about the same time, and this was a more disturbing one, for it was straight from the past she tried so hard to forget. A newspaper reporter, checking up on details in Norma Jean's official studio biography, discovered that a number of details were not true. Whether Norma Jean fabricated them or the studio flacks simply decided to devise a more palatable biography, I never knew. In any event, the reporter discovered that although Norma Jean was supposed to be an orphan, in fact her mother was staying in a state mental hospital in California.

"It all comes back, it all comes back," she sobbed

on the phone one night. "I can't walk away from my past. What do I do now?"

Actually there wasn't much she could do. The studio got her to issue a statement that, among other things, claimed, "Unbeknown to me as a child, my mother spent many years as an invalid in a state hospital." That was a flat-out lie, of course, but the studio was concerned that she would be portrayed journalistically as an unfeeling daughter. Norma Jean made no move to contact her mother but did arrange for her to be transferred to a private sanitorium. But to her distress, her mother's tortured brain made the connection between her daughter Norma Jean and the highly publicized starlet named Marilyn Monroe. Soon the letters started coming.

"Oh, my God, Eddie," she said, thoroughly upset. "I can't take this anymore. She clips stories about me out of the papers and magazines, and she writes me these letters. I can't handle it, I just can't handle it. I can't write to her. What am I gonna say?" The letters sent by her mother were heartrending. One that I saw some years later read this way:

Dear Marilyn,
   Please dear child Id like to receive a letter from you. Things are very annoying around here & I'd like to move away soon as possible.
   Id like to have my childs love instead of hatred.

                                        Love
                                        Mother

All this precipitated an even worse crisis in Norma Jean's life, for the encounter with the mother she had tried to forget somehow stirred her old dream:

meeting her father. Years before, she often mentioned to me about establishing some kind of contact with her real father, C. Stanley Gifford. She announced this plan to me one night on the phone, and when I tried to talk her out of it—I could not imagine what this man would do with a now-famous illegitimate daughter suddenly appearing on his doorstep—she insisted that there would be no problem.

I heard nothing more about it for some weeks, and then she called me again. She discussed a few matters, then suddenly blurted out, "I tried to see him, the bastard."

"Who?" I asked, playing dumb.

"Daddy," she replied, placing an ironic stress on the word. "You know, I hired this private investigator, and he found him out in Hemet [a community near Palm Springs]. He runs some kind of big dairy there, and he's been married twice since he left my mother."

"How does he look?"

"I didn't see him."

"How come?"

"I called him on the phone. You know, I just didn't want to barge in on him; he might have had a heart attack. I got this woman on the phone. I guess it was his wife. I said to her, 'I want to speak to Mr. Gifford.' She was cold as ice. 'Who's calling?' she said. I didn't want to tell her at first, but then I said, 'Tell him it's his daughter, Marilyn. His little girl.' Then I thought, Jeez, maybe he won't recognize the name. So then I said, 'Norma Jean, Gladys Baker's daughter. He'll know me.' She didn't say anything for a minute, then she said, 'Hold on a moment, please.' After a while she came back on the phone. 'He doesn't want to see you,' she said, real cold, just like ice. 'He says that you should call his lawyer in Los Angeles if you have a complaint. I'll give you the number. Do you have a pencil?'

"Jesus Christ, Eddie, do I have a *pencil?* What the fuck did he think I was doing, trying to get some child support out of him? What the hell is wrong? Was it too much for him just to see me? Was it too much just to say hello to me? I wasn't asking for anything, just to see me." She began to sob loudly.

What could I say? Not much, for the whole episode had reached the very deepest part of Norma Jean's psyche. All I could do was listen. I had no idea why Gifford was so frightened of acknowledging his own daughter. But I did know the impact it had on her: she was devastated.

No one who heard her wail about the abortive encounter could fail to be moved. (Yet, as was often the case, another of those Norma Jean contradictions came to play: some years later Gifford, apparently reconsidering his rejection, tried to contact his daughter. However, for reasons that I never understood, Norma Jean refused even to take his call.)

After a preview in Santa Barbara and other appearances throughout the country, *The Caine Mutiny Court-Martial* arrived in New York. On opening night I was surprised to receive a large bouquet of two dozen roses. Attached was a note that read:

To the only guy I met when I was a mere seed; the only guy who ever took the time to water my seed; the only guy with patience and love who never left or abandoned me while that seed took root and grew. To the only guy whose blood flows within my veins. My love forever.

Norma Jean

Fonda noticed the card. He picked it up and read it, then raised his eyebrows. "Hmm, Norma Jean. Isn't that . . ."

"Right," I replied. "One and the same."

"Holy mackerel," said Fonda, visibly impressed. "She a friend of yours?"

"You might say that," I answered, reluctant to get into any prolonged discussion about it. At that point I figured the relationship was pretty much over anyway. Why bother having to explain so much?

Sensing my reluctance, Fonda dropped the subject, but for the rest of the play's run, I was the constant subject of everlasting attempts to draw me out on the subject of Marilyn Monroe. A number of the attempts bordered on leering; some of them figured that I was trying to protect what they imagined must have been a relationship of incredible passion. There were plenty of Hollywood actors who fantasized about an encounter with Norma Jean.

What they did not know—and what I had begun to discover, by way of hints dropped by Norma Jean during our occasional transcontinental phone calls—was that Norma Jean was not having a hot affair with Ted Jordan. In fact, she had fallen in love with a man I would have thought held little appeal for her: Joe DiMaggio, the famed "Yankee Clipper."

The first clue came when she began to talk about Italians. "How's your mother, Eddie?" she asked by way of openers, then went on to talk about how warm and understanding she found her. "Italians are really great people. They're so warm, so friendly, so . . . *family*. They're like anchors, Eddie. Whatever's going on out there, no matter what the storm, they're always there for you, always keeping things right. You can depend on them. Once they like you, they'll do anything for you."

The next clue came when she talked about how Natasha Lytess worried about her reclusiveness. Or what she thought was Norma Jean's reclusiveness. My own experience was that Norma Jean had a horror of loneliness and would go to any lengths to be with people. At any rate, Natasha convinced other friends of Norma Jean of the necessity of dating. In turn, they pressured her to go out more often. One of them fixed up a date with DiMaggio.

"He's different than I expected," she said. "To tell you the truth, I never heard of him. I don't know anything about baseball. So maybe that was good, you know, because I wasn't too awed by him. Anyway, for such a big personality, he was pretty shy, I thought. Also very nice, very nice. He's so *warm*, just like all the Italians."

The more she talked, the more unhappy I became, for as the weeks went by, it was clear she was falling deeply in love with DiMaggio. In one sense I was happy for her. In another, of course, I was not, for I feared that even the thin connection we had now was about to end.

At the same time I began to wonder just how any permanent relationship could possibly work out. As I listened to Norma Jean talk about their life together, it occurred to me that they were two very different people. I heard about fishing (which Norma Jean did not particularly like), dancing (which DiMaggio hated), and social life in general (which DiMaggio generally disdained). I heard about how DiMaggio preferred the company of men, discussing sports and "broads," and how his idea of a big evening was to watch a ball game on television. I knew

Norma Jean well: she was a social animal and tended to wilt unless she was around people, preferably those who liked to have a good time.

I said nothing about any of these doubts and simply wished her the best of luck. "We'll always be friends, won't we, Eddie?" she asked. "Please swear to that."

"I swear," I said, convinced that it was mere rhetoric. The way she talked about DiMaggio, I assumed it was the end of whatever relationship we had. In fact, I had been going out with various women, but I felt vaguely bored with them. None of them, I realized, had that special spark of Norma Jean. Of course, they weren't as confused as she was, either, but then I had become convinced that all women fell into one of two categories—either they were normal and dull or they were a little crazy and very interesting. I never could seem to find anyone in the middle.

John Hodiak and Lloyd Nolan, two of the other actors in the *Caine Mutiny* cast, decided to take matters in hand. "A nice young fellow like you not hitched up with somebody?" Hodiak asked, with a twinkle in his eye. "Ho, ho, young Mr. Jordan, it's time we took care of this matter, right, Mr. Nolan?"

"Absolutely," Nolan replied, right on cue. "Mr. Jordan, Mr. Hodiak and I have decided to take matters in hand. Please put yourself totally in our hands. It is our mission, is it not, Mr. Hodiak, to fix this young man up with a beautiful woman?"

"Without question," Hodiak said formally.

I should have realized something was up, for both men were known as notorious practical jokers. But I decided to play along and found myself one night taken to a small nightclub called Le Boudoir. What I did not know was that the club was owned and run by Lili St. Cyr. Hodiak and Nolan were trying to fix me up with the legendary stripper.

They had an odd way of trying to accomplish that end. We watched her show, another stunning example of how to be sexy without a single overt move, following which Hodiak and Nolan sent word to Lili that there was an "ardent young admirer" just dying to meet her. Lili had heard more than her share of these messages, and she dispatched her maid to stiffly inform our table that Miss St. Cyr deeply regretted being unable to honor our request.

All the while Hodiak and Nolan, giggling, were plying me with drinks and encouraging me to be aggressive, to demand a meeting with the beautiful St. Cyr. "Listen, don't take no for an answer," Nolan advised, pouring me another drink.

By the time Lili's maid arrived at our table with the message from her boss, I was feeling no pain. "Look," I told her with all the obstinate courage alchohol provides, "I want to meet Miss St. Cyr. If I have to sit here all night waiting for her, that's what I'll do. Now, you tell her that. If she doesn't come out here to talk to me, I'm gonna get on my flying saucer, come back here, pick her up, and take her the hell out of here."

The maid shrugged and left. Little did I know that Lili had an obsession about flying saucers—she firmly believed that extraterrestrials were invading us at that very moment—and the mention of such craft apparently piqued her curiosity. A few moments later she came out and sat at my table. Hodiak and Nolan, having achieved their goal of setting up the meeting, quietly left, hardly able to restrain their laughter.

"So what's this about flying saucers?" she asked, staring at me.

The eyes that looked at me were among the most beautiful I had ever seen. They reminded me of a cat, vaguely Eurasian in set, an astonishing shade of green in color. They were practically hypnotic.

"What flying saucer?" I said stupidly. "Oh, yes, now I remember. I got it parked outside. Probably got a ticket on it by now. Anyway I want to take you to my planet."

"And what planet is that, may I ask?"

"Hollywood."

She laughed. "Oh, yes, Hollywood. Well, that is a very interesting planet."

"I work there. I'm an actor."

"Ah," she said. "An actor. And your name?"

"Ted. Ted Jordan. You don't know me, but I met you once. I didn't say anything then, but I had a friend with me. She talked to you. Now she's famous."

"Really?" she said, intrigued. "What is her name?"

"Marilyn Monroe. Oh, excuse me, Norma Jean Baker. That was her name then."

Lili reacted as though she had actually seen a little green man from Mars. "Oh, my God," she said, flabbergasted, "this is the most incredible coincidence, just absolutely incredible. You must be Eddie."

"One and the same," I said with a crooked smile. I felt somewhat naked sitting there as Lili stared at me. It was gradually dawning on me that Norma Jean, who had the habit of total frankness, probably told Lili just about everything there was to know about me. I could imagine there was not much Lili did not know about me at that point.

"Well, well," Lili said, shaking her head at the

astounding coincidence of it all. "You know, I have not spoken with Marilyn in a while. How is she?"

"Don't you read the papers?"

"Sure, but I was just wondering—"

"Well, Norma Jean and I aren't, you know, really together anymore. But we're still good friends."

"I'm sorry."

"It's okay, just one of those things. She's always been a very big fan of yours. She told me how much you helped her. She's very grateful. She learned so much from you." I diplomatically omitted mentioning the more intimate details of their relationship I heard from Norma Jean.

"Yes, well, I really didn't do much," Lili said, basking in the glow of the compliment. "I just gave her a few little tips, girlie-type things, you know, to highlight herself. She is really an extraordinarily beautiful woman. Whatever help I gave her, believe me, was inconsequential. Tell me about yourself, Ted. Or is it Eddie?"

"Ted, I guess. Most people call me by that name now." I was sobering up fast, noticing the exquisite beauty seated across from me. The parallels with Norma Jean were striking: the same rampant sexuality that oozed from every pore, the same stunning physical beauty, the same striking figure. The difference was sophistication: Lili was entirely self-controlled, aware every moment of exactly what she was doing. I felt a strong attraction.

I don't know how many hours we sat there in that little club, exchanging gossip about show business and assorted anecdotes about Norma Jean, the person for whom we both seemed to have an abiding fascination. Finally we left the club. On a whim, we hailed a hansom cab and took a slow ride through Central Park.

By now thoroughly sober—or at least I thought I was—I found myself almost in a sweat as I sat beside her. Those eyes, that throaty voice, that delicious little laugh, and the sheer physical beauty had begun to captivate me totally. This is a woman I must have, I told myself.

The next night at the theater I found a picture of Lili taped on my dressing-room mirror. "All right, who's the wiseguy?" I demanded.

"Why, Mr. Jordan," Hodiak snickered. "Mr. Nolan and I were just wondering how long it took, following our departure from Le Boudoir, before Miss St. Cyr's bouncer threw you out in the street."

"He didn't. As a matter of fact, Miss St. Cyr and I had a great time. We went home through Central Park. In a carriage."

Hodiak's mouth dropped open. "Also," I said, rubbing it in, "Miss St. Cyr will be going out on a date with me tomorrow night. Why don't you stop by and say hello?"

Hodiak began laughing. "Why, Ted, you old son of a gun!" The news spread fast among the cast, and I was soon approached by several of them—sometimes leeringly—who wanted to know all about the woman who at that time was probably the leading sex fantasy for an entire generation of American men. (Until she was replaced, eventually, by Norma Jean.)

If they were curious, Norma Jean herself was positively flabbergasted. *"Lili St. Cyr?"* she nearly shrieked several nights later on the phone. "Jesus, Eddie, that is absolutely unbelievable! Holy smoke! Tell me every detail. Don't leave anything out."

I recited the sequence of events with as much detail as I could recall. All the while, Norma Jean could not stop herself from giggling hysterically. "Who would believe this?" she said. "Christ, how many years ago was it when we saw her outside that theater? You remember that? You remember when we bought that greasy chicken?"

"Sure, sure. You know, Norma Jean, she remembered that night. She remembered you exactly. She also said she remembered me, although I think that's bullshit. I think she was just being polite."

"Well, now, Eddie," Norma Jean said in a purr. "Things go around, things come around. We'll all get together, right?"

"Right," I replied, wondering: what does she have in mind?

Chapter fifteen

BEFORE
THE
FALL

By any standard, Norma Jean was the most meteoric success story in the history of American movies. Like everybody else who knew her, I was stunned by it all, not only by the blinding speed of her rise but also by its impact.

In financial terms—the only ones studios really understood—the impact was unbelievable. Norma Jean's parts were steadily enlarging, and by the time she made *Niagara* in late 1952 (it was released early the next year), she was pure box office. The movie, the studio moguls noted satisfactorily, had cost about $1.5 million to make. But it earned just over $6.5 million—meaning that their contract player, the woman primarily responsible for moviegoers' interest in the movie, was almost directly responsible for a $5-million profit. And at that point she was earning a total of $750 a week.

No wonder the money men like Skouras in New York ordered her to be treated with kid gloves back at the studio. It was a bad mistake, for the treatment simply encouraged her lazy habits. Soon she was appearing chronically late on the set and generally acting like a spoiled brat. According to my friends who were working at the studio then, she was known there as "the bitch."

None of this animosity seemed to reach her. During the telephone calls she made to me, she seemed as gaily lighthearted as I had ever heard her. Her conversations were dominated by studio trivia and details of her relationship with Joe DiMaggio. He was living with her, and they were seriously considering marriage.

"I don't know," she said with a sigh one night. "He's really a nice guy, but Jesus, is he *dull*. I mean dull, dull, dull. He's so quiet sometimes, I hardly know he's there. You know me, Eddie, I like a little excitement. But he hates just about everybody I know. 'They're all phonies,' he says. Yeah, well, maybe some of them are, but they're a lot of fun, too. So what if they're phony? Hell, it's a phony business I'm in. I've tried to make him understand. Look, I told him, this is what I do for a living. These are the kind of people I deal with. You know, sometimes I get the funny feeling that after we're married, he wants us to move to San Francisco. His family's from there. Then maybe I'd quit the business. Oh boy, no way. Can you just see me, Eddie, a little housewife in an apron? Forget it."

She was right, of course, and I wondered how they could possibly work it out. Obviously DiMaggio was something of a traditionalist, and I had the feeling that he really wanted Norma Jean to play the traditional role of loyal little wife waiting at home for her man to arrive. That was about as far from Norma Jean's psyche as anything that could be imagined.

I was thus shocked when I got another call from

her sometime later. She didn't bother to identify herself, but the voice was unmistakable. *"Tum, tum, de tum. Tum, tum, de tum,"* she pronounced, without preliminary. It was the notes of "The Wedding March." I could guess the rest.

"I'm getting married, Eddie!" she squealed.

"Congratulations," I said, trying to put as much genuineness as I could into my voice.

She gushed on for nearly the next hour about how wonderful life would be with Joe DiMaggio. As she often did when entering a situation for the first time, she tended to see it with starry eyes. There were no clouds on the horizon, everything was absolutely wonderful, life was peaches and cream. When reality inevitably set in, the impact on her was all the greater.

"We'll always be friends," she cooed toward the end of our conversation. "Always, always."

I was more disturbed than I showed. There was, naturally, my own ambivalent feelings about her upcoming wedding—I always wanted to marry her, after all—but I also remembered all the things she had told me about DiMaggio, the things she didn't like. Why in God's name, then, had she decided to marry him?

There was no easy answer to this question. Primarily it centered on her obsession with Italians. I had my mother to blame for precipitating it back in Ohio nearly a decade before, and it had been further accentuated during Norma Jean's encounters with DiMaggio's typical extended Italian family. Norma Jean had always had a great hunger for a "normal" family with its attendant psychic comforts; large Italian families were to her the ultimate expression of that ideal. Half-Italian myself, I understood to a certain

degree why she sought the all-embracing warmth of
the people she considered the warmest on earth.

Among the contradictions that helped make Norma
Jean tick was her confused attitude toward various
races and ethnic groups. By 1953, when she had just
about achieved the pinnacle of her success, Italians
were at the very top of her list of "good people." At
the same time, however, she could be virulently anti-
Semitic (a prejudice that grew as she got older). To
my discomfort, she would sometimes refer to Joe
Schenck, the mogul, as "that Jew shit," and to other
Hollywood personalities as "Jew" this or that.

Occasionally I would have to remind her that I
was half Jewish and that that kind of talk made me
uncomfortable. She would immediately apologize, then
flit off, to alight on some other group, such as blacks
or Mexicans. Largely uneducated (she never got
beyond the eighth grade), she retained all the typical
prejudices of her lower-middle-class upbringing in
white California.

As I feared, trouble between Norma Jean and
DiMaggio began almost immediately, for not too long
after they were married, she began working on *Gentlemen Prefer Blondes,* the movie that would make her the
biggest star in Hollywood. From my friends at the Fox
studio, I heard stories of her lateness and the titanic
temper tantrums they caused in the director Howard
Hawks. He had plenty of cause: lateness on a big-
budget movie musical, with battalions of dancers,
musicians, and extras standing around, can cost a
bundle.

I also heard stories about arguments between
Norma Jean and DiMaggio, who occasionally visited
the set. He was plainly put off by what he saw of the

tinsel world of movies, and he made his feelings clear: he wanted her out of it. His motive, simply, was that he loved her. And because he loved her, he did not want to see her destroyed by that world.

On the set Norma Jean was a nervous wreck. Aside from her insomnia—despite DiMaggio's anger about it, she was drinking more and taking larger doses of pills—she was chronically late, precipitating all sorts of tensions. Sets are generally madhouses anyway, but with Norma Jean around, the atmosphere could only be described as complete chaos. To make matters worse, there were a number of little habits of Norma Jean that drove people up the wall. Such as directors: they confronted the unsettling sight of trying to direct a very nervous Norma Jean, while in the background lurked Natasha Lytess, coaching her with hand signals. Even the simplest actions required massive numbers of takes ("Diamonds are a Girl's Best Friend", from *Gentlemen Prefer Blondes*, required over ninety takes before Norma Jean finally got it right.)

The stories I heard from the Fox studio worried me, for they indicated a clear trend: Norma Jean was getting worse. And the studio wasn't helping things with their attitude of treating her with kid gloves, the better to protect their most valuable property—for which read "money-producing." Norma Jean needed discipline, not coddling.

DiMaggio was appalled by the kind of life-style she preferred. There was, for example, the incident in February 1953, when Norma Jean, named *Photoplay* magazine's "best new star of the year," arrived at the awards ceremony. Accompanied by Sidney Skolsky—DiMaggio refused to attend—she proceeded to pull a routine that wiped out every other female star in attendance.

Among the more infuriated was Joan Crawford, who had arrived a regal five minutes late, ensuring that photographers would notice her. She had no sooner assumed she had everyone's undivided attention when there was a hubbub. Norma Jean entered the room, wearing a stunning, skin-tight gown of gold lamé, with plunging neckline. It looked as though she had been sewn into it and it just about put every man in the place on the floor. While Crawford and other cinema queens seethed, all attention was focused on Norma Jean. Men among the audience of nearly four hundred people made fools of themselves, actually whistling, while comedian Jerry Lewis hopped atop one table and pawed the tablecloth, acting like a dog in heat.

Crawford subsequently gave an interview in which she pointedly mentioned Norma Jean's entrance, noting, among other things, "The publicity has gone too far, and apparently Miss Monroe is making the mistake of believing her own publicity." If Crawford intended this as a squelch, she badly underestimated Norma Jean's capacity for bitchiness.

"I've always admired her [Crawford] for being such a wonderful mother," Norma Jean said in a statement intended as a reply, "for taking four children and giving them a fine home." It was perfect, for people in Hollywood understood the subtle thrust of what Norma Jean was saying: contrary to her image as a perfect mother, Crawford was a child-abuser, beating her children with wire coat hangers. (This fact did not emerge publicly until many years later, with the publication of *Mommie Dearest* by Crawford's daughter.)

"That cunt," Norma Jean snarled during one of her phone calls to me, still angry at Crawford. "Who the fuck does she think she is? Did you know, Eddie, that bitch is actually forty-seven years old? *Forty-seven years old!* They use all those goddamn diffusion lenses to make her look much younger. Get up close, though, and you see she's a goddamn old lady."

"For heaven's sake, Norma Jean, forty-seven isn't old."

"It is if you're still trying to play the kind of roles she's trying to play. How dare she criticize me! What does she think, that I haven't heard all the stories of how she beats the shit out of her kids? That's why I made that statement. It was just right, Eddie. Boy, you should see how she shut up after that. You know what else? I found out that she said a whole lot of bad things about me that the reporter didn't write. He told me a few. He told me how she said, 'Well, there's nothing wrong with my tits, but I don't stick them in people's faces, like that hussy does.' Can you beat that? That bitch; she's got a nerve, talking about her tits. Hey, whatever she's got—and I don't see much—they're hanging down to her belly, guarantee you. But you know what really gets to me, Eddie? One time I went to see her, you know, like the peasant girl visiting the queen. She was pretty nice to me, but the next thing I know, she's coming on to me. She wanted to fuck me! And now she's saying bad things about me? See, that's the way she plays: if you don't fuck her, then she'll dump on you later on."

I quietly listened to this tirade, for Norma Jean, whenever she felt wronged by somebody, would at some point babble on like this, venting her anger. I learned to wait it out, until, exhausted, she would finally drop the subject. Then she would go on to more serious subjects.

"So how's married life?" I asked, when I thought the tirade was finally over.

"Oh, he's a lot of fun," she said, bitterly, referring to DiMaggio. "Like a funeral."

"Oh, come on, you can't mean that."

"I'm not kidding, Eddie. Guess what he said to me the other day? He told me to cover up. You know, he thinks everybody's looking at my tits. I said to him, 'Well, for Christ's sake, Joe, of *course* they're looking at my tits. That's the whole idea!' What does he think I am, Mother Hubbard? And then they're gonna have this ceremony outside Grauman's Theater, some big publicity for the preview of *Gentlemen Prefer Blondes*. Jane [Russell, her co-star] and I are supposed to put our hands in wet cement. So I said, 'Hey, there's a better idea: how about if Jane and I put our tits in that cement?' I thought it was a pretty good idea, but he just looks at me like I was a murderer or something."

The indictment she had prepared against her husband was long and detailed and centered on the one thing that had hopelessly divided them from the beginning: her career. Simply put, he had no interest in it, and the long hours of bullshit that delighted every man and woman who worked in the movies bored him to tears.

"Let me tell you something, Norma Jean," I said after she ended her list of complaints about DiMaggio. "You used to tell me how well you got along with him, how much fun the two of you had. I'll tell you truthfully, if you two had remained just best friends, we probably wouldn't be having this kind of conversation now."

"You're probably right," she sighed. "Speaking of friends, Eddie, I see you have an interesting one."

"What do you mean?"

"Don't give me that crap. I read the columns. What's this I read about you and Lili St. Cyr in Earl Wilson's column the other day?"

I confessed it was true. Since that first encounter with Lili, we had become, in the words of the gossip columnists, "an item." I avoided discussing Lili in too great detail with Norma Jean, for I sensed a slight edge of disapproval. Why exactly she felt that way I couldn't understand, but I continued to tread carefully in that area.

As so often happens in such things, before I knew it, Lili St. Cyr and I began to talk about getting married. How I actually got to that point, I really don't recall. All I know is, the more time I spent with Lili, the more drawn I felt to her. In those days, when you felt strongly drawn to someone, marriage was the natural next step.

It was also part of a general restlessness I was feeling. I was bored with *The Caine Mutiny,* and life with the woman then called the "Anatomic Bomb" promised an exciting new direction. Almost before I knew it, I had made the decision: I would leave the show, marry Lili, and begin a whole new life as her impresario, or some such.

It was one of the stupidest moves I ever made.

"Hello, *jewlopi!*" The voice could only belong to one person, and the phrase, her own invention, meant me. It was her odd construction signifying my half-Italian, half-Jewish makeup (don't ask how she got "jewlopi" out of that fact).

"You sound close," I said. For a wild, brief moment, as I looked out the window of Lili's room at the Astor Hotel, I imagined Norma Jean was calling me from a phone booth on the corner. Just as quickly I dismissed the thought. Norma Jean was in Hollywood, making movies and trying to salvage her marriage. It was the summer of 1954, and there were persistent rumors that Mr. and Mrs. DiMaggio were "splitsville," to use another popular columnist phrase of the time.

"I am close," she said, with a little giggle. "I'm right around the corner." She dropped her voice an octave, sounding more serious. "Listen, I'm gonna be here a while. They're filming *The Seven-Year Itch* in the city."

I felt my mind suddenly spin in some turmoil. At some level there was also a sickly fear: with Norma Jean on the scene, a hurricane force had arrived. There was no telling what would happen. Most importantly, I had managed to stay away from her. Now, with her in the same city, I was very much afraid of how I would react. I did not want to see her, yet I knew there was no way I could resist. God help you, I told myself.

It began almost immediately. Returning to my hotel one night, I found ten telephone messages piled up. All were from Norma Jean. As I began leafing through them, the phone rang. On the other end I heard that distinctive sound of racking sobs I had heard occasionally from her when she was very upset.

"I have to see you, Eddie," she said, about the only sentence I could understand from a jumble of sobs and broken phrases that poured out of the phone.

I began to recite several places we could meet the following day. All were selected for their privacy, since I assumed she did not want DiMaggio to know about it. (And for that matter, I didn't want Lili to know, either.)

"No! Now!" She was practically screaming.

"Okay, okay. Jesus, calm down, Norma Jean." Thinking quickly, I named a restaurant some distance away and gave her the address.

The restaurant was the perfect place to meet if you didn't want anybody to observe you. It was loaded with palms that hid most of the customers, who could then carry out their little trysts, or whatever, in almost perfect secrecy. I spotted her sitting far back in one corner, at one of the marble tables. She was wearing dark glasses and had a large scarf wrapped around her head. Even with that disguise, she was unmistakable. I felt my stomach give a little turn and the hairs on the back of my neck stand up. There was a distinct electricity in the air.

"Hello, Norma Jean," I said, with what I realized was a slight quaver in my voice. I gave her a quick kiss on the lips. To everyone else in the place, we must have looked like the typical couple having a clandestine affair.

She smiled wanly. "Well, well," she said. "So here's the man who's in all the columns. Wow, it sure is neat to meet such a big star. A big, hot thing with Lili St. Cyr, the 'Anatomic Bomb,' eh? Naughty, naughty, Eddie."

In spite of myself, I began chuckling. "How did you get out?" I asked her.

"I just went out," she answered, with a slight shrug of her shoulders. I was looking around nervously, worried that someone might recognize her. I pictured myself on the front page of the tabloids the following morning, neatly skewered by a photographer's flashbulb.

I ordered a chicken sandwich, but Norma Jean waved off all talk of food. "A split of champagne," she told the waiter, who slightly arched his eyebrows to indicate his surprise. Still, this was New York, and he had probably heard just about everything at that point.

"Eat something," I pleaded. She waved her head no.

I moved my hands across the table and took hers in mine. Her hands were ice cold. I noticed beads of sweat on her mouth and chin.

"Jesus Christ, what's wrong with you?" I asked. She did not reply. As her champagne arrived, she suddenly pulled a bottle of pills from her pocket-book, popped two of them into her mouth, and washed it down with a swig of champagne.

"Are you out of your fucking mind?" I hissed at her. "What the fuck are you doing taking downers with alcohol? How many goddamn times do I have to tell you, never mix the two together! Keep that up, and you're gonna wind up in the morgue!"

"Oh, Eddie, stop lecturing me," she said. "Listen to me carefully. I've known you all my life, it seems, longer than anybody. But most of all, I trust you. I hope you and Lili have something really nice. I only hope and pray you don't get hurt and go through what I'm going through with Joe."

So that was it. "Tell me," I said.

Norma Jean claimed the marriage was a disaster from the start. "I just can't get to his way of thinking. He likes to stay at home and watch television, and he still loves his baseball. But, my God, how much of that can I take? He's as sweet as sugar, really he is, and I know I've hurt him very badly, but I just can't go on living like this. Joe's love for me is stronger than my love for him. I never saw a grown man cry until the day I told him we would have to get a divorce. Oh, dammit, I've got to end this."

She recited some more grievances she held against her husband, including a real knockdown fight they had had just a few days before. She had been filming the famous subway-grating scene for *The Seven-Year Itch*, the one where the air blows her skirt around her waist. Crowds had gathered to watch the shooting, and DiMaggio was infuriated at the sight of his wife, her legs and panties visible, squealing with delight as all those people gawked. Some of the men made wolf whistles. To make matters worse, the movie publicists, knowing a good thing when they saw it, decided on a bold plan: a huge, eighty-foot blowup of that scene would be erected above Times Square, for all to see. It was too much for DiMaggio; he had a wife who was public property.

As she talked, I could see that Norma Jean was in bad shape, much worse than I had ever seen her. I was convinced her pill popping was the major cause, and when she casually put two more into her mouth in the middle of one sentence, I almost exploded.

"I thought that shit was gonna stop!" I nearly shouted at her. Several restaurant patrons turned to stare.

"You don't understand how I need them, Eddie. I can't sleep and I've got all kinds of problems. I'm working myself to a frazzle, and you tell me not to take anything to help me?"

To my distress, I noticed that she was slurring some of her sentences. "I thought Uncle Ted was gonna stop giving these goddamn things to you."

"Eddie, I think he tried. Don't blame him. I pressured him. I was the one. Christ, the poor old guy is so lonely. He told me he hasn't touched his wife in years. He practically begs me. What am I supposed to do, tell him no? Listen, thank God I came here to New York. I was running real low, so the other day I went to see him, and he got me some more. Don't blame him, Eddie. You know, he asked about you. He's hurt you haven't visited him."

I suddenly felt very tired. "If he wasn't my uncle and an old man, I'd punch his head in," I said. "What the hell is the matter with you, using him to get pills? What are you doing, eating them by the carload?"

She was under great tension, and I watched her make her characteristic nervous movements with her mouth and tongue. "Eddie, I don't need sermons, I need help."

"All right, I'll try. What is it?"

"Listen," she said, drawing closer and dropping her voice to a whisper. "You remember when Lili got into big trouble out in Hollywood some time ago?" She meant a rather sensational case in which Lili had been arrested for obscenity after part of her costume slipped during a performance at Ciro's. Part of her nipple was exposed. It seems incredible today that she was arrested for such a "crime," but things were different then. Fortunately Lili was a friend of the ace defense lawyer in Hollywood, Jerry Geisler. After a two-week trial, he won an acquittal.

"I don't understand," I said, puzzled.

"I need a divorce lawyer."

Now I understood. "That's ridiculous, Norma Jean. You don't need a guy with Geisler's reputation for a divorce."

"Listen, Eddie, I want him." The voice was low now: Norma Jean the lady with a steel inside.

"So why don't you just call Lili and ask her?"

"Eddie, I want you to help me. I want you to ask Lili to intervene with Geisler to become my lawyer. Also I want Lili to be a witness for me."

None of this was making any sense. Why did she want Lili as a witness in a divorce proceeding? I decided, finally, that I was hearing the pills and booze talking. She had no idea, really, of what she was talking about. We parted with my promise to intervene with Lili.

"So she's back." Lili, sitting in the hotel room, said it as a simple declarative statement, but I detected something more subtle in it. Things became clearer when Lili showed me a small pile of short notes she had received. They were all from Norma Jean. They were, to my shock, mash notes, gushing about the love and admiration and deep affection she felt for Lili. In other words, the kind of notes sent by a lover.

I hardly dared to ask. My God, I asked myself, what have you gotten yourself into?

Chapter sixteen

"IS THE POPE JEWISH?"

Somebody once said that Norma Jean played the best game with the worst hand ever dealt in the game of life. Perhaps, but I never thought the phrase "best game" was quite suitable for her.

Actually the problem was much more complicated than that—and at the same time simpler. Reduced to its essentials, the more fame she got, the less able she was to deal with it. The drug habit, the drinking, the self-destructive behavior were all part of it. They increased in direct proportion to her fame; the more famous she got, the more she tried to destroy herself.

This was not a popular deduction. To others who knew her, Norma Jean struck them as a beautiful woman pursued by demons. In this view, she did what she did to kill those demons somehow, not realizing she was destroying herself in the process. But I always thought the only demon she had to cope with was herself. As Tennessee Williams once said, "Hell is yourself."

The problem was that Norma Jean had the tendency to involve those who knew her in the maelstrom that was her life. So it was, I thought, in that year of 1954, when she directly reentered my life—and Lili's.

Lili agreed to talk Geisler into handling Norma Jean's divorce case, but made it clear she wanted nothing to do with the crackpot idea of becoming a witness. "Norma Jean," Lili said, "I don't want to be involved in any way in your divorce proceedings. I've had enough of courts, believe me."

While Norma Jean was getting divorced in the midst of a media extravaganza, Lili St. Cyr and I were married. The ceremony took place at the El Rancho Vegas in Las Vegas, where Lili often appeared. She was noted there for a trapeze routine during which she swung out over the audience gradually shedding her clothes just short of nudity. (I still treasure a photograph, taken during one of those performances, clearly showing an actor and occasional Las Vegas performer named Ronald Reagan staring up at Lili on the trapeze.)

A bouquet of roses arrived just before the wedding ceremony. These were from Norma Jean, expressing her hope for much happiness and so forth. They arrived at a somewhat piquant time, for I had had several long discussions with Lili on the very topic of Norma Jean. Among other things, I discovered that Lili and Norma Jean had occasionally enjoyed intimate relations. Lili was perfectly calm about it, for, like Norma Jean, her approach to sex was perfectly natural and relaxed. An incredibly sensual woman, Lili regarded sex as the most rewarding activity in human existence, with very few boundaries.

"Sex is free," she said with a wonderful Gallic shrug (although she was actually half Dutch). "If you like someone, whether it's a man or a woman, it seems to me that sex is a perfectly natural way to express your affection. I don't see any difference whether you're married or not, or whether you're in love or not. It's just a natural expression of how you feel."

It was the kind of sweeping argument hard to refute, and my experiences with Norma Jean had taught me that sex in its natural state was probably the way it was meant to be. Still, what about the question of marriage and commitment and so forth?

"Simple," Lili said. "Everything is all right so long as it does not upset the person you are with or your wife or husband. Hell, Ted, I know married couples who for years switch around with others. They're perfectly happy doing it. Who am I to condemn them?"

In other words, like Norma Jean, I had married a woman who was equally omnisexual. I was not especially disturbed by that, but I could not quite remove from my mind the image of Norma Jean and Lili making love. However sophisticated I considered myself at that point, for some reason the thought bothered me.

I was still in occasional phone contact with Norma Jean and learned she was about to enter still another one of her phases. In many ways, it was to be the most significant. First, she had decided to cut her ties with Hollywood, despite the fact that she was always very much a child of that strange place. Second, she had decided to cut her studio ties. With the aid of photographer Milton Greene (a friend of playright Arthur Miller), she would form her own company, Marilyn Monroe Productions, which would produce her future movies.

"What does Fox think about that?" I asked her.

"Fuck Fox," she snapped. "I'm tired of being exploited. I've been just a goddamn piece of meat to them. I want control over my own life. I want to be an actress, and I can't be one at the studio. Eddie, you wouldn't believe some of the shit they offer me. It's always the same: dumb blonde with big tits gets involved with man; man is mixed up in a funny situation; dumb blonde with big tits misunderstands; finally it all works out. I'm so tired of reading shooting directions that have the camera up my ass or between my tits. I just gotta have some respect."

In other words, she wanted to be a serious actress. She had publicly signaled that intention on the Edward R. Murrow TV interview show. The show, which earned some of the highest ratings in the series, showed Norma Jean with Amy Greene, Milton's wife, at their Manhattan apartment. To the viewers, Norma Jean seemed almost ethereal; she was vacant and appeared terribly nervous. Those who didn't know better assumed this was the typical Monroe persona, that vulnerability that aroused in so many men the desire to take care of her.

But what I saw were the symptoms I recognized so well: she was zonked out on drugs. Apparently, as I watched her almost lose any sense of where she was or whom she was talking to, she had been using even more pills, washed down with even more Dom Perignon.

I also heard the same symptoms during our phone conversations. Sometimes she was quite lucid and organized and seemed to have a firm grip on her life. At least she had set herself a goal: she would live in New York; study acting seriously for the first time in her life at the Actors' Studio, with its famous director, Lee Strasberg; perfect her craft; and make only quality movies under the aegis of her own production company.

Other times, however, I heard the disjointed thoughts, slurred speech and general vacuousness of a woman who had become a pure narcotics addict. At such times her conversations hardly made any sense. She would alternately lament the course of her life, then suddenly switch into a snarling attack on the "bastards" who she felt had tried to destroy her. One minute Joe DiMaggio was a great man, a wonderful lover, a terrific father; the next minute he was a no-good sonofabitch who frightened her because, she claimed, he beat her up. From there she would make the grand psychic tour: her mother, her father, the men who screwed and abused her, all the people who took advantage of her, the studio chiefs who hated her, the men who kept pursuing her, why we should have gotten married, why we shouldn't have gotten married, and on and on. Sometimes, simply unable to stay fully awake during these wee-hour phone calls, I pleaded fatigue and cut the conversations short.

Generally the phone calls were made on the run, for Lili and I were almost constantly traveling. I quit the *Caine Mutiny* cast (a serious mistake) and began a new life as a sort of impresario and manager of Lili St. Cyr, the world's most famous striptease artist.

What I realized, only belatedly, was that I could not travel with Lili and maintain an acting career—a career in jeopardy, in any event, since I had walked out on a hit play. And the travel, at first glamorous and exciting, soon settled into a grind. All the while I read in the trade papers of the successes of my contemporaries. I was delighted to hear of some of the nicer ones, especially a young actor from the

Caine Mutiny cast named James Baumgarner, who changed his last name to Garner and wound up in a hit television series named *Maverick*. There was also the success of my old friend James Arness.

Their success, I realized, was because they had stuck to it, patiently paying their dues during years of obscurity and struggle. I had cut myself off from that process and was now . . . what? Mr. St. Cyr was one answer, and it was an answer I didn't like; who I was had a direct relation to my connection to Lili. On top of that, we were living, I thought, out of a suitcase. It didn't bother Lili; she had been living that way for years. But it bothered the hell out of me. I was approaching the point in life where I wanted some kind of roots.

Life on the road, I finally concluded, was no life. At some places where Lili appeared, I was the singer, standing at the side of the stage while the girls in the supporting cast went through their routines (Lili's shows were fairly elaborate production numbers). In Las Vegas I played the straight man to the comedian Hank Henry. Other times I did the lighting for the shows, or worked on the sets, or scored the music.

Everywhere we went, the phone calls followed. Usually they would come very late at night, during the hours when Norma Jean, unable to sleep, ran up huge long-distance phone bills calling her circle of confidants.

"Eddie, you don't sound happy," she said one night.

"I'm not," I confessed. "Look, Norma Jean, this isn't working out. I can't help feeling like I'm a kept man. It's not Lili's fault, but we're arguing and snapping at each other all the time, it seems. I just didn't realize what kind of a life this is. I wanted to be an actor, and here I am, working the fucking lights for my wife, the stripper. Shit."

"How bad can it be?" she said, beginning to giggle. "Think of the compensations."

"What compensations?"

She began giggling loudly. "Jesus, Eddie, you can be really dumb sometimes. Don't you realize how many men in America would give their right arms to go to bed with Lili St. Cyr? Holy shit, if I were you, I'd be walking on air most of the time. Hey, I know she ain't frigid."

"Yeah, well, it isn't everything."

"Maybe, but think also of all the money you've got now."

I snorted. "Money? Yeah, there's a lot of money being made, but I'll tell you something: she spends it just as fast as she makes it, believe me. Get this: did you know she has a limousine on call twenty-four hours a day? I mean, twenty-four hours! A lot of the time she doesn't even need it, but she's just got to have the damn thing always around. She's got this place at the Astor; she keeps it, no matter where she is. A lot of the time the place isn't even used. But I can't change her. This is the way she likes to live."

She considered this awhile, then said, "You know what's funny, Eddie? We keep winding up at the same place. We run around, do all kinds of crazy things, then, in the end, we're right back where we started. How come we can't find happiness?"

"Maybe it's not meant to be."

"Fate, you mean? Could be. Are you happy?"

"Not really. How about you?"

She laughed. "Is the Pope Jewish?"

Now I was laughing, in spite of myself. "Well," she said, "I think there's only one solution. The next time you're in New York and we've got some time, we have to get together and talk over old times."

I hesitated. "I'm not sure that's a good idea, Norma Jean."

"Oh, don't be so goddamn stiff on me. Hey, we're good friends, aren't we? So what's wrong with us getting together, hoisting a few, and reviewing our lives? We can cry on each other's shoulders."

In the end, as always, she was impossible to resist. We made a date to see each other when I returned to New York.

Not too long after that, Lili took off on another tour. I decided not to accompany her, and I was alone at the Astor for two weeks. When Norma Jean heard that, she announced that she was coming over to see me.

I felt like a kid on his first date. Nervous, I paced the room, my mind swimming with conflicting feelings. I did not really want to see her again, and yet I did. I was angry at her, and yet I wasn't. I didn't love her anymore, and yet I did. I sat in a chair, my head in my hands. *What the hell is wrong with you?* I asked myself. *You've got to stay away from this woman, and yet, at the first opportunity, there I am, inevitably involved again.*

She arrived in the standard disguise of her New York period: dark glasses, a black wig, and large scarf.

"And now," she announced with a flourish, "we see the unveiling of the real Norma Jean!"

She did a striptease routine, shedding the wig, glasses, and scarf as she loudly hummed bump-and-grind music. "Ta-da! Well, what do you think?"

She was gorgeous, although, I noticed, she had

put on a few pounds. Possibly she sensed that thought in my mind.

"Oh, damn, he thinks I'm fat," she said, frowning.

"No, no," I protested. "Really, you've never looked better, really fabulous, Norma Jean." We embraced.

"You do not look happy, Mr. Friedman," she said, mock-seriously. "Well, lucky for you, the famed Dr. Monroe has arrived. Put your fate in her hands and you'll feel much better. Now, then, the first thing to do is to order the proper, um, refreshments so that the doctor can properly work."

I had anticipated that, and almost as soon as she said it, room service was at the door with the champagne. "You're such a good patient, Mr. Friedman," she said, pouring a glass of champagne. "Oh, excellent, Dom Perignon. However did you know?"

I was sitting in a chair, absorbing this performance. A natural comedienne, Norma Jean's little performance was hysterical.

"Ah yes," she said, "we appear to be ready. Oops, one small matter: the doctor is not properly attired for this treatment. Would you excuse the doctor a moment, Mr. Friedman? She appears to have overlooked the matter of proper attire." Then, in a flash, she took off all her clothes. She stood there naked, sipping her glass of champagne.

"Is something the matter, Mr. Friedman?" she asked. "Is there something bothering you? You appear to be having difficulty keeping your composure. Please don't stare so at the doctor; it makes her extremely nervous. All right, let's get serious here. Your treatment is about to commence." She reached into her pocketbook for something and, holding it concealed in her hand, walked over to me.

"First, I regret to tell you, Mr. Friedman, that all

my patients are required to strip. I believe in treating the whole person. None of that clothing stuff here." She helped me take my clothes off.

"Now I want you to close your eyes. No peeking; just trust me." I closed my eyes tightly and heard the sound of something plastic being snapped. I sensed her moving something under my nose. Then I felt some sort of fume entering my nose, and I had the sense I was roaring off the planet in a rocket ship.

"Jesus, what the hell—" I started to say, hearing my words as if in an echo chamber.

"Sssh! Keep your eyes closed and inhale. I told you, trust me."

I was floating now, in some sort of strange state. Everything seemed to be spinning around me. I became aware only of Norma Jean and her body, and how hungrily I devoured her. There was not an inch of her I did not explore, and the only sounds I heard were the sounds of passion. We were both like rutting animals.

I was not certain how much time had gone by, and I didn't much care. Through the window I noticed that night was falling.

"Feel much better now?" she asked as we lay together, exhausted, in bed.

"Sure do," I said.

"Boy oh boy," she said, the giggle beginning again, "you don't know how lucky you are, Eddie. Do you realize you've fucked the two biggest sex queens in America? Jesus, if I were you, I wouldn't complain about *anything*."

"I'm not complaining."

"Sure you are. You bitch all the time how you want to be an *actor*."

"You're a fine one to talk; all you've ever talked

about is becoming an *actress*." I laid the same sarcastic stress on the word as she had.

She giggled again. "That's true, but you know what I've learned? Christ, you have to pay one hell of a price. Sometimes I wonder if it's been worth it. Think about this, Eddie: go back to when we first met, way back in Hollywood. Suppose you knew then what you know now? Would you have done the same thing?"

"Who can answer a question like that? Shit, none of us can see into the future. You just do what you think you want to do, and that's it. Later you can drive yourself nuts trying to figure out if you did the right thing. But there's no point to it. What are you going to do, kick yourself the rest of your life?"

The conversation studiously avoided something that was on my mind: that little capsule she had broken under my nose. When the various topics of our conversation finally ended, I brought up the subject.

"Since when are you using poppers?"

She shrugged. "Oh, I just use them once in a while. You know, when I'm really in bad shape. One pop, boy, and you go to heaven. The only problem is I get nosebleeds once in a while."

"That's a warning signal: you have to stop using that stuff."

"Oh, stop talking like I'm an addict or something."

"Aren't you?"

"No, goddammit!" She was in that low voice of hers, and very angry. "For Christ's sake, Eddie, every time we're having a nice time together, you spoil it! You start all this shit about my pills! I'm sick of hearing about it!"

For a full minute there was silence between us. "Look, Norma Jean, I'm not trying to give you a hard time. How many times do I have to tell you, I'm just worried, that's all."

"Well, stop worrying; I have it under control." She began to cry. "Oh, you don't understand. I'm so confused, I'm so mixed up, I just can't find happiness. I get a little nice time with you, and what happens? You spoil it. Everybody wants to spoil it for me. See, it's just temporary, Eddie. I just need to get myself settled down, you know, and then I won't need it anymore. Hey, you'll see; I'll just quit, just like that."

I held her in my arms. "Are you still having trouble sleeping?" I asked her.

She laughed. "Trouble? That's an understatement. I can't sleep *at all*. Not without my friends, that is." She rose out of bed and returned with her pocketbook. From it she extracted two dark-colored bottles. She emptied the bottles and arranged the large pills in rows, like soldiers on a parade field.

"My friends," she said, "the only ones who are always loyal, never try to change me. See all my yellow friends? They hold me in their arms and gently rock me to sleep. It's a very deep sleep, Eddie, and when I'm that way, there are no memories to pursue me, nothing bothers me. But then it's time to wake up, time to fight and kick and scratch during a new day. That's where my red friends come in. They snap me right up, Eddie, wake me up so I can handle the day. 'Wake up, Norma Jean!' they yell at me, and then they start to shake me. When I don't want to get up, they get real nasty: 'Hey, cunt, get the fuck up!' Then they kick my ass out of bed. Oh, I also have some black friends. Sometimes, when I feel my clock running down, when I'm dead on my feet, they help me out. They run all over my body, turning all my switches on. They make me alive again!"

I was staring at her. I had never heard her talk that way. Christ, I thought, she talks like a junkie. Worse, she seemed to have no idea of the extent of her dependency. What was she talking about when she said she could just end her habit anytime she chose?

"You know, it wasn't too long ago," I reminded her, "that I thought I heard promises that you and Uncle Ted would stop this crap."

"Oh, I don't need Uncle Teddie anymore," she said brightly. "I got plenty of people who'll help me out." She made a face. "Besides, he was beginning to get on my nerves anyway. I met him the other day at the Central Park Zoo. Jesus, he's falling apart. You remember how well dressed and everything he used to be? Well, you should see him now. He's not really taking care of himself; his clothes are a mess, and I saw these stains on his tie. He's pathetic. He began to get the idea, I think, that he could own me. He'd wave those little bottles in my face and say, 'Look what I've got for you, Marilyn.' It was like some dirty old man showing candy to some little girl whose cunt he's trying to feel. I told him, I've had enough. He got tears in his eyes."

She saw me sitting there, morosely. "Oh, stop looking so goddamn gloomy. This is me. Take me as I am, Eddie, or don't take me at all."

And I did. I felt myself once again drawn into her vortex, the disorderly magnetism that seemed to capture anyone who knew her. In truth, I acted like a jerk.

There was the day she took me to the apartment

of one of her closest friends, the tortured actor Montgomery Clift. He was a brilliant actor, but his head was on very loose.

"You're not gonna believe this, Eddie," she said giggling, "but you're about to meet somebody who's even more screwed up than I am."

Indeed, Clift was pretty fouled up, a large part of it having to do with his homosexuality, which he tried to deny. It just made him even screwier. During our meeting with Clift, I discovered just how complicated Norma Jean's sex life had become. At some point there was another of those black capsules broken under my nose, and when I finally snapped out of it, Norma Jean was practically in hysterics, while Clift was sitting around zonked out, grinning stupidly.

"Congratulations," she said. "You've just gotten a blow job from Montgomery Clift." She collapsed in giggles.

The Norma Jean force field finally extended to Lili, and all three of us wound up in bed.

"This has to stop," I announced. But how?

Chapter seventeen

THE LADY OF
THE FLOWERS

Just when I thought I would never be able to put some space between myself and Norma Jean—as much as she talked of us being just friends, there was something quite different going on—fate intervened. She met another man.

Actually she had met this man quite some time before. At first glance, he did not seem quite the type who would turn Norma Jean's head. Owlish, a pure intellectual, Arthur Miller was America's greatest playright. He moved in circles about as far from Norma Jean's world as anyone could imagine.

Yet, there was some sort of chemistry. She had first met him, she later told me, even before she met Joe DiMaggio. "He squeezed my toe," she said of her first encounter with Miller at a Hollywood party—Miller was good friends with the director Elia Kazan—and for the life of me, I could not understand what she was talking about.

Apparently, however, the toe-squeezing did the trick, for she and Miller had an affair. She once mentioned this casually to me, then dropped it, and I assumed it was just another of the brief flings she seemed to have in those days. (Norma Jean was a woman who would simply have sex with just any-body she liked, and the men who enjoyed her favors amounts to a pretty long list.)

I never heard another mention of Arthur Miller for years until, at the height of our reinvolvement in New York, she suddenly brought it up again, in typical Norma Jean fashion.

"What would you think of me as Jewish?" she asked one day when we were sitting in the rear of a quiet Eighth Avenue bar-restaurant. She was in her scarf and dark glasses.

"Jewish? Wouldn't make any difference to me, but why are you thinking of taking up religion?"

"It's not the religion itself; it's the religion of a man."

I began to see. "So that's it. Which man?"

"Arthur Miller. You know, the playright."

"I've heard of him." I was somewhat astonished, although in the present context of her life, it made sense. Norma Jean had totally immersed herself in New York, particularly its cultural and intellectual milieu. In many ways, she was a chameleon, assum-ing the coloration of whatever surroundings she was operating in. In New York she had shed, at least outwardly, all traces of her Hollywood upbringing.

What resulted was the emergence of a very curi-ous amalgam. She was reading books now, going to plays, dipping into New York's amazing cultural stew, and generally acting like a typical New York culture maven. Her talk was beginning to become laced with assorted expressions meant to signify her new intel-lectual bent. At the same time, she had shed much of her Hollywood flashiness, signified, I noticed, by dressing more circumspectly and using a lot less makeup.

Yet, there was still a lot of the old Hollywood Norma Jean there, if you listened closely enough, some of that empty-headed chatter and sometimes-vapid approach to life New Yorkers associate with people from California.

The biggest influence on her life in New York was the Actors' Studio, the famed organization under Lee Strasberg and his wife, Paula. This was the site of the notorious Method acting theory, the place where a coterie of devoted students absorbed Strasberg's theories about "getting in touch with yourself" and "grasping the inner key" of a scene. In other words, it was part psychoanalysis and part acting instruction, and very much at the upper reaches of the New York intellectual world.

In that context, the reestablishment of a relationship with Miller made sense. Still, I wondered, how could the relationship survive? Norma Jean was on an intellectual kick now, but she had the bad habit of a short attention span. How long would this particular infatuation last?

"Oh, Eddie, he's such a wonderful man," Norma Jean was saying.

"I'm sure he is," I replied noncommittally.

"You'll never guess what really attracted him to me."

"Uh, his brain?"

"Well, yes, that," she said in the breathy voice she used when she was infatuated with somebody or something. "But I'll tell you what I really liked about him. He looks so much like Abraham Lincoln, you wouldn't believe it."

I was flabbergasted. I knew she always had a great admiration for Lincoln, but I was having trouble seeing the connection between him and a Jewish intellectual. Was I missing something?

"And he talks just like Lincoln," she said. "Very wise, very deep, you know. I tell you, it's uncanny."

Maybe so, but it seemed to me that it was not a very good basis for a relationship, especially when Norma Jean began to talk of marriage. I did not raise too many questions, for again I saw the classic Norma Jean pattern: total infatuation, to be followed, I was sure, by the inevitable letdown. No man could have lived up to the starry-eyed rapture Norma Jean felt about Arthur Miller before she married him.

In this early euphoria Norma Jean seemed not to have a care in the world. She was going to marry Arthur Miller, she was going to star in a "serious" movie (*Bus Stop*, which turned out to be her greatest performance), and her new outfit, Marilyn Monroe Productions, would prevent her ever being exploited by a studio again.

While the gossip columns were preoccupied with her romance with Miller, the studios were paying attention to more important things, most notably the deal Norma Jean's new production company negotiated with Fox. It caused a revolution in Hollywood, for no movie star had ever been able to extract such a deal from the all-powerful studio system.

Friends of mine in Hollywood talked of nothing else. The contract gave Fox Norma Jean's services for the next seven years and obligated her to do only four pictures. The indentured servants at the studios, worn to a frazzle by being cast in movies almost without letup, practically went into shock over that provision, and there were further shocks to come. The contract also was "nonexclusive," an unprecedented clause that would allow Norma Jean to work on her

own productions, television, theater—just about anything, including, incredibly enough, making films
for other studios. Additionally she was given director
approval.

In sum, Norma Jean had single-handedly destroyed
the studio system that had been the bedrock of the
movie industry for nearly forty years. And on top of
all that, Fox would pay her $100,000 per picture, an
astounding sum in those days. Compared with today's standards of megabuck deals between actors
and production companies, of course, Norma Jean's
deal seems modest. But back in 1956 her contract
with Fox was revolutionary and marked a watershed:
from then on, the most bankable actors and actresses
demanded similar deals, and in the end the studios'
system of formalized slavery was shattered forever.

Sitting there, in that Eighth Avenue dump, it was
hard to believe that the woman sitting opposite me,
in nondescript clothes, scarf, and no makeup, had
created this revolution. Despite all that had happened, she was still Norma Jean to me, the screwy,
maddeningly contradictory girl from the wrong side
of the tracks. I never could match the popular image
of sex goddess Marilyn Monroe with the astonish-
ingly vulnerable girl I had always known.

Still, the combination of good personal and professional fortunes seemed to have effected a transformation in her. The sweating, haunted persona
had suddenly disappeared. She was back to normal—if
that word really could ever apply in full measure to
her—full of life again, happily looking forward to
the future.

In that mood her concern turned not to herself

but to me. In a reversal of roles that had occurred so often during our lives, she now acted as my mother confessor. She wanted to hear everything that was going on in my life, then offer advice on how I was to solve my problems.

In truth, nothing much good was going on in my life. My marriage to Lili turned out to be a bad mistake, and I was completely miserable.

"Eddie, I never thought she was for you," she said. "I didn't say so at the time, but I never saw much future for the two of you, to tell you the truth."

"Well, you turned out to be right." We were sitting again in the far reaches of that Eighth Avenue place. It was early afternoon, and the place was practically deserted. I was drinking, but to my surprise, Norma Jean was not. Even more amazing, not once did I see her reach for a pill.

"So what's the problem?" she asked.

"It's pretty simple. I'm just tired of being Mr. St. Cyr."

She frowned. "Hey, that's a problem I'm familiar with. I think that was the problem with Joe, even though he was pretty famous himself. It's the problem any famous woman has with a man."

"Yeah, well, I'm really feeling it with Lili. You know, the other day, we had a hell of an argument. I said to her, 'Jesus Christ, Lili, the way you throw money away needlessly is criminal.' Boy, did I get it. 'Look,' she said, 'it's *my* money, and if I want to throw it away, that's what I'll do.' Boom! You know how that made me feel?"

"Like shit."

"Right. You know, she always has to be in the spotlight. When we're together, walking someplace, she always has to be walking a few steps in front of me. I mentioned it to her a couple of times, and she said, 'People know me. They don't know you.' What am I, some kind of valet? When we're alone together privately, everything's okay, but the minute we get out in public, it's like she feels the spotlight has to be on herself. And she doesn't want me in that spotlight. I'll tell you what else bothers the shit out of me. She doesn't want to have anything to do with my parents. Every time I suggest we pay a visit, she makes this face, like I'm asking her to walk on hot coals or something. Jesus, she wants to be a goddamn queen. When she's not working, her idea of a good time is to lie in bed all day, having breakfast served to her. She likes to lie there watching television. What a life."

It all came tumbling out of me: every resentment, every marital problem, every grievance I had. Norma Jean listened quietly, every so often making sympathetic noises.

"I haven't seen Lili in a long time," she said. "Is she still beautiful?"

"Are you kidding? She's gorgeous, but after a while it's just not enough."

"Don't I know it," she said with a little giggle. "But you know, Eddie, I get the funny feeling there's really something else bothering you. Something more serious."

"Not really."

"Hey, this is old Norma Jean, remember? How well do I know you, old friend? So tell Norma Jean."

I was hesitant, for what I had not yet revealed was in a very delicate area—especially with Norma Jean.

"She's been fooling around with other women," I finally blurted out. Norma Jean did not appear to react, and I went on. "I found out that she was friends with this actress in Hollywood. She wanted Lili to teach her how to do a real professional strip-tease, and the next thing you know, they're in bed together having a great old time. The next thing I know, there was this woman who came over to our place, and Lili says to me, 'Ted, why don't you go out for a few hours? We have a little girl talk we have to do.' Girl talk! The minute I left, they were screwing their brains out."

Norma Jean began to smile. "Hey, Eddie, what's happened to you? Are you becoming square or something? I hate to bring this up, but you remember you weren't exactly forced to go to bed with Lili and me. I don't remember you telling me that you had a bad time."

"That was different."

"Oh, different, I see. Well, you have different views than I do, I guess. To me, what's the big problem? If she wants to do it with girls, so what? So join in, Eddie, and maybe that'll solve the whole problem."

"You don't understand."

"Okay, so I don't. Shit, I've been to bed plenty of times with more than one person at the same time. If you like the people, what difference does it make? Men and women have screwed me all my life. Okay, so it feels different, you know, but the basic thing is there. Sex is the expression of how they like you, how they feel about you. I don't see what you're so upset about. You knew before you married Lili she liked girls too."

"Look, I'm not really into that kind of stuff."

Norma Jean shrugged. "Then you have a problem."

As was often the case, Norma Jean saw the whole matter as very simple: whatever somebody she liked wanted to do sexually, that was perfectly all right with her. There were no limits whatsoever. Despite a veneer of sophistication, however, I was different. Norma Jean had taught me about the joy of pure sexual expression, but at some level I was still Middle West in attitude. I could still be shocked when I saw, through an open door in Lili's dressing room one night, a famous woman entertainer trying to kiss her passionately. Or her devoted following of women, who would send her flowers and mash notes begging for a chance to be alone with her. (And, at the same time, there were battalions of men trying to achieve the same result.)

In essence, Norma Jean's advice to me was simple: go with the flow. It was not a solution I was prepared to accept, and my relationship with Lili continued to go downhill.

Thus, I was not exactly looking forward to a cruise to Europe Lili and I were scheduled to take. It was to take thirty-eight days, but considering the mood I was in, the whole trip seemed pointless.

"Take it, take it," Norma Jean advised. "Jesus, you know how much I yearn to take a trip like that? I can't. But for God's sake, Eddie, what a golden opportunity. Take the trip, and who knows, maybe it'll all work out. And even if it doesn't, you got a nice trip out of it. And while you're gone, don't even think of me. While you're away, Arthur and I are going to get married."

I almost went into shock. As she occasionally did, Norma Jean had slipped this bulletin into the end of a conversation on a totally different topic. "You're sure, right?" I asked.

"Eddie, I've never been so sure in my life," she

replied, firmly. "This is it. I just know it. Finally my life has changed. I've waited years for this."

I expressed my happiness for her and prepared to leave on the cruise. At dockside I was delivered a batch of two dozen roses, and although there was nothing written on the card, I knew who sent them. So did Lili.

"Are you still talking to that little bitch?" she snapped. Apparently she and Norma Jean had some sort of falling out. Its exact causes I never did find out, since neither of them ever discussed it again.

If ever there was a totally miserable trip, the cruise to Europe was it. Every passenger, save Lili and myself, seemed to be considerably over the age of fifty, and the ship had all the excitement of a senior citizens' outing. The only action seemed to be bingo, but after the second night at sea, whatever excitement was in the game had long paled.

After two weeks I felt as though I was going out of my mind. Lili and I were hardly speaking, and I found myself spending most of my time among the younger members of the crew. When we arrived in Southampton, the final disaster struck. Lili and I mutually agreed that one of us had to go, and I decided it would be me. I moved to another hotel, and it was there I hit the low point of my life.

I desperately needed someone to talk to. Actually I needed Norma Jean, but she was a continent away, getting ready to marry Arthur Miller. I didn't want to bother her with my troubles. What I finally wound up with was an English prostitute, who, after announcing that it would cost me fifty dollars American for a maximum of forty-five minutes, stared at me in shock when I told her I did not want her to take her clothes off. What I wanted, I told her, was to sit there and listen as I talked to her.

She shrugged and listened, totally puzzled, as I poured out an account of my current troubles. Occasionally she would say, "Oh, *right*, love," in a heavy cockney accent, although she couldn't even begin to follow what I was saying.

The cruise back home was even more miserable, highlighted by a heart-to-heart talk with Lili, during which it was decided that we would get divorced. "We'll remain friends, won't we?" she asked, and I agreed. (We have remained friends right to this day. As was the case with so many other show business marriages of those days, we made the mistake of spoiling a perfectly good relationship by getting married.)

I was feeling a terrible vacancy in my life at that point, and I knew exactly what it was. Desperate, I used the transatlantic telephone to call Norma Jean.

"Hi!" she said brightly when I finally tracked her down in Hollywood, where she was finishing work on *Bus Stop*. "What's up?"

Shouting to make myself heard, I quickly told her how badly I missed her, and that Lili and I were getting divorced. "Oh, that's terrible," she said over the line filled with static. "It didn't work out, huh?"

"No," I shouted. "We have to talk."

We arranged to meet after the ship returned to New York, where her permanent home now was, a beautiful apartment on ritzy Sutton Place in Manhattan.

After arriving in New York, I didn't hear from Norma Jean for more than a week. She was still in Hollywood working, and I was determined not to bother her there. I would wait until she got back.

The phone call came one night at 5:00 A.M. "I told

you so," a low, whispery voice said, without preliminary. None was necessary, for it was followed by that giggle.

"Hello, Peanut," I said, an occasional pet name I used for her. I had invented it as a description of her shape.

"Well, I hate to say this," she said, "but it's just like I figured. It didn't work out."

I began to talk about her now-worldwide fame and new respect as an actress, but she cut me off. "Never mind that shit. Listen, I want to hear all the dirt. I want to hear how you and Lili broke up."

"There's nothing to tell," I said, disappointed that I couldn't fulfill her constant need for inside gossip, the more sexual and bizarre the better. "We weren't twenty-four hours out of port when we realized we had done something pretty stupid. We hardly spoke. That's it."

"*That's it?*" She was palpably disappointed. "Eddie, you're not holding out on me, are you?"

"No, no, I swear. It's just that there was no big blowup or anything. We just drifted apart. I don't blame her, really. She can be a terrific lady: she's smart, she's sexy, she's got a lot going for her. We don't get along as man and wife, that's all. She doesn't have a boyfriend, and I don't have a girlfriend."

"Oh, yes, you do," she said, giggling. "Me."

"You know what I mean. You know, you're not my *girlfriend*, the way people define the term."

"Uh-huh," she said, giggling again. "Sure, Eddie, just keep telling yourself that. You just have platonic feelings about me, right. Sure."

"Why are we bringing this up now, Norma Jean? We've been through this before. Let's just ignore the topic. If I start thinking again about how I've felt about you all these years, I'm going to drive myself crazy. So I don't think about it if I can help it."

"Fair enough," she said quietly. We made a date to see each other three days hence.

Our rendezvous was a small restaurant that we had been in a few times before. Norma Jean particularly liked the place because it was famous for its chocolate souffle; she had a mad passion for the stuff.

Again, although she was dressed in her New York disguise, I recognized her immediately; she could not hide that distinctive figure. After the greetings and preliminaries were over, she got right down to brass tacks.

"So what's the next step?" she asked. To my surprise, she had just turned down a chocolate soufflé. ("I'm getting too goddamn fat. That thing has about three pounds staring me in the face.")

"I'll tell you," I said, beginning a somewhat lengthy monologue. "I'm tired of being Mr. St. Cyr, jack-of-all-trades, master of none. I'm a goddamn gelding. I was whipped from the beginning, but I didn't have the brains to realize it. You know, it all looked so damn glamorous at the very beginning, all that glamour and excitement. Then I suddenly realized what it was all about, and it's not so glamorous anymore. As a matter of fact, it stinks."

She was nodding her head up and down, recognizing the symptoms.

"I'll tell you," I continued, "I must have had my head up my ass. There's only one thing to do, Norma Jean. I've thought this out. I think I'll go back to Hollywood and start all over again. And this time I won't be shooting for glitter and glamour, because they're not worth a shit."

I must have gone on like that for nearly an hour. All during my tirade Norma Jean said practically nothing. Later that afternoon we wound up in my room at the Astor.

For the first time our lovemaking was *pro forma*. There was hardly any spark in it, as though we were both too distracted to care.

Later I stood by the window, looking out over New York. "I used to love this city," I said, "but now, it's a goddamn jungle. You can't walk the streets anymore, the place is crawling with Puerto Ricans, it's filthier than I've ever seen."

"You think Hollywood's any better?" she said. She was lying on the bed, her famous body sprawled among several pillows and the bedsheets. "Let me tell you, Eddie, you wouldn't recognize the place. First of all, it's getting so goddamn crowded, you can't move. *Everybody* wants to live in Los Angeles, I guess. The air stinks now; you can hardly breathe half the time. You can't move, either: I never saw so many goddamn cars in my life. Ugh! Believe me, New York is the place to be."

At that moment we recognized jointly what was really happening in that conversation: we were trying to recapture the past. We wanted to recapture that time of the golden sunshine and clean air; that old car I had that sputtered along; the beautiful nights; the time we met Howard Hughes (who sat down on his hat and never said another word for three hours); the homosexual comedian in the little nightclub who did an incredible impersonation of Charles Laughton in *Mutiny on the Bounty;* the guy in the audience at another place who would sing while people threw money on the floor (he later became Frankie Laine); and the magic of that first day at the studio, the sheer wonder of it all.

With a whoop, Norma Jean suddenly launched herself off the bed. Fishing in her pocketbook, she emerged with her red diary.

"It's all here," she said, leafing through the early pages. We spent the next several hours reading over her entries for those earlier years, swathing ourselves in the memories.

Later she stopped, and her face grew dark. "It's like they say out there," she said. 'Nobody in this gets out alive.' "

Chapter eighteen

THE FALL

In the weeks that followed, Norma Jean seemed to have dropped out of sight. She was in New York, I knew, still living at Sutton Place, but for some odd reason I did not hear from her. I toyed with the idea of calling her, but the task of getting through the madhouse that was her life—to say nothing of avoiding the problem of her husband—made me hold back.

And then, after what seemed a long time had passed, I got one of those predawn phone calls. "You still together with Lili?" the voice of Norma Jean asked.

"Sort of. We're separated, but not really divorced yet." Having been awakened from a sound sleep, I was trying to collect my thoughts.

"Well, it looks like we may be in the same boat before long," she said, and I noticed that she was slurring her words. So that was it: her marriage to Miller was coming apart.

"Are you drinking?" I asked.

"Goddamn right I'm drinking," she said. "I've got my champagne, and I've got me, and there we are."

"What happened?"

Norma Jean did not answer directly. She began a rambling discourse on the Italian cook she had hired, the proper way of making Italian sauce, how much she liked my mother, the travails of making movies, and a dozen other topics. It was almost impossible to follow.

Suddenly she said, "I have to talk to you."

"So come on over."

"No, I don't want to go to the Astor. I don't think that's a good idea anymore. Listen, tomorrow I have a hairdressing appointment right near Columbus Circle. Afterward let's meet in the park there. You know, the entrance to Central Park?"

I knew it, and the following day I found her seated on a park bench. As usual she had on a dark wig, dark glasses, and a scarf, but I noticed a shocking change. Her skin was chalky white and blotchy, and she looked drawn and pasty, like someone who has been in the hospital or a prison a long time.

"Prison is right," she said when I mentioned it. "I'm in a fucking prison, Eddie, and my jailer is named Arthur Miller."

I could hardly believe what I was hearing. It seemed like only yesterday when she was rhapsodizing about this man.

"You know," she said, with a heavy sadness in her voice, "it's funny how life is. Now, I've got everything, right? I've got the career I always wanted, plenty of money, I'm my own boss in a lot of ways, I got a beautiful place to live in, I've got a maid and a cook, and I've got a husband. And I've got nothing."

"What are you saying, that he locks the door and keeps you penned up or something?"

"No, but he might as well. Every morning he goes into that goddamn study of his, and I don't see him for hours and hours. I mean, what the fuck is he doing in there? And there I am, just sitting around; I haven't a goddamn thing to do."

It all sounded rather bizarre. "I don't want to sound stupid, Norma Jean, but why can't you just do anything you want to do? Just go out."

She gave a sarcastic, bitter laugh. "Just go out? Are you crazy? Look at me: this is the way I have to dress so I won't get mobbed on the streets. You don't understand how it is. I just can't go into a store or something like normal people do. I'm a prisoner, don't you understand that?"

I nodded my head yes, although the suspicion grew that the situation was not precisely as she had described it. Seeing the sweaty upper lip and hearing the slightly slurred speech, I came to my own conclusion. Norma Jean was in fact more a prisoner of herself than anything else. When not working on a picture—and four pictures in seven years was not exactly a taxing schedule—she had only her own resources to fall back upon. But those resources were thin, especially in New York, where she did not have the Hollywood circles in which she once hung around. I suspected she was back to her pill-popping habits, combining it with the champagne she drank even during the day; she was again destroying herself.

"He's a cold fish," she complained, renewing her attack against Miller. "I thought he was Lincoln, but Lincoln had a great sense of humor. Arthur's got no sense of humor. I'm living with a dead man. You know the most frightening part? He reminds me now of a Nazi."

"Oh, come on, Norma Jean, he's not—"

"No, listen! Every time I look at him now, I think

of Rudolf Hess. That's right, he looks just like Hess to me."

"I thought you once told me he looked like Abraham Lincoln."

"I know I said that, but I was wrong. I'm telling you now, he looks like Hess."

I was hearing almost pure irrationality, and I don't think I had ever heard her so divorced from reality. For reasons that were not clear to me, the love she once felt for Miller was now completely extinguished, and she was turning on him. The vehemence was almost frightening; she actually hated the man. Meanwhile, whatever his faults, he was busy in his study every day trying to put together a screenplay just for her. It was called *The Misfits*.

I was not the only one to notice Norma Jean's sudden and rather obvious mental deterioration. Laurence Olivier, for example, the distinguished British actor with whom Norma Jean starred in *The Prince and the Showgirl*, openly referred to her as "schizoid" (his own wife, Vivien Leigh, had gone insane a short while before). Other friends of Norma Jean worried about what was happening to her, and there were rumors that she had tried to commit suicide at one point while living at Sutton Place.

At times she seemed to be descending into paranoia. "They screwed me!" she yelled at me one night during a phone call. "The sonsofbitches screwed me!" She meant Milton Greene and Arthur Miller, whom she accused of stealing money from Marilyn Monroe Productions.

"You don't have any proof of that," I said, trying to get her back to reality. "You can't just say things like that, Norma Jean. You have to have evidence. Where's the evidence? What do the accountants say?"

"Fuck the accountants! I'm telling you, they're screwing me! Arthur just married me to get at my money; I know that now. He and that other Jew sonofabitch Greene were in on this plan together!"

"Norma Jean, you've got to stop talking like that, because the next thing you know—"

"Bullsht! All those fucking Jews are alike. They're just out to grab the money!" She began sobbing. "Jesus Christ, why did I ever get mixed up with these Jews?"

I was angry now. "Listen, lady, don't start that anti-Semitic garbage with me. I warned you about that stuff before." Then I hung up on her.

Several hours later she called back. "Hey, Eddie, I'm sorry. You know how it is, honey, I just get all worked up sometimes and I say things I don't mean. Forgive me?"

"Yeah," I said, not really meaning it.

"So, look, let's forget about all this. Tell you what: let's get together again and we can talk over old times. How's that?"

"Okay," again without too much enthusiasm.

Several days later we were sitting in the Astor room sipping champagne. I stared at her while she sat on the edge of the bed naked. We had made love, but it was the most unsatisfying I had ever experienced with her. Something had come between us, and I had the strong feeling it would never be the same again.

"He doesn't like our poems," she said, slightly tipsy. "One night I tried to make him look at them, but he didn't want to bother even. He just said, 'Marilyn, I don't really have the time right now.' The sonofabitch."

"Let's not talk about your husband, if you don't mind," I said.

"Okay, we won't," she said, pouting. She stretched herself languidly on the bed and slowly spread her legs. "Hey, big man, it still looks pretty good, huh?"

"Yeah, terrific."

"What's wrong with you?"

"Nothing. I just don't feel right, that's all."

She took another long sip of champagne. "Turn the radio on," she ordered.

"Turn it on yourself," I snapped at her.

"Hey!" she growled in the low voice. "I told you to turn the fucking radio on!"

"And I'm telling *you*," I yelled at her, "to turn the fucking thing on yourself! Ever since you came here today, you've been ordering me around, like I'm your goddamn servant or something!"

"Well, fuck *you*!" She was nearly screaming.

"Yeah? Well, fuck you *too*!" We were both suddenly silent, spent by the flashes of anger.

She began to cry. "Oh, Jesus, Eddie, who'd ever think we'd be talking to each other like this? I thought we always loved each other."

I went over to the bed and held her in my arms. "We do, Peanut," I said, "but you keep acting like you're trying to kill it."

"I know I am," she said, the tears running down her face, "but I can't help it. God, I'm going crazy, just like my mother, I just know it. Somebody has to help me, Eddie. I'm going to pieces."

"Okay, okay, Peanut. Listen, aren't you seeing a psychiatrist?"

"I am, for all the fucking good it does me. I know all about my past and all that, so what's the point? I want to know how to get cured, not the reasons why

I'm going crazy. Shit, I already know all about my childhood. I don't need some guy at a hundred bucks an hour to tell me I'm screwed up because of my childhood."

During the next several hours there were flashes of the old Norma Jean. We sat together and recited some of our favorite poems together. But she popped a couple of pills and would periodically descend into a form of paranoia in which everybody—her husband, her friends, the director of her latest movie, her fellow actors—were all part of a massive conspiracy to mock her and make her unhappy.

It was not true, of course. In fact, according to the stories I heard, Norma Jean had severely tested everyone's patience, long past the point of ordinary human endurance. Everybody in the movie industry, for example, had heard the stories of Billy Wilder, himself in severe pain from bursitis, patiently waiting on the set of *Some Like It Hot* while Norma Jean blew scene after scene, then huddled with her newly hired drama coach, Paula Strasberg (who, to everybody's shock, was getting three thousand dollars a week). It was simply not done to have a director of Wilder's stature stand around while an actress "consulted" her drama coach on how to play the scene.

Nor was Jack Lemmon, a highly capable actor and Norma Jean's co-star in the movie, to blame. Patiently he, too, endured Norma Jean's increasingly bizarre behavior, at one point standing in his costume of dress and high-heel shoes while Norma Jean flubbed forty-seven straight takes. A man who stands in women's high-heel shoes for forty-seven takes is a very patient man.

Actually everybody was trying to protect her at this point, for however infuriating her behavior, she appeared so fragile and so near the edge, men especially sought to do everything to help her. Tragically, Norma Jean interpreted all this as a huge conspiracy of people trying to destroy her. (There were a few exceptions in this ring of protection, among them a man I never had much respect for, Tony Curtis. He also worked with Norma Jean on *Some Like It Hot*, but regaled the Hollywood party circuit with stories of her problems and claimed that kissing her was "like kissing Hitler.")

I tried, as best I could, to point out how many people were actually trying to help her, but it did not do much to pull Norma Jean out of her deepening depression. She lay on the bed, occasionally drying her tears with the edge of the blanket, as she recited the signs she saw pointing to her inevitable madness.

"I want you to know the whole truth, Eddie," she said, "so you understand what I'm telling you. You have to understand how lonely I am now. I just don't have enough people I know around me. I have to have people around me! All day I don't have anything to do, and if I'm not at the Actors' Studio, I just sit around. See, you don't know that right outside the apartment building, there's this group of six kids. They're like some kind of super fan club of me. They just wait there, around the clock. If they see me coming outside, they follow me, like little dogs, no matter where I go. So I have to be careful in disguising myself. Late at night the disguise usually works.

"I take these long walks, Eddie, all over the place. Sometimes I walk across the bridge all the way into Brooklyn. I just stare at the water and the lights. Do you know how many times I've thought of just jumping into that water and ending the whole problem?

Once I met this cop there, who was worried about this woman out there that late. We had a very nice conversation, about two hours long. I figure that when he got back to the precinct, he told everybody he'd just met Marilyn Monroe and they probably thought he was nuts.

"Anyway, sometimes when I go out, I just pick up guys. Doesn't matter, as long as they're guys. Then I fuck them. Afterward I really feel like shit, and I tell myself I'll never do that again. But a few days later I'm seized by this overwhelming urge to do it again. Hey, you know one day I went out in my disguise and I went into this bar and just picked up this guy. He took me to this hotel room, and then he fucked me. Afterward I told him he'd just fucked Marilyn Monroe. He absolutely didn't believe it, and who can blame him? He figured I was just some cheap pickup who looked like me. See, that was the thrill for me, telling this guy who I really was and him not believing it, but then, the more I said it, he maybe started to believe it. See, the whole thing was a kick to me, just watching the expression on his face while he tried to figure it all out. Christ, that's sick, but I just can't stop it. You see what I mean, now?"

I certainly did, and what I heard had confirmed my worst suspicions: she was falling apart. I had noticed the other signs, too. For the first time since I knew her, she was beginning to show signs of aging. There were crows'-feet around her eyes, and her body's once-perfect shape was beginning to show the ravages of all the abuse to which she had subjected it. I did not mention it, but she must have seen me looking closely at some parts of her.

"Oh, Jesus, don't look!" she cried. "I'm becoming an old hag!"

Far from it, but the signs of physical deterioration were there nevertheless. I feared that in combination with her pronounced mental deterioration, she would crumble fast.

"So, when are you going back to Hollywood?" she suddenly asked.

"I'm not sure," I replied, not wanting to be specific. I was afraid that if I left New York soon, she might fall apart further: another friend had abandoned her.

"Too bad about you and Lili," she said distractedly. "Too bad about Arthur and me. Too bad about you and me. Too bad about everybody." She began weeping again.

"Look, Norma Jean," I said, "I don't have to go back there right away. I mean, I could stay here a little while longer, and that way—"

"No, no, no," she said, shaking her head. "You go, because I'll tell you a big secret: I'm going back there myself, just as soon as I can. There's no way I can be happy here, Eddie."

"Norma Jean, maybe that's not such a hot idea. Maybe that's not the place for you. Let me be honest: you may not be in shape to handle Hollywood anymore."

"I don't care," she said defiantly. "If I'm gonna fall apart, I might as well fall apart out there, among my friends."

I heard from Norma Jean only irregularly when I returned to Hollywood. Divorced from Lili, I took a small apartment just off Doheny Drive and set about to restore a movie-acting career.

I discovered that movieland was buzzing with gossip about Norma Jean's latest escapades, including her public stammering during the premiere of *Some Like It Hot,* ironically one of her greatest triumphs. Increasingly out of touch with reality, she seemed to be in another world at times. Many of the phone calls I got were nearly unintelligible: part paranoia, part fantasy, part self-pity, and part something almost other worldly. Often I could hear the slurred words and thickened syllables revealing the combination of champagne and those pills. There were flashes of assorted developments in her life. Despite the fact that her marriage to Miller was dead in the water, she told me she was desperately trying to get pregnant but had suffered two miscarriages.

"Too many abortions, I guess," she said, my first clue that the abortion of our child was not the only one she had had.

By early 1960 she seemed to be spinning totally out of control. How else to explain her highly-publicized romance with the French star Yves Montand during the making of *Let's Make Love,* a fling so flagrant—at one point, she followed him across the country—Miller must have felt like a fool. I took the whole episode as a sad symptom in her mental decline, and I was to receive another piece of evidence from Lili St. Cyr.

Lili and I had, as we vowed, remained friends, and I had just settled in Los Angeles when she visited me. During the visit she asked me about Norma Jean. I told her of the precipitate decline.

"I sort of figured that," she said, "because I saw some evidence myself." She proceeded to tell me that some time before, when I was not with Lili at the Astor, Norma Jean had come to see her. Norma Jean hoped that she had nothing to do with the divorce of Lili and myself, and after Lili assured her that she did not, Norma Jean discussed me, mentioning what a close friend I had been to her since 1943.

"And then," Lili recounted, "things began to get very strange. I was trying to keep some distance between us, but she suddenly started telling me how she used to masturbate just thinking of having sex with me. She started coming on very strong to me, and to tell the truth, I was not in the mood. But she was very insistent, and finally I had to tell her to back off. Then she started telling me about Natasha Lytess: 'Natasha and I were *very* close, just like Siamese twins joined at the stomach.' Then she started to giggle. I figured she was trying to tell me something, but I just didn't want any part of her at that point. My God, she is so terribly mixed up!"

Very true, I admitted, and I was now feeling a very strong pity for Norma Jean. I continued to get the phone calls, but they were stranger than ever. Once, while she was working on *Let's Make Love*, she came over to see me.

"What the hell is the matter with you, with this Montand stuff?" I accused her, pointing at the headlines in that day's paper. "You're making a goddamn fool of yourself."

"Oh, shit, you too," she said, collapsing in a chair. She looked pathetic. "Nobody understands. Can I help it if I fell for my co-star? Big deal."

"It *is* a big deal. For Christ's sake, if you want to have a fling with this guy, at least do it in private. Don't do it in public like this, with everybody in the world seeing you throw yourself at his feet. What kind of a way is that to act?"

"I want a drink," she said, and that was the end of the discussion.

No wonder the director, George Cukor, was publicly calling her "reckless." It went some distance beyond that, as I was to discover in the summer of 1960.

I had no connection with the filming of *The Misfits*, which was due to begin shooting in Reno that year, but I was going to be there working for Lili St. Cyr. Actually it was a favor: Lili had been pressed into service as a last-minute replacement for an act that suddenly canceled at the Mapes, and I agreed to go to Reno and give her a hand setting up her act.

"Hold on to your hat," Lili said when I arrived there, "but you're not going to believe this. Guess who's occupying the suite we use to stay in when we were here."

I shrugged in puzzlement. "Mr. and Mrs. Arthur Miller," she said with a grimace. "Isn't that nice?"

Not really. I was so aggravated with Norma Jean at that point, I did not really want to see her. I had the feeling that, given her current condition, the making of *The Misfits*—it was being shot at Pyramid Lake, in the desert north of Reno—things were going to be somewhat unpleasant.

Sure enough, the second night I was there, I saw the exhausted crew from the movie trooping into the hotel after a hot day of shooting. "How's it going?" I asked several of the crew members I knew.

"Don't ask," one of them said. Then the stories began: Norma Jean was impossible, Norma Jean was chronically late, Norma Jean was driving everybody nuts, Norma Jean was zonked out all the time, Norma Jean looked like she would die at any minute. Things were so screwed up, it looked as though the picture never would be finished. Clark Gable, the matinee idol making his last movie, was the very model of patience, but everybody had the feeling he wanted to kill her. The other male star, Montgomery Clift, was so drunk on his favorite concoction of grape juice and vodka, he didn't seem to notice much of anything.

I was busy helping Lili's act and was making an effort to stay away from Norma Jean. Sometime after 2:00 A.M. one night, however, I was awakened by the sound of heavy thuds, loud voices, and crashing glass from the Miller suite. One of the crew members rushed upstairs, pounded on the door, and then heard everything go quiet inside. He left, but a few minutes later, there was the sound of a scream from the room, a door opening, and the unmistakable voice of Norma Jean yelling, "Get out or I'll throw you out, you sonofabitch!" Then all was quiet again.

Nobody wanted to talk about the episode, but I had the uneasy feeling that there was something seriously wrong with Norma Jean. Against my better instincts, I called her. I got what sounded like a zombie on the phone. She was just coming out of a pill-induced stupor.

"I have to see you," she said in a thick voice. Her room or mine was out of bounds, considering the potential trouble that could be caused if we were seen together at that point. We decided to meet on the hotel rooftop.

At 10:00 P.M. that night I met her on the rooftop— or rather, I should say, encountered her, for the moment she caught sight of me, she fell into my arms and began sobbing. When she finally was able to speak, I heard a long, rambling story about the collapse of her marriage to Miller, the affair with Montand, and how Miller, in a fury, had pushed her over the bed and onto the floor the previous night. "He called me a no-talent pill-popper," she said.

Perhaps shock therapy would be best at this point, I decided. "Maybe he's right," I said, as she looked at me in shock. "This movie's your really big chance to prove yourself the great actress you want to be, and what are you doing? You're taking those fucking pills, fucking up your life, fucking up the movie, fucking up everybody around you. You know why I didn't call you here until after a couple of days? Because I don't really want to talk to you. Look at yourself!"

"I thought you were my friend, Eddie," she said, weeping.

"I am, and that's why I'm talking to you like this. Jesus, what the hell are you doing?"

She did not answer, and for a while she stared out toward the desert. Far away, the sky was lit bright red with the forest fires that had been burning for some weeks.

"If only I could sleep," she said dreamily. "Look at it out there, Eddie. It looks like the end of the world. Maybe this is the way it all ends." She turned and stared at me intensely. "Eddie, come with me to the edge of the roof. Hold my hand, Eddie, and let's jump together. Let's give them something to *really* talk about."

This had to be handled carefully. She was balanced right on the edge of life and death. "No," I said quietly, turning to walk away. "You jump yourself. I'm not going with you, Norma Jean. I love you in life, not in death."

I walked away, praying that it had worked. To my relief, I heard the steps of someone running behind me. She clung to me.

"I can't do it, not by myself," she said.

Later I went back to my room and began packing. "Leaving?" Lili asked.

"Yes, it's time," I said. "We're finished here, and I don't want to stay another minute. If I stay any longer, she's either going to kill herself or break my heart."

I left a one-word note on Norma Jean's door: "Good-bye."

Chapter nineteen

AN
UNQUIET
DEATH

My return to Hollywood after the Reno incident was fortuitous, for I immediately encountered my old friend James Arness. I went to visit him in a trailer, where he was resting between takes of a new television series, a Western called *Gunsmoke*.

I wasn't looking for a job in a television series, but Arness gave me one anyway. I discovered it was a high-quality show, and I now faced the prospect of steady work, something of a novelty for a journeyman actor.

I was determined not to call Norma Jean, despite my worry about what was happening to her. In sum, just about everything seemed to be going wrong, as I learned when the phone calls began. The calls were even odder than before.

"You know why I was so upset in Reno?" she said. "Clark Gable. You remember what I told you about Gable when I was a kid? Well, Jesus, there he was, live in the flesh, right in front of me! My God, Eddie, I almost melted. We had this kissing scene, and I could see the look in his eyes: 'Honey,' those eyes said, 'we're going to bed after this movie is over.' I just couldn't wait. But then . . ." Her voice trailed off.

Gable had suddenly died, and to Norma Jean's mortification, his widow blamed the death on the strain of working with the very difficult Norma Jean. The accusation was shattering, and I heard in the phone calls the unmistakable sound of a woman retreating further into madness. It was confirmed when she had a nervous breakdown after the movie was finished and was rushed to Payne Whitney Psychiatric Clinic. It was a terrible mistake: Norma Jean saw the men in the white coats, and the nightmares of her childhood suddenly came flooding back. She became nearly unhinged until Joe DiMaggio, still her great friend, pulled some strings and got her released.

It was her last experience in New York, and the next thing I knew, I received a call from her. "Hi, neighbor!" she said, the old giggle suddenly returned.

"Neighbor?" I said, not knowing what she was talking about.

"Didn't you know? I bought my first house, and guess what: it's right near you! So we're neighbors now!"

The news aroused mixed feelings. With great pride she showed me her new place, a small, one-bedroom house in the Spanish style. It had a swimming pool out back, an addition I found rather odd, since Norma Jean seldom swam, and hardly ever went near a swimming pool. The place was surrounded by a ten-foot-high wall. She furnished it sparingly inside: a few pieces of furniture, some books, several sculptures (including one of her favorite poet, Carl Sandburg).

"It's a new life for me here," she said, more in hope than in fact. "I'm going to get all straightened out, just you see, Eddie."

But, as I feared, Hollywood was about the worst place in the world for her at that point. She no longer had the power to discriminate between friends and leeches, and her first serious mistake was to become involved in the infamous Hollywood "rat pack" headed by Frank Sinatra.

For some years Sinatra had been a friend of Norma Jean's, but the other people in the rat pack were no friends. To them, Norma Jean was a dizzy blonde good for parties, fun to have around, a kick to watch her in action. They were pure hedonists, and to them a troubled lady like Norma Jean was just another source of amusement.

The most dangerous, in my view, was Peter Lawford. His connections ran both ways: to the Kennedys, via his wife, Pat, JFK's sister; and to the Hollywood establishment, through Sinatra's crowd. Worse, Lawford was a notorious drunkard and narcotics user who read Norma Jean's code immediately: he became her new drug supplier for her constant need of downers and uppers. In return, Norma Jean—although she had no awareness of the fact—became a glittering plaything for Lawford's frequent parties.

But there was something much more dangerous going on at that house, and I heard the first clue one night in a phone call that woke me up sometime around 4:00 A.M.

"Who's the most desirable man in America?" the familiar breathy voice asked.

"Norma Jean," I said sleepily, "I don't want to play guessing games at this hour."

"C'mon, think. Who's the one man just about every woman in America wants, the one man they can't have?"

"Um, me."

"Very funny. No, silly, it's . . . John F. Kennedy, president of the United States! And guess what woman's got him?"

I was suddenly alert now. "What are you trying to tell me?"

"I made it with the prez."

I felt my blood run cold. "Norma Jean, are you sober?"

"Compared to what?"

"Listen, are you trying to say you have a thing going with the president?" At first I thought she was mad, but I was beginning to believe what I was hearing.

"Sure did. We made it out at Bing Crosby's house, in Palm Springs. I was real good for his back." There was a long giggle.

It was insane, but things actually got worse. A few weeks later she was reporting that the relationship between Kennedy and herself had "deepened," by which she meant that the president had confessed his love to her.

"I'm the one he wants, I know it," she said. "He wants me to live with him."

"Where?" I asked, afraid of the answer.

"In his house, of course, the White House."

It was worse than I thought. "Look, Norma Jean," I said, "you have to forget that idea. In the first place, he's married to another woman. Secondly, there is no way the president of the United States is going to get divorced. I don't care what he told you. Forget it."

She was adamant. "You don't know what's happened between us, Eddie. You don't know what he feels for me. Anything's possible. What are you trying to tell me, that dumb old Norma Jean hasn't got what it takes to be the First Lady?"

There was not much point in continuing after that, and following a few more attempts to give her a dose of reality, I gave up. I tried a shock treatment: the truth. Lawford was infamous for keeping a "stable" of nubile lovelies for the amusement of himself and his friends, I told her, and his prime service to his brother-in-law, at that point, was keeping him in female flesh.

"Norma Jean, you're being used," I said.

She paid no attention, and there was to be further alarming news. JFK, having amused himself sufficiently, dropped her, and as casually as though they were changing a tire, Lawford and Kennedy arranged for Bobby Kennedy to step into the president's place.

What was even more extraordinary was that Norma Jean hardly seemed to notice the change. Apparently without noticing any difference, I began to hear talk of how wonderful Bobby Kennedy was, how he had pledged to marry her (with a wife and ten kids?), and how she was studying up how to be a Washington hostess. Nothing I said seemed to make the slightest dent in her.

The slide was ever downward, and tragically enough, it seemed that nothing would stop it. As a supplement to the phone calls, occasionally she would come to see me during the year 1962.

I wished she hadn't, for to look at her was enough to break my heart. I could not help contrasting the vibrant, very different teenager I had met nearly twenty years before, a short distance from where I was then living, with the wreck of a human being I was now seeing. She would walk to my place in the wee hours dressed only in her kimono, carrying a bottle of Dom Perignon.

"Is Mr. Jordan at home?" she would ask, smiling, as I answered the doorbell. I never hesitated to let her in, for I thought that so long as she was talking to me, at least she was alive.

But there was not much left. Her face and figure were falling apart. At thirty-six she was beginning to look somewhat older. Her rear end, once her most noted feature, was spreading. Overall, she looked blowsy.

"What are you looking at?" she asked, sipping her champagne.

"I'm looking at you, Norma Jean," I said with a sigh. "I've been looking at you for almost twenty years."

"And what do you see?"

"Not the Norma Jean I once knew, that's for sure."

"Well, a lot of water's gone under the bridge." She was curled up on my couch. I noticed that she occasionally spilled champagne from her glass and often had difficulty holding it steady.

"Well, now see here, old boy," she said in an imitation of Lawford's English accent, "I think we'll have to have a chat on this."

I shook my head. "Really, Norma Jean, what's to talk about? We've said it all many times. All I'm going to do is repeat myself."

"You're right. So will I."

When she had finished most of the bottle, she rose and announced she was leaving. I made a move to walk her back home, but she pushed me away. "Nothing doing," she said, giving me a crooked little smile. "I walk alone now." She left, and I watched her walk down the street, singing some song to herself I couldn't recognize.

What had happened to her and the Kennedys I did not know—in fact, I was afraid to ask. The Hollywood scuttlebutt, usually fairly accurate, said that they had dropped her, afraid that her habit of telling everybody she knew might get them into trouble. (In fact, J. Edgar Hoover found out because somebody anonymously sent his agents a five-page letter revealing the whole thing. It gave him wonderful leverage over the president.)

The scuttlebutt also reported that Norma Jean was just about finished. Society and the movie business that it spawned were changing, and Norma Jean was rapidly becoming an anachronism. Fox, to whom she was obligated for another movie, had prepared a comedy called *Something's Got to Give* for her. She had started work on it, but Lawford insisted that she play hooky to sing at the president's birthday party. She called in sick and staggered out to center stage at the Kennedy birthday gala to sing "Happy Birthday." To the laughter of those in attendance, she stumbled over the words; a drug-fogged brain couldn't even remember the words to a simple song.

Not unreasonably, the studio chiefs were irate over this incident, and she was unceremoniously canned. Fox was already in big trouble with its $20-million flop *Cleopatra* and was not about to buy more trouble with the troubled Marilyn Monroe.

No one knew it then, but her string had run out.

It was the first day of August 1962. On a warm evening, when the hum of the night insects could be heard, I was sitting by an open window. I heard a new sound: the sound of a whispery human voice, singing snatches of a tune I couldn't recognize. She was standing at my door, dressed, as always at that hour, in her kimono. She carried her usual bottle of champagne, but in the other hand she was holding what appeared to be a stack of papers.

"Why, hel-l-l-o-o there, Mr. Jordan," she trilled as I opened the door. "I thought I'd pay you a visit." She was slurring her words and appeared to be very tipsy.

She handed me the stuff she had been carrying in one hand. I recognized them instantly. "Why are you giving me these now?" I asked.

She shrugged. "Because maybe it's time to."

I looked at the material. Included was the diary she had been keeping, some costume jewelry she wore during *Gentlemen Prefer Blondes*, a framed picture of myself that I had given her, twin lockets with our pictures inside, copies of various poems, and a few trinkets we had picked up in our travels years before. It amounted to what we called our "treasure chest," a collection of keepsakes in her possession that we once promised would remain forever as a repository of memories.

I leafed through the diary. She had not made any entries for quite some time. "No time," she said, as if reading my mind.

"What's going on here?" I demanded. "I thought you were going to keep our stuff."

"I think you ought to hold on to it from now on," she said, and refused to discuss it any further. I was puzzled and a little hurt.

"I got an idea." she said, "Let's recite one of our poems. Gee, we haven't done that in years, Eddie. Get that Indian love thing, whatever it's called."

I searched through the papers and found it. The paper was well worn, as though handled many times. "Together," she said.

I began to recite "Whether I loved you who can say . . . ," when I noticed she was stumbling over the words. We had recited this, our favorite poem, so many times together; how could she have forgotten the words?

> *Whether I drifted down your way*
> *In the endless River of Chance and Change*
> *And you woke . . .*

"Oh, shit," she said, "I can't remember it, Eddie. Look, let's forget it. I just can't go on. It's no good. I can't do poetry anymore. Maybe if I took a little something to help me along—"

"Goddammit, Marilyn! What the fuck is the matter with you? Have you forgotten everything that meant something to us? Can't you do anything without sticking some chemical in yourself?

"What did you call me?" She was looking at me in what appeared to be sheer terror, her eyes wide.

"What do you mean, what did I call you? I didn't call you anything."

"Yes, you did!" she screamed. Her eyes were full of tears. "You called me *Marilyn!*"

"Oh, sorry. I meant Norma Jean. Now—"

"You shit! You meant that deliberately! You know

how I hate that name now! You know it's a fucking albatross around my neck! I never thought you'd do that to me, Eddie."

"Look, Norma Jean—"

"Don't touch me! Get away from me!" Weeping, she picked up her bottle and with surprising speed ran out of the apartment. I ran after her, but she refused to stop. She went into her place and slammed the door in my face. I knocked, but no one answered. Later I wrote a note and slipped it under the door.

I was still waiting for a reply to that note when my phone rang early in the evening of August 4, a Saturday. It awoke me from a nap. Norma Jean was on the other end. I apologized for sounding fuzzy, but explained I had just awakened. She gave a little laugh, appreciating the irony: usually it was her voice that was a little woolly.

"Hey, I'm sorry about the other night," she said. I noticed that her voice was especially slurred; momentarily the thought crossed my mind that she seemed to be in a narcotic daze somewhat early. Usually she began to take pills and drink champagne much later in the day, when she could not sleep.

"I just wanted to say so long, Eddie."

"So long? Where are you going?"

"Oh, on a trip."

In my drowsy state it did not occur to me to question her further. She seemed to want to cut the conversation short, and she hung up a moment later. I had been very worried about her and was grateful merely that she had contacted me. For the moment I attached no other significance to the call.

"Take care of yourself," she said as she hung up.

Again, despite the fact that I had never heard her conclude a conversation with me that way, I did not see anything significant.

At 8:00 A.M. the next day I was up early, preparing for a date. I was not feeling especially alert, for I had spent a sleepless night. Something was beginning to nag me: was there something different about that phone call the previous evening?

I left my place and got into my car, then headed for Malibu. I turned on the car radio and switched to a news station to catch up on the latest developments. I heard the words ". . . and police have ruled it preliminarily an apparent suicide." I wondered what prominent person had committed suicide, then felt a hot rush to my body as I heard the next sentence: "Police said that Miss Monroe was alone at the time of her death."

I drove the car off the road, nearly ramming a tree. For a full minute I sat there in shock, unable to believe it. Then I drove back toward Los Angeles, heading for her house. It was a madhouse of police cars, curiosity seekers, cameramen, photographers, and reporters.

All the way there I hoped against hope. I prayed that there was some sort of mistake, that the radio had gotten it wrong somehow. She would be at home. She would not be awake that early in the morning, of course, but sometime later that evening, perhaps, I would hear from her. That drowsy voice would come on the line and I would hear "Hi!"

But it was true; she was gone. I saw one of my neighbors standing outside the house. "You okay, Ted?" he asked, noticing I looked white as a ghost.

"Yeah," I said vacantly, and then I started to sob like a baby.

*   *   *

On the morning of the funeral I dressed in a somber black suit with a subdued tie. I looked at myself in the mirror and suddenly, as though she was in the room with me, I laughed. I looked like a funeral director. I could picture her sitting there in that room, or perhaps lounging on the bed, nearly doubled over with a fit of the giggles.

"Jesus, Eddie," she would say, still giggling, "what a sight! Hey, what are you so gloomy about? Boy, you midwesterners are all alike. Don't you people ever have any fun?"

On my way to the cemetery I could not shake the feeling that she was somewhere around me. It got stronger as I entered the cemetery. What a circus! There were mobs of people, a huge crowd of reporters and cameramen, and a contingent of police trying to prevent what seemed at moments to be an incipient riot.

How Norma Jean would have loved it. She always loved the big crowds, the grand show, and the sheer sweep of such scenes. It was, of course, the greatest exit of her career, and no scriptwriter could ever have improved on it.

There was Joe DiMaggio, in tears, along with his family. Through it all, they had always loved the Hollywood waif he had married, and to the end they were loyal to her memory. As the casket was slowly carried to her crypt, DiMaggio began weeping with greater force. "I love you, I love you," he repeated over and over again as she was taken to her final resting place.

I wept that day like I have never wept before. I loved her, too, of course, and I knew she was the one woman who had dominated my psyche for most of my life.

Somehow I became convinced that she was there. She was in that blue bathing suit I saw her wearing the first moment I laid eyes on her, smiling that little smile that was at once friendly and uncertainly vulnerable.

At some point I swear I saw her standing at the entrance to her crypt, flashing that dazzling smile to the crowd.

"Take it easy, folks!" she shouted. Then she laughed.

EPILOGUE

I thought that Norma Jean would rest in peace, but I did not anticipate the extraordinary industry that would spring up centering on the question of her death.

This vulturelike business, picking at the bones of a woman in no position to defend herself, always struck me as among the lowest forms of behavior. More importantly, it angered me. Again she was being put in the position of helpless pawn in still another game. Again she was regarded as the dumb blonde, incapable of mastering her own fate.

The basic thesis of the minor necrophilia devoted to examining Norma Jean's death can be summarized fairly easily. Norma Jean was the unwitting subject in a series of complex plots. In a word, say the conspiratorialists, she was murdered. Depending on your pick of conspiracies, she was murdered by the Mafia, by Jimmy Hoffa, by the CIA, by Bobby Kennedy, or by all of the above.

Let us now demolish all of these once and for all. Hopefully she will then be able to rest in peace, at last.

*   *   *

Norma Jean Baker, a.k.a. Marilyn Monroe, committed accidental suicide sometime during the late hours of August 4 or the early hours of August 5, 1962.

The death climaxed a period of approximately ten years in which, for various psychological reasons, she was preparing to kill herself. No one had to murder Marilyn Monroe, for she was intent on murdering herself. Toward the end of her life she had become so self-destructive, it was simply a matter of time before she committed the one act that would give her the final release from the tortures that afflicted her mind.

I continue to believe, however, that she did not specifically plan to commit suicide on August 4. As she had done so often in the past, she made preparations to kill herself. On previous occasions, she had either been rescued from death at the last moment or had suddenly decided not to go through with it.

It is clear that her death was an accidental suicide. On the previous day she had obtained a large drug supply, in preparation for the possibility of ending her life. At some point during the night of August 3, she decided that it was time to commit suicide. We still do not know exactly what triggered that final decision, but during the afternoon of August 4 she began the process, filling her body with drugs in sufficient amounts to induce a slow, gradual, and very deep sleep that would result in death. Clearly, toward the end, she suddenly changed her mind. Frantically she began to reach out by telephone to those she knew, trying, in the deep fog of the narcotics-induced drowsiness, to warn them she was slipping away. None of the recipients of those calls, including myself, picked up the warnings of what was happening.

"The strongest memory is weaker than the palest ink," Norma Jean would say sometimes, quoting the old line. Unfortunately her own death proved what the line meant. The drumfire of conspiratorial literature over the past decade has raised, in many people's minds, at least the possibility of an intricate murder plot.

The assorted theories advanced as fact by the conspiratorialists and, to a much more cautious extent, by Anthony Summers in his flawed biography, are simply drivel. They rely, largely, on skewered evidence, questionable interpretations, selective citations, and plain sloppiness.

Unfortunately it has also proven profitable, and for some years now, the conspiratorialists have made a tidy living out of the ghoulish hashing and rehashing of the circumstances of Marilyn Monroe's death. The low point in this tragicomedy took place in 1982, when several of them managed to pressure the Los Angeles district attorney's office to reopen an investigation into the death. The fact that the D.A.'s investigators ultimately concluded that there was no evidentiary basis for reopening the original verdict of probable suicide has not dampened the conspiratorialist movement; in fact, it is stronger than ever.

It would take many volumes to fully discuss some of the trash they have written, but let's dispose of some of the more prominent pieces of "evidence" they have advanced to support their fanciful theories of murder conspiracies.

Marilyn Monroe kept a red diary, in which she wrote down many secret things, including top-secret information on CIA and other activities, which she got from Robert Kennedy: This diary, which some conspiratorialists allege was stolen from Norma Jean's bedroom the night of her death, does not exist. The only red diary that exists is the one she gave me shortly before her death. It contains a number of intimate thoughts, but it does not contain any secret information. For the last year or so of her life Norma Jean was in very bad shape psychologically and could not perform even the simplest functions without help. She certainly was in no shape to keep a diary.

Bobby Kennedy visited Marilyn Monroe's home shortly before she was found dead. Wrong. Bobby Kennedy did not visit her home. In fact, he was in San Francisco. The records of toll calls made by Norma Jean during her final hours reveal that she was desperately trying to reach him via the Justice Department switchboard in Washington, D.C., not realizing he had left the capital and was in northern California. She would hardly have tried to call him if he had already visited her.

The autopsy of Marilyn Monroe was a cover-up designed to conceal evidence of foul play. Nonsense. The original autopsy was reviewed by other prominent pathologists, all of whom found it was conducted scientifically and perfectly within accepted standards.

Marilyn Monroe was murdered by an injection given to her before her body was discovered. Impossible. The pathologist conducting the Monroe autopsy—the medical examiner, Dr. Thomas Noguchi—found no evidence of needle-puncture marks anywhere on the body, despite an examination by magnifying glass.

According to the ambulance driver who first arrived at the Monroe home, she was still alive and was killed by an injection performed by another man in the house. This ex-ambulance driver's story does not jibe with the facts. For one thing, Norma Jean's body was found in a state of rigor mortis, a process that takes from two to four hours. Thus it would have been impossible for her to have been alive when he arrived at the home. Further, the autopsy report clearly states that no needle mark was found anyplace on her body.

Marilyn Monroe's phone was wiretapped by several government agencies. Not true. The original source of this assertion was a convicted illegal wiretapper allegedly employed by Jimmy Hoffa to gather defamatory material on the Kennedy brothers. However, the wiretapper was later exposed as a liar and never did have any so-called "Monroe tapes," recordings of intimate conversations between her and Robert Kennedy.

And on and on it goes, a tissue of suppositions, rumors, pseudofacts, and, sometimes plain downright dishonesty.

Will it ever end? Probably not, for so long as Marilyn Monroe exerts her extraordinary pull on the popular imagination, there will continue to be a little industry of moles, occasionally surfacing to pronounce the latest "exciting discovery" in their never-ending quest to prove how Marilyn Monroe was murdered.

Shortly after midnight on June 5, 1968, Senator Robert F. Kennedy acknowledged the cheers of Democrats after winning the California presidential primary. His loyal crowd of supporters cheered themselves nearly hoarse in the ballroom of the Ambassador Hotel in Los Angeles.

Moments later, as he walked through the hotel kitchen on his way out of the hotel, a man named

Sirhan Sirhan fired a shot into his brain. The shooting took place less than fifty feet from the spot where Norma Jean Baker was one day posing in a bathing suit for a modeling assignment when a lifeguard at the pool spotted her.

In 1979 Fred Karger, the musician who was among the first men in Hollywood to be smitten by Norma Jean, died on the exact anniversary of her death.

On August 4, 1982, I was in Westwood Village Memorial Park, putting flowers on the crypt of Norma Jean. I gradually became aware of a large group of people who were watching me. Several of them were young girls. To my disquiet, they were dressed in a perfect imitation of Norma Jean, the cultural hero of a whole new generation of young Americans.

One of the young women, who had been watching me for some time, approached me.

"Hey, mister," she said. "Did you know her?"

"Yes, in a way," I replied.

About the Author

Actor Ted Jordan likes to say that he is the only man in Hollywood who has been shot to death at least ten thousand times. His repeated death occurs when, as the bad guy in black, he is outdrawn and shot down by Marshal Matt Dillon (James Arness) in the most famous opening sequence in television Westerns history—the High Noon gunfight in the streets of Dodge City that begins each episode of *Gunsmoke*.

Jordan also played the freight agent during the show's twenty-year run, capping a career as a noted supporting actor in such classic films as *Wing and a Prayer, Guadalcanal Diary, Mother Wore Tights, Sierra, The Wild One, My Six Convicts,* and *Walking Tall.* His television credits include several episodes of *Dallas, Bonanza,* and *Mission Impossible.*

Now retired, he lives in California.